Supervising Student Teachers

The Professional Way

6th Edition

Marvin A. Henry   W. Wayne Beasley   Kenneth L. Brighton

Supervising Student Teachers
The Professional Way

A Guide for Cooperating Teachers

Sixth Edition

by

Marvin A. Henry, Ed.D.
Professor of Education Emeritus
Indiana State University

W. Wayne Beasley, Ed.D.
Professor of Education (Retired)
University of South Florida

Kenneth L. Brighton, Ph.D.
Associate Professor of Education and
Acting Chairperson
Department of Education
Johnson State College
Johnson, Vermont

Sycamore Press
P.O. Box 552
Terre Haute, IN   47808
Phone-Fax: 812-235-6440
e-mail: sycamoreh@aol.com

MARVIN A. HENRY, Professor of Education Emeritus and former Chairperson of the Department of Curriculum, Instruction and Media Technology at Indiana State University, has supervised hundreds of student teachers throughout his professional career. He has written and consulted in the areas of field experiences and student teaching. He was involved in developing a model teaching intern program in Indiana which was awarded the Distinguished Program in Teacher Education by the Association of Teacher Educators. He is a former President and also a Distinguished Member of the Association of Teacher Educators.

W. WAYNE BEASLEY, Professor of Education (Retired) at the University of South Florida, is an experienced educator who knows the real world of student teaching. He has been a public school teacher and administrator as well as university supervisor and professor of supervision and leadership. His extensive contacts with school personnel in these varied roles have given him insight into the need for cooperative relationships between the public school and the university.

KENNETH L. BRIGHTON, Associate Professor of Education and Acting Chairperson, Department of Education, Johnson State College, Johnson, Vermont, is a former middle school teacher and is presently active in higher education as a teacher, student teacher supervisor, middle school expert, and Professional Development School coordinator. His considerable experience has been valuable in keeping this edition updated to reflect current trends in student teaching and teacher education.

Dedication

To the Numerous Student Teachers Who Have Meandered Throughout These Pages:

May your journey have helped create a straighter path for those who are following you into the profession.

MAH
WWB
KLB

Preface to the Sixth Edition

The sixth edition of Supervising Student Teachers the Professional Way, like the previous editions, is written with the intention of providing a practical reference for supervisors of student teachers. The authors define the terms in the title as follows:

Supervising means facilitating the growth of a future teacher through observation, analysis, conferences, and information sharing.

Student Teachers are those teacher education candidates who are completing their final directed field experiences prior to completion of the sequence of professional study.

The Professional Way is considered to be a systematic process based on scientific knowledge, theoretical constructs, and accepted professional practice.

This edition continues to emphasize the belief that student teaching involves development in the interpersonal, cognitive, and instructional processes. Student teachers must grow in attitudes, values, and feelings as well as in the thinking processes, the selection of content and the determination of teaching strategies. A cooperating teacher plays a key role in seeing that these domains are successfully developed throughout student teaching. In addition, student teachers must become familiar with the complete scope of the mission of teacher education.

Changes that have occurred in professional education since the last edition are reflected in these pages. The emphasis on accountability and criteria for effective teaching remain, but other movements are now taking center stage. One of the most encouraging developments is the advent of Professional Development Schools. Public schools and universities are joining more closely for teacher preparation, inservice education, and research. Student teaching has always linked the university with the public school, but now more extensive formal agreements through Professional Development Schools have given it more credibility. All this points toward the goal of improved learning for pupils and educators as well. Supervisors of student teachers may note that candidates are keenly aware of current educational issues. This is due to the fact that they generally have had a substantial number of contact hours with students in the classroom during their pre-service training.

The rapid growth of technology as a tool in teacher education cannot be ignored. The computer with its multiple capabilities can be used in numerous ways by teachers, student teachers and teacher educators in enhancing the effectiveness of student teaching.

The changing nature of our society as it reflects on the school is probably most notable in Chapter Ten. Due to the increased activity in legal aspects of teaching, Chapter Ten has been extensively revised. It also includes a section on ethics for the first time. Teacher educators, along with student teachers, should know Chapter Ten is not only for cooperating and student teachers, but also for those who want to see that future teachers and teachers are aware of the law.

Emphasis on cooperative and other types of student-centered activities should also have reached student teachers. As a result they should be more prepared for group dynamics and risk taking rather than relying on more conventional teaching styles. Additionally, alternative assessment techniques may have become a part of their lives in teacher education. They should possess a working knowledge of such innovations as portfolio development and implementation of state standards.

The obligation for cooperating teachers to provide a more sophisticated approach to supervision is obvious as we view the more complex nature of teacher education. Training in supervision is no longer an added benefit but a necessity. And, as usual, cooperating teachers may find themselves learning from their student teachers.

Case studies have been revised and increased in order to reflect typical problems of the present educational scene. The cases presented are either actual vignettes or composites of similar situations that have happened in the classroom. The case study method is now in the mainstream of educational thought and is being touted in some circles as a way of developing a set of recommended procedures based on prevailing practices. Case studies have always been a vital part of this book because they focus on specific vignettes which guide supervisors and future supervisors in thinking about the appropriate procedures for dealing with problems. The questions that follow each case study are written with the specific intent of encouraging the reader to think about case practice that has application beyond the immediate context of the problem situation.

Each chapter begins and closes with the imaginary Brian Sims and Elaine Bennett, student teacher and supervising teacher respectively. The introductory anecdote points to a problem relating to the chapter study and the closing narrative implies that the situation has been resolved. The chapter content is organized into sections with an attempt to provide practical information for the busy cooperating teacher. Throughout the chapters, the authors have summarized salient points from research and practice into lists of criteria. Supervisors should find them helpful for checking procedures or generating ideas. A summary set of principles closes each chapter, reiterating the major ideas of the section.

The references at the end of each chapter will provide assistance for the individual who wishes to investigate the chapter topic in greater detail. The reader will note a wide range of citations in order to meet the interests and needs of the cooperating teacher as well as the more serious graduate student who is studying the field of student teaching. Instructors will particularly find it beneficial to have their students review some of the citations at the end of the chapter in order to provide a more comprehensive treatment of each topic.

The book is primarily designed as a textbook for university courses in principles and techniques of supervising student teachers with the intent that it will accompany teachers into their classrooms where they supervise student teachers. However, classroom teachers can effectively use it as a reference in the event that they are asked to supervise student teachers without the benefit of a formal course in supervision. Public school administrators and college supervisors will find that it is valuable as a reference for overseeing student teaching programs. Student teachers should find the book to be of value in that it will give them a perspective on the expectations of student teaching as well as review teaching criteria that will guide them in becoming more competent. Their familiarity with the various topics should enhance communication with both the supervising teacher and the university supervisor.

The reader should be aware of the authors' use of certain terminology in the book. The profession has never agreed as to whether the public school teacher who supervises a student teacher is a supervising teacher or cooperating teacher. However, the present trend is to refer to that individual as a cooperating teacher. As a result, that term will be used consistently in this book. The profession is still uncertain as to whether the higher education representative is the "college supervisor" or "university supervisor." In deference to this, the terms will be intermixed. The problem of pronouns which refer to both males and females has been met by using "he" and "she" interchangeably when referring to the student teacher and supervising teacher.

The sixth edition has been enriched by the contributions of newest author, Dr. Kenneth L. Brighton, who brings recent experience to the complex task of revision. His role was that of updating the research, adding new case studies and updating current ones, and reviewing the entire text for relevancy in the current world of teacher education in general and student teaching in particular. Also, Ruth Henry and Maryanne Newsom Brighton used their considerable editing skills to made this a more readable book.

When we initiated the project of writing the first edition of this book, we were convinced that a practical, straightforward reference book for cooperating teachers would be beneficial in the educational field. The continued interest that has been shown in the book seems to substantiate that premise. We believe this edition keeps pace with new developments in the supervision of student teaching.

Marvin A. Henry
W.Wayne Beasley
Kenneth L. Brighton

Contents

Supervising Student Teachers
The Professional Way

1

Before The Student Teaching Experience Begins

Elaine Bennett checked her school mail and found an invitation to supervise a student teacher from the neighboring university. She was surprised because she had no training or experience in supervising field participants at any level. After carefully studying the request, she consulted with her principal who stated that he believed she was capable of such a responsibility because of her reputation as a teacher and her skill in working with young people. She reluctantly agreed after he promised his complete support.

Even though she consented to be a supervisor, she knew that she was unprepared for the task and hoped that she could learn something quickly about what it means to guide a student teacher. Her principal suggested that she secure ideas from some of the other teachers in the building who had supervised student teachers. She learned from the university correspondence that the student would make a visit to the school prior to the beginning of the experience. She wondered what she should do to prepare for this meeting.

A few days later, Brian Sims, a teacher education student at the university, was informed of the school where he was to student teach. He stared at the contents of the assignment form and with a puzzled look inquired to all within hearing distance, "Can anyone tell me anything about Central City?" He later received a briefing on student teaching responsibilities in a meeting with a university supervisor. The advisor concluded by saying that the student teaching candidates should visit their assigned schools as soon as possible in order to become familiar with the teaching situation and to meet the cooperating teacher.

Brian wrote a note to Miss Bennett suggesting that he visit on a specific day. He raised several questions in the letter and indicated that he wished to learn more about his responsibilities, the community, the school, and the students.

Miss Bennett carefully folded the correspondence and began to consider what she could do to help this stranger become acquainted with the school, with the class, and with her . . .

Student Teacher Supervision
Presiding Over a Professional Transition

In the few short weeks of student teaching a college student completes the final required experience necessary to become a certified teacher. This is the last opportunity to develop and refine the skills and attitudes that will inaugurate a teaching career. This transformation occurs not on the college campus under the watchful eye of a professor but in an elementary, middle, or high school under the direction of a classroom teacher.

A teacher who agrees to supervise a student teacher has consented to assume one of the most responsible, influential and exciting roles in teacher education. This brief period in the life of a college student may have greater impact on professional skills and potential than any other segment of undergraduate study. There is evidence (Brodbelt 1980) which shows that the teaching model established by the cooperating teacher becomes the actual pattern followed by the student teacher. Yamashita (1989) reviewed the literature on cooperating teacher effectiveness and concluded that the cooperating teacher has a significant impact on the attitudes and teaching behavior of the student teacher.

It can be a stimulating experience for a teacher to have a student teacher in the classroom. Gibbs and Montoya (1994) found that cooperating teachers perceive that student teachers play a significant role in the professional development of cooperating teachers as well as providing benefits for the classroom students. Ganser and Wham (1998) reported that cooperating teachers often felt personal satisfaction by giving professional guidance, providing an arena for beginning teachers to try their wings, being a role model, and contributing to the teaching profession. In spite of the increased responsibility involved, the experience of student teaching is a winning proposition for all parties.

The period of student teaching may be the only time that a teaching candidate has the benefit of individualized instruction. This offers a unique opportunity for the cooperating teacher to demonstrate one-to-one teaching, one of the most highly respected of all strategies. Student teaching also may be one of the few times during an educator's career when she can observe another professional at work. The hours together provide time for information sharing, planning, analysis, feedback, and evaluation.

These activities are the nucleus for effective learning and they can be adapted to the student's individual needs.

A classroom is changed when a student teacher arrives. A teacher who has been solely in charge of a class will be working jointly and sharing responsibility with a person who is learning to teach. A student teacher will assume much of the responsibility that has previously been the prerogative of a teacher. Eventually a teacher surrenders a great amount of teaching activity and autonomy to this neophyte and assumes the role of supervisor and counselor. Turning over the role of instructional leader to a student teacher may be disconcerting in this day of increased scrutiny and accountability, but it is necessary in order to prepare future teachers. This change of roles places the supervisor in a new, exciting, and challenging position.

Experience--The Key to Success

The objective of a professional certification program is to prepare a teaching candidate to be minimally competent in specialized knowledge, human relations, and professional skills. The final development of these proficiencies ultimately involves experience as a student teacher in a classroom setting.

When a teaching candidate is learning to teach, the classical process of experience should be followed. The procedure should involve direct reflection upon the activity (Barnes 1984). When a problem arises, reflection begins. A student teacher should learn to analyze the problem and to consider alternatives that should improve the situation. A plan of action is carried out and the results are observed. An effective student teaching program will be structured in such a way that a teaching candidate can develop and initiate a plan, reflect upon the experience, and develop alternatives which may be more successful in guiding learning experiences in the future.

A student teacher develops the ability to function in the world of the first-year teacher through guided activity. It is a challenging responsibility and may well be the main reason why teachers are willing to work with student teachers.

An Enriched Professional Atmosphere

While still an emerging professional, a student teacher should be well enough grounded in theory and practice to be an asset from the outset. Trenfield (1971) summarized eight specific ways in which a student teacher's presence may improve classroom instruction. The possibilities seem to be as apparent today as when they were first written.

- The presence of a student teacher in the classroom frequently is stimulating to both pupils and teacher.
- The presence of a student teacher requires the cooperating teacher to examine critically his own objectives and teaching strategies.
- The student teacher is sometimes a valuable source of ideas about instructional techniques and materials.
- Until the student teacher assumes responsibility for most of the instruction, there are two teachers in the classroom, enabling them to work as a team to plan and conduct activities.
- While the student teacher conducts class, the cooperating teacher is able to observe his students from a different perspective, perhaps gaining valuable insight into their interests and learning problems.
- While the student teacher conducts classes the cooperating teacher may work with individuals and small groups who need more special attention than he can normally find time to give them.
- As the student teacher assumes more responsibility the cooperating teacher is freed to consult administrators and colleagues, to accumulate instructional materials, and to plan instruction for the future.
- Occasionally a pupil will relate much better to one adult than to another. The presence of a student teacher gives this pupil additional opportunity to form a meaningful relationship with an adult.

In a more recent study at Brigham Young University, Moore (1995) found four distinct growth areas as the result of mentoring student teachers:

- Cooperating teachers can gain new ideas for innovation in the classroom.
- The student teacher helps create time to apply, analyze, and reflect on new experiences.
- The presence of the student teacher in the classroom causes the cooperating teacher to plan more effectively, teach, and evaluate that teaching with a more discerning eye.
- A reflective perspective on classroom relationships develops between the cooperating teacher, student teacher and the students.

The presence of a student teacher presents an excellent inservice activity for the cooperating teacher. If student teaching is approached by both parties as an opportunity for growth, the possibilities for improved instruction are countless. The cooperating teacher should start to develop ideas before the student teacher arrives.

Case Study No. 1: What Challenges Will Occur?

Mr. Jones was looking through the portfolio of Barry Johnson, the student teacher assigned to his classroom. He was delighted with Barry's credentials yet was uneasy about what changes would occur in the classroom when a new teacher appeared on the scene next month. Will he and his student teacher be able to communicate openly? Will he be able to balance the needs of his students while providing an arena for the novice teacher to explore and practice his ideas? Will Barry be able to establish a good rapport with the students? How long will it take the students to adjust to another person in the classroom and to his absence at the end of the term? What steps should Mr. Jones take to ease his concerns?

1. Evaluate the pros and cons to determine if supervising a student teacher is worth the effort.
2. Ask Barry to come for an interview so the concerns can be discussed.
3. Begin to make plans for sharing responsibilities with a student teacher.
4. _____

Comment:

It would be highly unusual to invite a guest into your classroom for an extended period of time and not have some concerns. It is important for the supervising teacher to know that while hosting a student teacher is professionally and personally rewarding, the experience can have its negative sides as well. But in most instances, the benefits of mentoring a beginning professional far outweigh the inconvenience.

Questions:

1. What other concerns might a cooperating teacher have about serving as a supervisor for a student teacher?
2. What could be done to relieve the anxiety and have some of his questions answered?

The Cooperating Teacher's Role
Do Your Traits Meet the Image?

Those who are privileged to work with student teachers have both a great opportunity and an enormous responsibility in pointing the way for future educators. Costa and Garmston (1987) suggest that there are three major contributions which cooperating teachers and other educators can make to student teachers. The first is modeling. Cooperating teachers should model instructional and classroom practices such as teaching standards based content, using time and resources productively, using a variety of instructional strategies, providing a safe and healthy learning environment, engaging students in active learning, and employing traditional as well as authentic methods of assessment.

Teachers also present a series of images of professional behavior that student teachers examine at close range. Student teachers are continuously studying their cooperating teachers and will likely emulate their behaviors in the classroom, on the playground, during faculty meetings, at conferences between teacher and parents, and other activities. Their movements, questions, responses, techniques, attitudes, relationships, degrees of participation, and leadership will impact student teachers and help to determine how they will approach similar processes.

The second contribution is passing along tools of the trade. Much has been learned about how certain teacher behaviors impact student learning. Judgments must be made about the amount of instructional time allocated to various needs, such as how to give directions, elicit attention, handle distracting behavior, and manage classroom skills. Cooperating teachers have the opportunity to help student teachers develop these skills and techniques.

Thirdly, Costa and Garmston indicate that the intellectual process of teaching must be developed. Superior teachers perform a complex pattern of intellectual functions that are basic to these teaching behaviors. Superior teachers make decisions about the instructional process including what to teach and what questions to ask. It is the distinction between "know how" and "know why" that separates the professional educator from the novice teacher. Cooperating teachers should focus some of their energies on developing teacher thinking on the part of student teachers. Simply stated, this means that cooperating teachers should work with student teachers in guiding their thinking about planning, teaching, analyzing and evaluating what happened, and applying what they have learned to future actions. These teaching processes are taught, modeled, coached, and refined by cooperating teachers.

Barnes (1984) studied cooperating teacher styles and found a number of characteristics that distinguished between most and least effective supervisors. Findings indicated that certain beliefs about teaching and practices of interaction during student teaching were associated with more productive experiences. The five beliefs listed below were characteristic of the more accomplished supervisors:

- Learning by experience is necessary but not sufficient unless accompanied by directed reflection upon the experience.
- Teaching includes the enculturation of morals and values and community mores to include awareness of and respect for varying beliefs and perspectives.
- Motivation is better than discipline.
- The workplace norms that must be attended to include recognition of organizational complexity and requirements.
- Professionalism means assumption of responsibility to include the right to make decisions and have a degree of control over circumstances as well as acceptance of blame.

Supervisors who were considered to be not as effective displayed the above characteristics to a lesser extent. The findings also indicated that certain practices of interaction during the student teaching experience are more likely to be related to the development of the student teacher's ability to successfully assume teaching responsibilities.

Cooperating teachers in the more effective experiences:

- Were more proactive than reactive.
- Were more specific in their communication.
- Modeled the behaviors, teaching techniques, and attitudes they recommended to the student teachers.
- Exhibited greater consistency between their behaviors and their verbal expressions.
- Were more adaptable and flexible.
- Provided rationales for their actions and suggestions.
- Practiced self-reflection as an active learner.
- Employed positive, problem-solving approaches.

Grimmett and Ratzlaff (1986) investigated the role expectations of cooperating teachers over a period of time. Although they found that there was a disparity in findings between studies conducted a decade apart, they found five expectations for cooperating teachers that appear to transcend the bounds of time and content. These five expectations are:

- Providing student teachers with basic information (school rules, policies, physical arrangements, etc.) to enable adjustment to the situation.
- Ensuring student teacher's acquisition of resource materials (teacher's guide, teacher's manual, textbooks, teaching aids, etc.).
- Involving student teachers in planning and evaluating learning experiences.
- Conferencing with student teachers at regularly scheduled times.
- Evaluating student teacher progress and development through regular observation and feedback.

Conner (1993) asked student teachers and cooperating teachers to define the qualities of successful cooperating teachers. Student teachers report most frequently that successful cooperating teachers (1) gave helpful feedback, (2) shared files and ideas, and (3) allowed freedom to try new things. Cooperating teachers felt that the two most valuable contributions were (1) sharing ideas and methods in planning and management skills and (2) giving time and freedom to try new ideas.

Kahn (2001) used semi-structured interviews of cooperating teachers to develop a portrait of what it means to be a successful cooperating teacher. The attributes most commonly mentioned were:

- Flexibility, including allowing student teachers to fail on occasion.
- Ability to establish a good working rapport.
- Easy to talk with.
- Tact in constructive criticism.
- Ability to relate to the student teachers.
- Positive communication skills.

Nearly one-third of the participants commented that being able to learn from one another contributed heavily to a successful experience.

A cooperating teacher must be more than an exemplary classroom teacher. The responsibilities include modeling good teaching as well as using effective supervisory skills. In addition, a cooperating teacher must be willing to devote a great number of hours helping a student evolve into a teacher.

Preparing For A Student Teacher
Building a Good Beginning

It is just as essential to prepare for the arrival of a student teacher as it is to prepare to teach a new class. Adequate preparation reduces anxiety for both the cooperating teacher and the student teacher because advance preparation provides for a smooth induction of the student teacher into teaching.

A great number of arrangements will be necessary before a student teacher arrives. Effective preparation includes knowledge of the requirements of a student teaching program, making adjustments to allow for participation by a student teacher, and developing the concept of working on a team basis with a teaching candidate.

The cooperating teacher will have to be prepared to make modifications in order to assimilate a new personality into the classroom routine. The individuality of a student teacher is a variable that can determine the types of responsibilities that will be assumed. The confident, outgoing student may be able to readily adjust to most situations, but the timid or insecure person may need responsibilities that build confidence. An alert cooperating teacher will want to know something about the incoming student teacher in order to plan for the most appropriate initial activities.

Learning About a Student Teacher

A supervisor can become acquainted with a future student teacher through personal contact, written communication, and e-mail conversations. Some teacher education institutions require prospective student teachers to have an interview with the building principal and cooperating teacher prior to formal placement. The information learned should increase understanding and decrease the possibility of making incorrect judgments. The following list will be helpful in determining what is worth knowing:

- **Educational background**
  High school record
  College courses completed in major and minor areas
  General education
  Experiences with children or youth
  Prior field experiences
  Special honors or awards
  Extra-curricular involvement
- **General experiences**
  Employment

Community service
Leadership responsibilities
Travel
Recreational interests
Hobbies
- **Autobiographical statement**
- **Educational philosophy**
- **Professional goals**

A considerable amount of information is normally summarized by the student when application is made for student teaching. The university student teaching office typically forwards this resumé to the school. If it has not been made available, it probably can be located by contacting the individual in the building or school district who coordinates student teacher assignments.

All information received in written form may be supplemented and interpreted through informal conferences with the student teacher and with those who know him at the university. Information should be secured only for more complete understanding and any sensitive information should not be shared with others.

Preparing the Class

A teacher should begin to establish a student teacher's status with the class before the arrival date. The pupils ought to know that a student teacher is coming and should anticipate this event with some enthusiasm. If pupils are provided with clear and accurate information about the purposes and processes of the student teaching experience, they can become partners in preparing future teachers. Typical preparation activities will include:

- Creating anticipation that more interesting, worthwhile experiences will be possible.
- Initiating correspondence between the class and the student teacher.
- Describing the purposes of student teaching.
- Explaining how the members of the class can help the student teacher.
- Assigning specific students to acclimate the student teacher to the school.
- Encouraging the student teacher to visit the assigned school whenever possible.

Case Study No. 2: We Want The "Real" Teacher

A few days after you have informed your class that a student teacher will be arriving during the second semester, Jason brings you a note from his mother that expresses concern that his education will be diminished and disrupted by the presence of a student teacher. As the week progresses, you receive more missives that carry the same basic message--the parents want the "real" teacher educating their children. The school board is becoming less supportive of accepting student teachers as the presence of a novice teacher may have a negative impact on test scores. Though the children had been excited when first informed that they would have a student teacher, the attitudes of adults have created concern and dampened their enthusiasm. What action will you take to address concerns of students, parents, and school board members?

1. Ignore their concerns and assume that the issue will disappear once the student teacher arrives.
2. Suggest that concerned parents request that their children be transferred to another class.
3. Inform the university supervisor that you cannot accept a student teacher.
4. Respond to the parents' notes and meet with those who have questions about the role of the student teacher.
5. Assure the parents and school board that you are ultimately in control and responsible for student achievement.
6. _____

Comment

Fear of the unknown may cause anxiety for some parents and students when a student teacher is to take part of the instructional load. Cooperating teachers should focus on the contributions a student teacher will make and emphasize the student teacher's qualifications and special talents. By doing this, the cooperating teacher may create enthusiastic feelings among even the most strident cynics. Some people may not be aware that the supervising teacher continues to play a vital role in the educational process during the student teaching experience.

Questions

1. What are some possible reasons that parents and students would resist a change of teachers?

2. What is the most convincing argument that you could make for having a student teacher in your classroom?

Preparing the Student Teacher

The feelings of a teacher candidate prior to and during student teaching range through a series of concerns (See Chapter Three). The initial ones are likely to center around issues such as compatibility between the student teacher and cooperating teacher, time management, and developing positive relationships with pupils. (Teacher Talk, 1995). Later, student teachers may have such concerns as whether the students will like them, how they can learn their pupils' names, and how to appear to be a mature person in a strange setting. University student teaching orientation may increase rather than reduce these worries because the explicit nature of the instruction can create more anxieties until student teachers have been able to experience the classroom.

Recognizing the above concerns, it becomes apparent that there are certain types of preparation that can only be accomplished at the host school and by the cooperating teacher. For example, the future student teacher may have questions about the activities and responsibilities of this new assignment. The following are typical:

- Where is the school located?
- Where should the student teacher park?
- When is the student teacher expected to be in the building?
- Where does a visitor report upon arrival at school?
- What is the school calendar?
- What is the nature and composition of the class or classes?
- What information about the community should be known immediately?
- What kind of preparation would be helpful?

A student teacher can benefit from having answers to the above questions before the initial visit. Correspondence that contains a set of directions to the school and stating where visitors report can be useful and reassuring.

There may be several creative ways to describe the class. A statement of class sizes and content being studied is a good beginning. Consider having students write a brief note of introduction or welcome and possibly include photographs or videocassettes of the pupils and classroom scenes. Such gestures can help to create a sense of belonging. If the school or class has a web site or e-mail address, send the student teacher the information and encourage her to visit the class electronically.

Finally, offer a few substantive thoughts that may cause a student teacher to perceive what contributions can be made. Encourage thought about teaching ideas or resources. Suggest that a real difference will be made if work is begun early on certain topics which are to be taught.

Case Study No. 3: Is It Normal To Be Anxious?

Your future student teacher came with all the qualifications that you had ever hoped for. She was an honor student competing to be the summa cum laude graduate from the college. Your preliminary assessment was that she had a superior grasp of the content that she was to teach. She had a charming personality and excellent recommendations. In spite of all her positive qualities, she confessed that she was apprehensive about this phase of her training and asked you if it is normal to be anxious about beginning student teaching. What do you say?

1. Dismiss it as a normal phenomenon.
2. Have a conference with her and try to determine if the concerns are more severe than one would normally expect.
3. Suggest that she talk with a first-year teacher or two or any other student teachers who might be in the building. Their comments might present some perspective on her feelings.
4. _____

Comment

Experts in student teaching would almost unanimously answer the question with the response that it is indeed normal to be nervous. Most new situations present initial anxiety as explained in Chapter Three. The critical focus for the cooperating teacher must be on how to help the student teacher become less anxious.

Questions

1. What would cause a student teacher who is apparently as qualified as this one to be anxious?
2. What helps you overcome new situations where you are likely to be somewhat apprehensive?
3. What experiences have you had that would help you relate to the apprehensions felt by the student teacher in question?

Providing Information About The School And Community
Preparing For More Than The Classroom

The school and community environment may be more strange to the student teacher than one would assume. A cooperating teacher who has lived in the community and taught in its school system for some time may fail to realize that the student teacher is not familiar with the school or the area. There is a considerable amount of information that will aid the newcomer in understanding the school community, and it will be helpful if the cooperating teacher is prepared to share this knowledge.

Depending on the individual situation, attention should be called to the following:

- **Information about the school in general**
  Type of population served
  Philosophy, goals, and mission statement
  School schedule
  Unique characteristics
  Facilities
- **School policies relating to the faculty**
  Arrival time
  Assigned responsibilities
- **School policies relating to students**
  Dress
  Discipline
  Student activities
- **Forms and reports**
- **Grade forms**
- **Attendance reports**
- **Accident reports**
- **Special Services requests**
- **Emergency procedures**
  Fires
  Weather-related incidents
  Natural disaster drills
  Violence prevention
  Conflict resolution
- **Specific information about students**
  Pupil records
  Personality characteristics
- **Schedule of classes**
- **School directory**
- **School calendar**

- **Location of key areas**
  Office suite
  Work rooms
  Cafeteria
  Teachers' lounge
  Library
  Media center
  Computer center
  Guidance office
  School
- **Service facilities**
  Procedure for reproducing materials
  Media resources
  Available computers
  Supplies
- **Responsibilities in the extracurricular program**
  Types of duties
  Expectations
  Compensation

There are various ways of acquainting a student teacher with the responsibilities of teaching prior to the beginning of the experience. A school handbook can be beneficial in helping a student teacher understand the school. In the absence of, or in addition to this information, some administrators provide orientation programs for prospective student teachers that expose them to many facets of the school. A good way to have student teachers learn about the various support staff responsibilities is to have them interview a variety of personnel about their role in supporting the mission of the school. Other faculty members may be willing to help with initial orientation. The pre-teaching visit provides a good opportunity for introductions to teachers who will voluntarily assist the student teacher in becoming acquainted with the school.

Any available community handbook can be useful as well. If such a publication is unavailable, the supervisor may want to describe those facilities that will be necessary or useful to the student teacher. The following list is typical of a student teacher's needs in learning more about a new area:

- Living accommodations
- Restaurants
- Available transportation
- Recreational facilities
- Places of interest
- Service facilities

- Location of shopping areas
- Unique features
- Community social structure

A checklist for student teacher preparation may be found in the Appendix (Worksheet Number One). Teachers may find it to be beneficial in completing the details that are necessary before the student teacher arrives.

Case Study No. 4: A Different Community

During Alan's pre-teaching visit he expressed concern about the community. He asked a number of questions about the poor appearance of the section of the city where your school is located and wondered what the students were like. He contrasted the school with his home school which he described in complimentary terms. He implied that his background was different from your students and wondered if he could communicate with them. How do you respond?

1. Describe the environment as best you can.
2. Ignore the comments and direct his attention to his new opportunities.
3. Arrange to have him meet some students and hope that this will relieve some of his concerns.
4. Suggest that a new situation normally causes some anxiety and that he will soon become accustomed to the school and community.
5. _____

Comment

Alan's feelings may result from more than one source of uncertainty. If he is unsure of his ability, he may be looking for reasons that would justify his performance. If he did not wish to be assigned to the school, he may be projecting unhappiness with university personnel who assigned him. His attitude will probably change through understanding and involvement with students. A warm greeting from teachers and students can be reassuring, and a newcomer's packet or personal contact of some sort could alter his opinion of the community.

Questions

1. What are some methods of introducing a student teacher to a different type of school community?
2. How can a supervisor deal with expressions of displeasure?

Brian Sims guided his automobile into the faculty parking lot and eased into a space reserved for visitors. After hastily checking some papers, he walked to the main entrance of the school and followed the signs to the principal's office.

A few minutes later Miss Bennett is greeted at her door by the principal who introduces the new student teacher. "Hello, Brian," said Miss Bennett with a smile, "welcome to Central City."

As the principal returned to the office, Miss Bennett and Brian moved into the classroom. "I'm glad you are here," began Miss Bennett, "I hope we can make some plans for your teaching and I would like to know something of your particular teaching interests. I also want to give you a tour of the building so that you will know about our facilities before you begin student teaching."

"I appreciate this opportunity," replied the visitor. "I still have several questions about my responsibilities and I would like to know about your students so that I can make some plans while I have university resources available."

The conversation continued until late in the afternoon. Brian was seen leaving the building carrying a stack of books and papers. His car moved smoothly out of the parking lot and turned into the main artery of traffic apparently headed for a quick tour of the downtown area before returning to campus.

Remember:

- **More anxiety on the part of the student teacher may occur prior to student teaching than during the actual experience.**
- **A supervisor cannot assume that a student teacher has received much information about the school or cooperating teacher prior to the pre-teaching visit.**
- **The cooperating teacher sets the climate for the student teaching experience prior to the time that the student teacher appears.**
- **The best orientation plans are designed to prepare a student teacher to be comfortable and informed at the beginning of the experience.**
- **Student teaching is a period of transition in which the teaching candidate changes from college student to beginning teacher.**

Useful References

Balch, Pamela M., and Patrick E. Balch. 1987. The Responsibilities of a Cooperating Teacher. Chapter 3 in *The Cooperating Teacher: A Practical Approach for the Supervision of Student Teachers.* Lanham, MD. University Press of America, Inc.

Barker, George P., and Cynthia G. Desrochers. 1992. A Head Start for Student Teachers. *Executive Educator* 14 (May): 23-24.

Barnes, Susan, and Sara Edwards. 1984. Effective Student Teaching Experience: A Qualitative-Quantitative Study. Austin, TX: Research and Development Center for Teacher Education. ERIC ED 251441.

Blank, Mary Ann. 1986. The Roller Coaster Ride of Student Teaching. *Tennessee Education* 16 (Fall): 21-23.

Brodbelt, Samuel. 1980. Selecting the Supervising Teacher. *Contemporary Education* 51 (Winter): 86-88.

Conner, Kathy, Nadine Killmer, Joane McKay, and Myrna Whigham. 1993. Cooperating Teacher Effectiveness and Training: Two Views. *Action in Teacher Education.* 15 (Summer): 72-78.

Copas, Ernestine M. 1984. Critical Requirements for Cooperating Teachers. *Journal of Teacher Education* 35 (November-December): 49-54.

Costa Arthur L., and Robert J. Garmston. 1987. Student Teaching: Developing Images of a Profession. *Action in Teacher Education* 9 (Fall): 5-11.

Fairley, Lesley Peebles. 1995. Student Teaching: A Student Teacher's View. Chapter 5 in Slick (Ed), *Making the Difference for Teachers: The Field Experience in Actual Practice.* Thousand Oaks, CA. Corwin Press, Inc.

Feiman-Nemser, Sharon, and Margaret Buchmann. 1986. When Is Student Teaching Teacher Education? East Lansing: Institute for Research on Teaching, College of Education. ERIC ED 274 654.

Ganser, Tom, and Mary Ann Wham. 1998. Voices of Cooperating Teachers: Professional Contributions and Personal Satisfaction. *Teacher Education Quarterly* 25 (Spring): 43-52.

Gibbs, Linda, and Alicia L. Montoya. 1994. The Student Teaching Experience: Are Student Teachers the Only Ones to Benefit? Research report presented at the Association of Teacher Educators Annual Meeting. Atlanta. ERIC ED 373025

Grimmett, Peter P., and Harold C. Ratzlaff. 1986. Expectations for the Cooperating Teacher Role. *Journal of Teacher Education* 37 (November-December): 41-48.

Hawley, Chandra, ed. 1995. Preparing for Effective Teaching. Teacher Talk: 3-1. Bloomington, IN Center for Adolescent Studies.

Kahn, Brian. 2001. Portrait of Success: Cooperating Teachers and the Student Teaching Experience. *Action in Teacher Education* 22:4 (Winter):48-56.

Koehler, Virginia-Richardson. 1986. The Instructional Supervision of Student Teachers. Paper presented at the annual meeting of the American Education Educational Research Association. San Francisco, CA. April 16-20. ERIC ED 271430.

Kronowitz, Ellen L. 1982. Views on Student Teaching. *California Journal of Teacher Education* 9 (Spring): 67-83.

Moore, Blaine H.(Brigham Young University). 1995. Inservicing Through the Back Door: The Impact of the Student Teacher Upon The Cooperating Teacher. Paper presented at the annual meeting of the Association of Teacher Educators. Detroit. February.

O'Bryan, Sharon. 1995. Can Every Teacher Be A Successful Mentor? Chapter 7 in Slick (Ed), *Making the Difference for Teachers: The Field Experience in Actual Practice*. Thousand Oaks, CA. Corwin Press, Inc.

Olson, Pennie M., and Kathy Carter. 1989. The Capabilities of Cooperating Teachers in USA Schools for Communicating Knowledge about Teaching. *Journal of Education for Teaching* 15:2. 113-31.

Rikard, G. Linda. 1982. The Student Teacher Practicum: Preparing Supervisors and Cooperating Teachers. *Journal of Physical Education, Recreation, and Dance* 53 (November-December): 60-61.

Smith, Janice P. 1991. Cooperating Teachers: Nurturing Professional Growth. *Music Educators Journal* 79 (October): 25-29.

Susi, Frank D. 1992. Using Clinical Supervision Techniques with Student Art Teachers. *Art Education* 45 (November): 45-51.

Trenfield, William. 1970-1971. Your Student Teacher: An Asset in the Classroom? *Supervisors Quarterly* 6 (Winter): 35-39.

Wood, Nancy L. 1988. Be A Super Supervising Teacher. *Instructor* 98 (August): 14.

Yamashita, Shirley. 1989. *Student Teacher Assessment of Cooperating Teacher Supervision*. Unpublished doctoral dissertation. University of Hawaii at Manoa.

2

The Student Teacher's
First Few Days

Brian Sims arrived early at the school on his first day of student teaching. Making his way down the hall, he came to Miss Bennett's room just as she was arriving. After the initial greetings, they engaged in small talk while they waited for the school day to begin.

Brian tried to look at ease, but he failed to conceal his anxiety. All the information given to him the previous week in orientation at the university seemed to whirl around in his head as the sounds from the Monday morning school rush surrounded him. There were so many things to think about! The new state performance standards! Assessment! Accountability! Requirements! Ethics! Teaching! Observations! Planning! Organization! The orientation instructions seemed even more obscure and abstract as the actual situation was about to begin, and he clenched the arm of his chair as the minute hand pointed to the top of the hour.

The complexity of the supervisory task became more apparent to Miss Bennett as she talked with her beginning student teacher. So much was at stake for him. She was a little uneasy herself since this was a new experience for her as well. Many details had to be attended to promptly, but the first task was to acquaint the class with the student teacher. The bell sounded and attendance was checked quickly. She arose from her desk more carefully than usual, looked at her pupils, and began to introduce her first student teacher to the class . . .

The First Few Days
Beginning the Developmental Cycle

The initial days of student teaching are vital to the development of the beginning teacher because new roles and expectations are being assimilated (NMSA, 1996). The advent of student teaching initiates a long anticipated learning sequence. The student may have participated in a number of exploratory field experiences, but student teaching is a step closer to reality. The first critical days of student teaching start the systematic development of the student teacher so that in a few weeks she will complete the experience with the skill and confidence necessary to independently direct a classroom.

Researchers have verified that student teachers tend to experience orderly stages of development. Three of the more popular theories about the stage of development are listed below.

Fuller (1967) and others found that students became less focused on themselves and more concerned about the pupils. Six stages of concern emerged as a "rough" index of the student's readiness to teach."

- **Stage 1: Where do I stand?** Students were curious about their role before teaching began.
- **Stage 2: How adequate am I?** Students questioned their adequacy to teach subject matter and manage classrooms.
- **Stage 3: Why do they do that?** Students share concerns about individual pupils and behaviors such as fear and withdrawal.
- **Stage 4: How do you think I am doing?** Students were concerned about evaluations from supervisors, principals, parents and others.
- **Stage 5: How are they doing?** Student teachers began to be concerned with the students' learning.
- **Stage 6: Who am I?** Student teachers' unconscious interactions arose to the conscious level as they became aware of their actions, behaviors and mannerisms.

After studying the research and conducting an independent study, Piland and Anglin (1993) identified four stages of student teacher development:

- **Stage 1: Fear/Uncertainty**. Student teachers experienced fear, nervousness, anxiety, frustration, and uncertainty prior to entering and during student teaching. They entered the experience with expectations, excitement, goals, and questions centered on the unknown and "how to."
- **Stage 2: Socialization**. Student teachers moved through a socialization process. It was important to be liked as an individual and respected as a teacher. It was important to be accepted by the cooperating teacher, pupils, and staff. Confirmation was obtained and confidence gained when the student teacher felt successful in the teaching of the lesson, received positive responses and feedback from the pupils and

from evaluations. Trust level began developing with the cooperating teacher. Knowledge base of content to be taught was reviewed. Classroom management began.

- **Stage 3: Autonomy.** Student teachers wanted control and the opportunity to take charge of the classroom and management of the pupils. They wanted to function in the authority role, to be able to discipline pupils and to make decisions regarding the planning of the lesson and the content to be taught. Received or wanted permission from the cooperating teacher to take charge of the classroom.
- **Stage 4: Affirmation.** It was important for student teachers to be affirmed by the pupils. Formal evaluation by the cooperating teacher and the university supervisor affirmed the student teacher's ability to demonstrate the knowledge and skills of teaching. Self-affirmation was obtained by meeting personal goals and expectations set at the beginning of the experience.

Kagan (1992) analyzed over 40 studies relating to teacher development and concluded that growth consists of at least five components:

- A developing awareness of initial and changing knowledge and beliefs about pupils and classrooms.
- A reconstruction of idealized and inaccurate images of students and a reconstruction of early images of self as teacher.
- A shift in attention to students and instruction upon resolution of one's own professional identify.
- Acquiring and becoming comfortable with standard classroom procedures.
- Growth in problem-solving skills.

A student teacher may be aware that changes are going to occur but may not be cognizant of what will take place. A cooperating teacher should understand the pattern of growth that is anticipated and be prepared to help the new student teacher keep in touch with his feelings as the experience progresses.

Changes in the Classroom
Adjustment, Learning, and Demands

The arrival of a student teacher brings about a change in the classroom environment that is sensed by both pupils and teacher. Pre-teaching visits and communication about expectations provide some degree of preparedness for the impending change, but only the physical presence of a student teacher provides the full impact of this different educational climate. For the cooperating teacher, Mari Koerner (1992) identified three negative aspects of hosting a student teacher in one's classroom that veteran teachers feared could hinder instruction:

- Student teachers interrupted the instruction of the class.
- Student teachers took longer to teach the curriculum.
- Student teachers shifted the teacher's time and energy away from the students and to the student teacher.

By examining the items cited above one can see that the concerns focused on issues that could detract from student teaching achievement. It is understandable that some teachers are apprehensive about allowing student teachers to take a major role in their classrooms in the current climate of testing and accountability. On the other hand, the well-prepared student teacher, appropriately involved in the classroom, and working in concert with the cooperating teacher, should be an asset rather than a liability to student learning. Change can and should be a positive element in the classroom, and different should not be construed as deficient. It is the duty of the cooperating teacher to provide an environment for the novice teacher to develop competency while maintaining the educational quality for her students.

The first few days are periods of adjustment and learning for the student teacher who is confronted with a series of tasks which may cause apprehension. If the early experiences of a student teacher are successful, subsequent responsibilities will pose much less threat. During these initial days the student teacher has a number of tasks to meet:

- To become acquainted with school personnel.
- To get to know the students.
- To become aware of unique needs and aptitudes of students.
- To become aware of the curriculum.
- To become familiar with the classroom and school wide routine.
- To assume some teaching responsibility.

Early experiences tend to set the mode of procedure for student teaching. In an investigation of teaching styles of student teachers and their cooperating teachers, Seperson and Joyce (1973) found that the relationship established during the initial part of student teaching continued throughout the entire semester. The tasks listed above appear more significant when one contemplates the impact that they have for the entire experience.

The pupils also will begin a period of adjustment to the new person in the classroom. What is the student teacher like? What changes will there be? What will be the cooperating teacher's reaction to the student teacher? Some pupils will vie for the attention of this new individual and the cooperating teacher may note that a few persons are acting differently. A new mood may permeate the classroom.

The cooperating teacher should be ready to accept additional responsibilities. The most apparent initial change may be an increased work load. During the first few days, the cooperating teacher will need to:

make her feel comfortable · *copy of preschool standards*

- Learn more about the university's student teaching requirements.
- Arrange initial teaching activities.
- Confer with the student teacher.
- Orient the student teacher to the school.
- Involve the student teacher in constructive activity.
- Introduce the student teacher to the faculty and staff.
- Confer with the college supervisor.
- Acquaint the student teacher with planning procedures.
- Determine a teaching schedule for the student teacher.
- Schedule classroom observations.
- Help gather materials and supplies for teaching.

· *Show curriculm & where things are located*

Quimby (1985) looked at student teaching from a principal's perspective and listed four tasks of student teaching. Recognizing that student teaching gives a student the first extended experience in teaching, he suggests that student teaching should strive to:

- **Bridge the gap between theory and practice.** The practical side of teaching should be made apparent so that the student teacher will know what it is like in the classroom.
- **Emphasize that knowledge alone will not guarantee teaching success.** Knowing how to teach is critical, but student teachers must also be able to relate to pupils.
- **Give student teachers experience in determining how they would teach students of various ability, learning style and interest level.**
- **Establish a foundation for growth.** Student teaching is not the end and student teachers should learn where they need to improve.

Quimby further states that new student teachers should have the following materials:

- Faculty handbook
- Student handbook
- School curriculum guide
- Grade book
- Lesson plan book
- Teacher schedule

Cotton (1981) presented advice to cooperating teachers on what and what not to do when a student teacher arrives:

- **Tell the student teacher what you are doing and why.**
- **Provide opportunities for the student teacher to plan lessons with you.** Gradually give the student teacher more responsibility for planning.
- **Observe the student teacher teaching.** Take notes on strong and weak points. Comment on strengths and weaknesses and give alternatives.
- **Listen to your student teacher and allow the student teacher to ask questions of you.**
- **Give your student teacher some ownership in the classroom.** A cooperating teacher can provide such activities as working with a reading group, preparing a bulletin board or taking attendance. Most importantly, the student teacher should have some definite space in the classroom.
- **Acquaint the student teacher with the rules and procedures used in the classroom and school.**
- **Share your personal style.** Inform the student teacher how you do things.
- **Do not undercut the value of a teacher preparation program.** It is not helpful to criticize the program that prepared the student to teach.
- **Do not compare one student teacher with another.**
- **Do not ask the student teacher to grade all papers.**

The change in environment encompasses the totality of the classroom. Be prepared to modify the way things are done. The investment now will pay dividends later and should not compromise the quality of your students' education.

Introducing The Student Teacher To The Class
Helping Strangers Meet New Friends

An introduction of a student teacher does more than present a name to a group of pupils or give the student teacher a chance to offer greetings to a sea of faces. It is a process of communicating feelings and ascribing status. This may be the most obvious clue for the pupils in perceiving their teacher's attitude toward this beginner. Certain words in the introduction can reveal what the cooperating teacher actually thinks of the student teacher. Select them carefully.

The introduction often is the activity that defines the roles of student teacher, cooperating teacher, and pupils. Since it may affect relationships during the entire student teaching sequence, it should be carefully planned. These considerations are worthy of emphasis in designing an effective introduction:

- **Welcome the student teacher.** Show sincerity and delight at having this person as part of the class. Use personal expressions to show a feeling of acceptance. Ask pupils to share in the greeting.
- **Recognize the competency of a student teacher.** Specify major areas of study and describe any unique experiences, special skills or achievements that she has.
- **Introduce the student as a teacher.** This will ascribe status and authority.
- **Indicate confidence in the student teacher.** Project the feeling that the classroom will be improved because of this new person's presence. Indicate some projects or learning activities that are possible now that you have extra help.
- **Make the introduction open-ended.** Give the student teacher an opportunity to speak to the class.
- **Allow time for the students to ask the student teacher questions.**

The student teacher should be introduced to the class in a way that gives status and conveys a feeling of acceptance. It may be a formal introduction or a more personal presentation, but it should contain appropriate elements of the above criteria. In either event, the student teacher should not simply enter the classroom and begin to teach. A good introduction will help to establish the person as a teacher in the class.

Case Study No. 5: A Timid Response

Kim has been timid in her interaction with you. She has answered questions quickly and looks away while talking. She indicated that she did not really want to give a response when you introduce her to the class, but you felt that an acknowledgment from her was necessary. After you introduce her, she mumbles a few words and sits down quickly. The students appear to be surprised and look at each other. Then they look at you. What do you do?

1. Continue as if the response were expected.
2. Attempt to involve her in conversation with you and the class.
3. Mention a specific topic that she is familiar with and ask her to talk about it.
4. Arrange for Kim to work with a small group of students as soon as possible.
5. _____

Comment

Probably everyone in the room, including Kim, will be wondering about the cooperating teacher's reaction. The teacher's next moves may determine the pattern of future reactions. In most situations the student teacher would be best supported by a teacher's acting as if the response were typical. However, this does not relieve the cooperating teacher of the responsibility of working to help this insecure person to relax in subsequent situations of this kind. Role playing or rehearsing the introduction ahead of time might have reduced Kim's anxiety in this situation.

Questions

1. Would a perceptive teacher have known that this situation was likely to have occurred?
2. What principles concerning an introduction should take priority in this case?

Case Study No. 6: A New Agenda

Your student teacher is confident and has her own agenda which reflects what she learned at the university. Although you and she had discussed some new ideas, you were surprised when she responded to your introduction by giving a long list of activities that are different from the present class routine. She tells them that discipline will be more strict and she continues by giving an outline of a grading system that is rather formidable and different from your procedure. She is in front of the class and you are in the back of the room. The students are going to be looking for your reaction. What kind of response will you make?

1. Ignore it for the present assuming the students will forget what was said and then discuss the matter with the student teacher before she assumes responsibility for teaching the class.

2. At the next opportunity, explain to the class that these were preliminary ideas and that some adjustment will be made.
3. Support the student teacher and observe what happens, assuming that both of you may learn something.
4. Under some pretense, change the student teacher's schedule so that she will not be working with that group.
5. _____

Comment

You may have just witnessed the more contemporary thinking of today's college students. The aggressive behavior might imply that the student teacher feels her rights and ideas come first. It also could reflect some insecurity on the part of the student teacher in that she fails to check with you and presents an agenda that would imply an effort to control the situation.

Questions

1. How could an introduction have prevented this kind of response from happening?
2. How does a supervisor respond to a more self-centered approach?

Introducing The Student Teacher To The Faculty
Meeting the Members of the Club

Interaction with the faculty can be as much a growth experience as many other activities during student teaching because relationships with other teachers help formulate professional behavior. Student teachers' previous contacts with teachers have been mostly as students; now they are associates. It may be a surprise when they find that most teachers are friendly and sincere and even possess human weaknesses. There is much to be learned about teaching through association with colleagues.

The encouragement and assistance of teachers in the school can be very helpful to a beginner. Teachers can provide instructional ideas for the student teacher. Some faculty members may have a special interest in the student. This would be particularly likely among those who graduated from the same university and those who teach the same grade levels or subject areas. A student teacher may be sought out to contribute knowledge and ideas to the instructional staff. Many teachers play a direct part in learning by allowing student teachers to observe them teach (See Chapter Five).

The introduction to the faculty should be made in a manner that provides recognition and acceptance of the student teacher. The following procedures may be of value in acquainting the student teacher with the teaching staff:

- **Make it known that a student teacher is coming to work with you.** The official school announcement or school newspaper can list the names and arrival dates of student teachers. The impending arrival of a student teacher can be mentioned in casual conversation with teachers as well.
- **Introduce the student teacher to the faculty.** If a faculty meeting is scheduled during the early days, this would be an appropriate time. Informal occasions where student teachers can meet the staff provide situations for closer personal contact.
- **Arrange for the student teacher to eat lunch with you and a small group of colleagues.**
- **Make comments that will help a student teacher know and remember a teacher.** For example, indicate a faculty member's responsibilities and make comments that will serve as cues in recalling that person.
- **Arrange a time to be spent with other teachers without your presence.**

Case Study No. 7: Still A Student

Your student teacher is a graduate of the school where you are teaching. During her initial visit, she explains that she is pleased to be back in her home school. She spends a considerable amount of time renewing acquaintances with former teachers and administrators. A few weeks into her experience, she approaches you with the observation that teachers in the school are not treating her as a colleague. She fears that her former role as a student in the high school has influenced their vision of her. What action should you take?

1. Tell your student teacher not to be concerned. The faculty will accept her new role eventually.
2. Explain that this is an inevitable consequence of a student teaching assignment in a school where she was a student.
3. Make sure that you have included her in faculty meetings, extracurricular supervisory responsibilities, and other activities that will allow teachers and administrators to see the student teacher in her new role.

4. Observe the student teacher's interactions with the faculty to discern if she is unknowingly contributing to their inability to perceive her as a colleague.

5. _____

Comment

Student teachers have the daunting task of formulating appropriate relationships with both students and adults in their educational environment. Often, the student teacher may be much closer in age to her charges, and, after sixteen years of schooling, she may have nearly perfected the role of student. Faculty members may not be the only ones having difficulty envisioning the student teacher as a colleague. The student teacher herself may not feel comfortable in the multiple roles often assumed by the classroom teacher. The cooperating teacher may facilitate the transition for both the student teacher and her colleagues by treating the student teacher as a valued member of the school's educational community. This can be accomplished by including her in the everyday activities of the classroom teacher, and in return, expecting mature behavior from the student teacher.

Questions

1. What specific actions might the cooperating teacher take during the student teacher's practicum to help her adjust to her new role?
2. What can you do to aid her in developing collegial relationships?
3. Should universities refuse to place student teachers in the schools from which they graduated?

Introducing The Student Teacher To Teaching
Cautiously Into the Classroom

The student teacher's initiation into the classroom is critical. The first few days can easily become boring and anxiety-producing for the student teacher, and these feelings may remain until she is convinced that she has been accepted and is working as a teacher.

Boredom can result from inactivity. Most student teachers have been active in college and teacher preparation programs require scores of hours of observation and participation in classrooms prior to student teaching. Most student teachers are ready to assume an active role early in their experience. A well-intentioned cooperating teacher can contribute to boredom by falsely assuming that a *actively involved play time*

student teacher should observe a while before any kind of classroom responsibility is given. A student teacher may lose interest in a matter of hours if there is nothing to do that seems to be of significance.

Anxiety can also result from inactivity. Tension will likely increase unless there is some opportunity for participation. The longer a person waits to become involved, the greater the likelihood that behaviors will result which are not growth producing. The best antidote for boredom and anxiety is meaningful activity.

The Initial Days

The first day of student teaching is not too early for the student teacher to be involved in classroom participation, however responsibilities should make a contribution to the class. There are many worthwhile teaching activities that can be performed without extensive preparation or orientation. Some of the more common early activities include:

- Carrying out brief teaching activities.
- Distributing and collecting papers.
- Checking attendance.
- Supervising study periods.
- Supervising a recess period.
- Administering tests and quizzes.
- Helping pupils with computer activity.
- Assisting with laboratory project work.
- Working with individuals or small groups. *help me*
- Operating equipment.
- Assisting the teacher with demonstrations.
- Explaining a specific procedure or technique.
- Planning and creating a display or bulletin board. — *artact* .

A student teacher will find it advantageous to be seated at a place in the room where eye contact can be made with all pupils. This helps to establish the feeling that a teacher, rather than a visitor, is in the room. It increases awareness of classroom dynamics and will facilitate learning the names of the pupils. A teacher is more likely to seek the assistance of a nearby student teacher in minor but necessary teaching tasks such as writing on the chalkboard or distributing papers. In effect, the student teacher becomes a second teacher in the room with correct positioning in the classroom.

The student teacher will be formulating impressions about the nature of the class during these first few days. She will observe the supervisor's procedures and probably start to develop her own style.

The student teacher will respond favorably to the supervisor's taking time to explain her actions or to analyze the results of a particular activity.

A suitable teaching schedule should be determined early. It will be helpful for the student teacher to know what has been taught previously, what is to be taught during the weeks of student teaching, and what the expected learning outcomes will be after the experience is over. Student teachers should know what resources will be available to them and how they may be secured. Obviously some early conferences on this topic are required.

There are many activities that must be completed by the cooperating teacher in the initial days. Some teachers feel a need to know what should be done and what has been done. Worksheet Number Two in the Appendix provides a checklist that can be used either for preparing for the initial days or for reviewing the adequacy of the orientation program.

Case Study No. 8: Getting Started

It is not an easy task to orient a new student teacher while continuing with the responsibilities of teaching a class. Since it was your student teacher's first day, you decided that she could best learn by watching you. In the brief moments you had, you showed her your lesson plan and gave her a few materials to look at that you would be using throughout the day. At first she seemed interested but before the noon break she showed obvious signs of distraction and boredom. You have no time to spend with her and have no idea of what you could do to get her more interested. What can you do to get her more involved?

1. Explain that it is normal for students to "watch and learn" at first.
2. Try to draw her into the classroom discussion.
3. Suggest that she might work individually with students.
4. Quietly ask her to move to another position in the classroom where she can see the students better.
5. At the first opportunity, explain what you are doing and ask her to look for indicators which will give you feedback.
6. _____

Comment

This vignette shows symptoms of a lack of preparation for the first day on the part of the cooperating teacher and the student teacher. An unstructured situation usually results in little or no growth. The student teacher probably would be willing to be more active if she knew what she could do. The situation also presents the complexity of having to integrate another person into classroom routine. The best solution is to have some sort of scheme in mind that will involve the student teacher. A detailed discussion concerning roles and expectations would go a long way toward averting such unfortunate situations.

Questions

1. What kinds of procedures can be used to involve a new person into meaningful participation in a class?
2. What are the priorities that a supervisor might determine at this point?

Case Study No. 9: An Eager Beginner

Cindy is enthusiastic. She says that she is excited about student teaching and wants to begin immediately. She asks if she can start by teaching her full load of assigned classes so that she will get as much experience as possible. You have serious reservations, but she is persistent. You do not want to crush her enthusiasm but your understanding of the first few days of student teaching is that there should be a more gradual induction process. You still have materials that you want to give and to discuss with her and you had planned to model some teaching strategies for her to observe.

You are in a dilemma about whether to honor her request or to stay with your original plan and have her assume teaching responsibilities gradually. What action do you take?

1. Grant her wishes and observe the results.
2. Propose that she begin with smaller amounts of activity and let her assume additional tasks as she demonstrates readiness.
3. Indicate that you want to share more materials with her and model some teaching strategies.
4. Refuse her request on the basis that your understanding of university policy is that this should not occur.
5. _____

Comment

One of the mistakes cooperating teachers commonly make is to wait too long before permitting a student teacher to become involved in teaching. But the problem which can be nearly as unfortunate is to give too much teaching responsibility too early.   Careful collaboration with the college supervisor and the student teacher should allow the cooperating teacher to find the appropriate balance. It is unlikely that a student teacher's enthusiasm will be dealt a permanent blow if she teaches less than she wants during the first few days.

Questions

1. How can one distinguish between enthusiasm alone and enthusiasm based on the ability to do the job?
2. What are some alternative ways of getting a student teacher involved in meaningful activity?
3. How can one channel exuberance and idealism without breaking spirit or stifling motivation?

Assuming Increased Responsibility

Cooperative teaching is one of the key methods for a student teacher to assume responsibility quickly without being held responsible. This arrangement allows both the cooperating teacher and the student teacher to share in guiding pupil learning. Pupils can observe that the cooperating teacher and the student teacher are co-workers. Several types of joint activities can be selected which will achieve such a goal with little advance organization or planning. The following have been practiced by successful supervisors:

1. **Cooperative planning.** A teacher may wish to elicit ideas from the student teacher. Another procedure would be for each to develop plans independently and then compare them.
2. **Team teaching.** There are several models that could be effective for initiating a student teacher. The class can be split with each teacher instructing a different group or the two can share an activity with the whole class. One teacher can teach while the other one assists. In the case of a cooperating teacher and student teacher, a cooperating teacher could begin with major responsibility and the roles could gradually reverse so that the student teacher assumes the major instructional role and the cooperating teacher assists.
3. **Share responsibilities.** A student teacher could assume responsibility for such things as keeping attendance records or other reports. Student supervision could be shared also.

The cooperating teacher can assign tasks that illustrate confidence in the student teacher. It can be an incentive for a student teacher when he is asked to work with pupils who need assistance or to perform tasks that demand special skills. Deborah Walker(1999) identified specific "Roles and Goals" that student teachers can realize early on in their experience:

- **Clarifier** - Restates ideas or directions to students who have difficulty staying focused.
- **Progress Coach** - Helps students master content by giving feedback concerning individual progress during lessons.
- **Individual Motivator** - Encourages students to maintain a positive attitude and to participate in class activity.
- **Taskmaster** - Continually monitors and keeps students on task and uses positive statements to re-focus student behavior.
- **Individual Facilitator** - Directs and guides an individual student throughout an entire activity.
- **Small Group Monitor** - Stays within close proximity of a group, observing and recording behavior that can be given as feedback to the lead teacher.
- **Small Group Facilitator** - Directs and guides group activities such as providing the group with materials, equalizing participation, clarifying directions, re-teaching skills or providing feedback.
- **Large Group Facilitator** - The class is divided into two groups following a lesson, and the student teacher acts as the facilitator of one group.

The student teacher can often be used as a resource person. The supervisor might rely on the student teacher's recent knowledge or special expertise and ask her to present a new idea or concept to the class.

Responsibilities should be challenging to the student teacher. Menial tasks may be interpreted as lack of faith in the person's ability which could affect self-concept and enthusiasm for performing more important tasks. Although routine tasks are a part of teaching, a student should be challenged with more demanding and more exciting teaching activities just as soon as possible.

A quick survey of the student teacher's activities gives an appraisal of progress toward initial adjustment to this new life. If the right proportion of responsibilities has been assigned, within the first two weeks a student teacher should:

- Be independent in moving about the school.
- Know the names of pupils.
- Have some professional knowledge about the pupils.
- Be able to make plans without the cooperating teacher's direct supervision.
- Have taken some responsibility for teaching an entire class.

- Have met a number of other teachers and feel comfortable with them.
- Have observed teachers including those in other grade levels or subjects.
- Have enough confidence to make minor teaching decisions independent of the cooperating teacher.
- Contribute valuable ideas during joint planning sessions.
- Have much to say about her work during supervisory conferences.

It is not unusual for beginning student teachers to report that they are fatigued at the end of the day. The pressure of adjusting to a new and demanding role such as this consumes more energy than one might assume. This situation will likely rectify itself in a few days but it might be well at this time to remind a teaching candidate that teaching can be emotionally draining and physically exhausting. The student teacher should not be overprotected, though, since being tired is a normal part of a teacher's life.

Many cooperating teachers wish to provide concrete requirements for a student teacher in order to insure that certain activities have been completed. Worksheet Number Three in the Appendix is an adaptation of one such list which was developed by a cooperating teacher. It may serve as a point of departure for the teacher who wants to develop a statement of requirements and suggestions.

Case Study No 10: Am I Qualified For This?

You have kept up with the latest advancements in technology and incorporate many sophisticated ideas into your teaching. Your students regularly use the Internet to research questions, scan data and photographs to supplement their own work, communicate with peers and experts from all over the world, and commonly create computer-generated presentations. Some students even keep a record of their work by constructing an electronic portfolio. When your student teacher observed your students at work and you further explained that you used differentiation of instruction and alternative assessment techniques, he seemed concerned. He remarked that he had been taught by traditional methods and was not familiar with many of the things that you were doing. He wondered aloud whether he was qualified to work in your classroom. How do you react to this?

1. Explain that he can use procedures that make him comfortable.

2. Provide him with learning materials and experiences that will enable him to work comfortably in this environment.
3. Promise to work with him jointly until he becomes comfortable with the technology.
4. _____

Comment

Innovative schools may be ahead of universities in newer teaching methods and technology. This is particularly true with secondary student teachers who may have been taught mostly by academic professors and who plan to imitate their styles. Johnson and Landers-Macrine (1998) stated that student teachers often will revert to methods and strategies they experienced as students, especially when they are faced with a classroom situation for which they are inadequately prepared. Student teachers may employ a traditional delivery system because this is all that they have seen or because they are impressed with one or two professors. The critical task is to see that the student teacher understands and wants to use some of the newer approaches.

Questions

1. What kind of rationale can you give to justify the integration of technology into the curriculum and for using newer approaches to teaching?
2. What would be a good way to help a beginning student teacher acquire some of these skills?

Case Study No. 11: An Impatient Student Teacher

After two weeks in the field, your student teacher expressed surprise at how little the pupils know and care. Her impatience shows frequently and she has commented to you that she cannot understand why they are not more attentive. The major problem is that she is not using appropriate techniques for the age level of her students. What can be done to help her reverse her feelings and to use more effective methods?

1. Plan a few lessons together.
2. Video tape a class and ask her to evaluate her performance.
3. Teach a demonstration lesson that would model the difficulties that she is experiencing.
4. Confer with her and analyze the appropriateness of her procedures in meeting the objectives she is trying to achieve.

5. Ask the student teacher to assess the level of active involvement her lessons require of her pupils.
6. _____

Comment

The fact that the student teacher is concerned about pupils not being as attentive as she would like may indicate there is much direct instruction and teacher-centered activity going on in the class. It has been said that education is not a spectator sport. The pupils' lack of attention could be attributed to little active involvement in the learning process. One of the most challenging tasks a student teacher has to meet is that of appropriately engaging the pupils and adjusting to their level of comprehension. A cooperating teacher should see that the student teacher makes adjustments that will help her to better communicate with pupils. This requires giving early attention to the problem.

Questions

1. What is the best way to expose a student teacher to a variety of good techniques?
2. What procedures are helpful in assisting student teachers to understand the attention spans and ability levels of their pupils?

Ten school days have passed. Brian Sims turns to his computer to enter the required portfolio data and begins a summary of his first days as a student teacher.

"I feel a little tired right now. I do not think that I have worked so hard or been under as much mental strain in my life. This has been a hectic period, but it has been most beneficial.

"My cooperating teacher is thoughtful and helpful. She has let me grade papers and kept me informed about all that was happening in the class. After each class she will answer my questions and we talk about everything that seemed significant.

"When I was introduced to the class, I spent the first few minutes telling the students about myself. In a few days I had assumed responsibility for teaching one group. I was surprised at myself the first day I taught. I was uneasy, but not like I thought I would be. As a matter of fact, I do not think I outwardly appeared to be tense. Miss Bennett seems to have confidence in me, and this gives me more assurance.

"I find that I am busy most of the time. When I am not teaching I am usually talking with my supervisor or planning. I take work home

most every evening. I have been to a faculty meeting, teachers' association meeting, and two sporting events. No time to get bored."

Remember:

- **The student teacher must be approached with trust and confidence.**
- **Emphasis should be placed on a team concept where two teachers work together.**
- **The student teacher should become involved in activities early.**
- **The most effective way of reducing student teacher anxiety is to provide teaching experience.**
- **The early resolution of small problems may prevent more complex ones later.**
- **A student teacher should be allowed to assume teaching responsibilities gradually.**
- **Every student teacher will be different.**
- **The student teacher should be viewed as an asset and as an additional resource.**

Useful References

Balch, Pamela M., and Patrick E. Balch. 1987. Preparing for and Surviving the First Day. Chapter 4 in *The Cooperating Teacher: A Practical Approach for the Supervision of Student Teachers*. Lanham, MD. The University Press of America, Inc.

Burstein, Nancy Davis. 1992. The Transition into Teaching and Supervision of Student Teachers: Implications for Enhancing Student Teaching Experiences. *Teacher Education Quarterly* 19 (Fall): 5-18.

Cole, Andra L., and J. Gary Knowles. 1993. Shattered Images: Understanding Expectations and Realities of Field Experiences. *Teaching and Teacher Education* 9 (Oct-Dec):457-471.

Cotton, Eileen G. 1981. A Student Teacher! What Do I Do Now? *Kappa Delta Pi Record* 13 (April): 100-01,120.

Fuller, F. F., G. H. Pilgrim, and A, M. Freeland. 1967. *Intensive Individualization of Teacher Preparation in Mental Health and Teacher Education*. pp. 151-187. Dubuque, IA. Wm. C. Brown.

Johnson, Virginia G. and Sheila Landers-Macrine. 1998. Student Teachers Explain Changes in Their Thinking. *The Teacher Educator* 31 (Summer): 30-40.

Kagan, D. M.1992. Professional Growth Among Preservice and Beginning Teachers. *Review of Educational Research* 62 (Summer): 129-169.

Koerner, M. E. (1992). The Cooperating Teacher: An Ambivalent Participant in Student Teaching. *Journal of Teacher Education* 43 (1) 46-56.

NMSA, 1996. Student Teaching at the Middle Level. *Fax on Demand* 1-888-FAX-NMSA, Westerville, Ohio 43081.

Piland, Diane E., and Jacqueline M. Anglin. 1993. It Is Only a Stage They Are Going Through: The Development of Student Teachers. *Action in Teacher Education* 15 (Fall): 19-26.

Quimby, Donald E. 1985. Student Teaching--A Principal's Perspective. *NASSP Bulletin* 69 (October): 114-18.

Seperson, Marvin A., and Bruce R. Joyce. 1973. Teaching Styles of Student Teachers as Related to Those of Their Cooperating Teachers. *Educational Leadership Research Supplement* 31 (November): 146-151.

Siler, Carl R., and George E. Swafford. 1987. The Student Teacher Awareness Program. *The Teacher Educator* 22 (Spring): 15-21.

Sparks, William G. 1987. The Student Teaching Partnership: Collaboration and Collegiality. Paper presented at the National Convention of the American Alliance for Health, Physical Education, Recreation and Dance, Las Vegas, 13-17 April. ERIC, ED 283 800.

Walker, Deborah, and Joanne Archer (Kent State University). 1999. Side by Side: A True Cooperative Student Teaching Experience. Presentation at the National Middle School Association Annual Conference, October 28 - 30, Orlando, Florida.

3

Personal Relationships In Student Teaching

Brian and Miss Bennett entered the teachers' work room and almost collided with Gordon Rogers, a student teacher from another university. "I've had it," he fumed, as he made a quick exit. "I simply cannot communicate with her."

When they walked in the work room area, they found an exasperated Sally Hawkins, Gordon's cooperating teacher, sitting alone at a table. Miss Bennett made a feeble attempt to ease the tension, but Ms. Hawkins only had the previous confrontation on her mind.

"I am thinking about calling the university and telling them that I can no longer tolerate this disrespectful young man."

"What is the problem, Sally?," inquired Miss Bennett. The response was more than she had anticipated.

"In the first place, he told me that he could be teaching effectively if I had taught the class better before he came. Imagine! This happened when I tried to tell him that the pupils did not understand his language in the new material presented in class today. If I had wanted my teaching criticized, I would have called my supervisor.

"The plans that he does manage to submit consist of a few topic outlines, and he dashes them off after he gets to school in the morning. He tends to confide in a younger teacher instead of trying to talk with me. He just will not listen to me at all. I make suggestions and all he does is argue. This young upstart is not the expert he thinks he is."

Miss Bennett and Brian exchanged glances but said nothing.

Ms Hawkins continued, "Furthermore, he has been acting very immaturely in class and tries to be too friendly with some of the students. His ego seems to exceed his ability. Two teachers have even asked me not to let him observe them any more because of his behavior."

Miss Bennett interrupted, "Have you discussed the problems with him or with his college supervisor?"

Ms Hawkins shook her head. "All our conferences become arguments. Just now I asked him to explain how two activities were related and he said, 'I don't need a cross examination. I'm not stupid,' and stormed out. I thought I would call his supervisor. What would you do?"

"I really don't know," responded Miss Bennett. "Fortunately, Brian and I have been able to communicate well during these first few weeks."

Ms Hawkins looked at her, but said nothing. . .

Effective Personal Relationships
Working Together Effectively

The influence of cooperating teachers on student teachers has always been considered significant. Karmos and Jacko (1977), in a landmark study in teacher education, found that cooperating teachers were far and above the most significant professionals who influenced student teachers. The authors found that the greatest apparent needs of students are for empathy, understanding, and release from the pressures and anxieties presented by student teaching. Student teachers have strong needs for professional guidance as well as emotional support. Cooperating teachers are a major source of this vital feedback. Success in student teaching is contingent upon the relationship between a student teacher and cooperating teacher. A student teacher may possess adequate skills in methodology and be sufficiently knowledgeable in subject matter, but the experience is not a complete success if the relationship with the cooperating teacher is less than desirable. A cooperating teacher must establish a supportive emotional and professional climate.

Williams and Graham (1992) found that there is a relationship between the student teacher's attitudes and the cooperating teacher's personal attributes. The prevailing opinion seems to be the one expressed by Fuller and Brown (1975) and Mahan (1977) who found that student teachers grew more conservative during student teaching. Their progressive thinking generated by preservice training undergoes a reversal beginning with student teaching and continues into the early teaching years. Some believe that the influence of the cooperating teacher is the cause of the reversal. Others feel that the direct influence of the classroom environment and a retreat into a "survival mode" leads to a more conservative stance. On the other hand, Woolley, Woolley, and Hosey (1999), found that most student teachers emerged from their clinical experience with more progressive teaching philosophies than those of their cooperating teacher.

Other researchers have suggested that the findings stated above are too simplistic, although they agree that change takes place and that a cooperating teacher is involved in the process. Tabachnick and Zeichner (1984) suggested that the pairing of student and cooperating teacher is related to student teaching outcomes. Bunting (1988) sought to examine the influence of teachers with differing views on the beliefs of their student teachers. Her findings revealed that many candidates emerged from student teaching with more liberal views and others with less liberal perspectives. She suggested that student teaching worked not to redirect the thinking of candidates, but to expand their perspectives to include a wider diversity of methods and practices. She recognized that the cooperating teacher is a central figure in this process and concluded that teachers who possessed more flexible, adaptable views more often witnessed change. Teachers with more extreme views more often witnessed no change in the views of student teachers assigned to them. Generally, professionals agree that the level of communication and the personal connection established between the student teacher and cooperating teacher is vital to a positive experience.

Positive Traits of Cooperating Teachers

Looper (1999) asked student teachers to list qualities and traits of cooperating teachers that they highly valued. Sixteen items that student teachers wished their cooperating teachers would keep in mind as they work through their practicum experience are listed below:

- Provide encouragement.
- Avoid putting student teachers in difficult situations.
- Provide honest and timely feedback.
- Communicate often and freely.
- Share insights about the students.
- Discuss successful teaching techniques.
- Allow student teachers to experience the excitement of learning as well as the mundane tasks.
- Let student teachers "try their wings".
- Set regular times to conference with student teachers.
- Give suggestions about planning.
- Be as flexible as possible.
- Listen to the student teacher and be as receptive as possible to his ideas and concerns.
- Instruct the student teacher about classroom management.

- Show the student teacher how to organize time and space for effective instruction.
- Share tips for success.
- Be a positive role model for the student teacher.

Other studies of student teacher-cooperating teacher relationships show a similar pattern. Zerr (1988) found that student teachers reported that cooperating teachers provided:

- Help with their relations with students.
- Aid and encouragement with initial planning and teaching.
- Initiation into teaching.
- Help in assuming additional responsibility for class.
- Suggestions for improving plans, sources of materials, etc.
- Guidance with child study, classroom management, and professional growth.

Stahlhut and Hawkes (1990) reported two teacher leadership behaviors which are positively related to student teacher success: (1) behaviors which give a student teacher freedom to make decisions and take action, and (2) behaviors which encourage the student teacher to make contributions to classroom procedures. Finally, Enz and Cook (1991) presented findings of mentoring functions that revealed that critical areas of concern could be subsumed into personal, instructional, and professional. There was agreement between student teachers and cooperating teachers that their relationship should be congenial and collegial.

Sudzina and Coolican (1994) queried student teachers and cooperating teachers about roles of cooperating teachers. Student teachers saw the ideal cooperating teachers as supportive role models. Their biggest fear was that their cooperating teachers would not let them try new ideas or "let go" of the class. They were additionally concerned that their cooperating teachers would not be open and honest or communicate clearly with them. Cooperating teacher responses either saw mentoring student teachers as an enterprise in which student teachers needed "to do more" and follow their lead in the classroom or as a shared enterprise between the cooperating teacher and student teacher. Their preliminary results suggest that cooperating teachers tend to function as advisors to student teachers rather than mentors.

Coolican, Giebelhaus, and Sudzina (1997) later reported a number of stances cooperating teachers could take in regard to hosting a student teacher, some of which were detrimental to professional growth. The authors saw the most productive relationship between the cooperating teacher and the student teacher to be that of a mentor-mentee. Head, Reiman, and Thies-Sprintall (1992), found the genuine mentor-mentee relationship exists when both parties are equally committed to the goals of the enterprise and when the mentor possesses broad career and personal influence over the mentee. Mentoring activities are more valued because mentoring involves support, encouragement and understanding.

Kahn (2001) interviewed cooperating teachers and found that the qualities they possessed that enhanced their supervision were flexibility, ability to establish a good working rapport and positive communication skills. This study, along with the others mentioned, builds a profile of what is considered to be a successful student teacher.

The above studies generally agree with Karmos and Jacko (1977) regarding the importance of the relationship between the student teacher and cooperating teacher. They also reinforce the notion that the student teaching experience is a period of adjustment for both student teachers and cooperating teachers.

Case Study No. 12: Poor Communication

While you and your student teacher seem to be communicating well, another cooperating teacher within your department feels that her student teacher is avoiding sessions that could lead to her growth as a classroom teacher. Your colleague, who is very self-confident and direct, sees no reason why her student teacher should be unwilling to confront her problems. During your discussion, your colleague adds that she gave the student teacher a list of her weaknesses, since the two had not been able to conduct a meaningful dialogue, and that during their lone meeting since that time, the student teacher had been monosyllabic, at best. What advice should you give to the cooperating teacher?

1. Ask the cooperating teacher if the list included the student teacher's strengths, as well as areas targeted for growth.
2. Suggest that the student teacher might respond better to a more empathetic approach.
3. Encourage her to ask for advice from the university supervisor.
4. _____

Comment

Some student teachers, whose self-concept may already be shaky at this pivotal point in their lives may find the blunt criticism of a cooperating teacher to be a shattering experience. Conversation about the student teacher's performance should begin with a "strength analysis" - observations and specific mention of components of sessions that were taught well. Areas of deficiency in the student teacher's performance also need to be addressed but tempered with empathy. Specific examples of both positive behaviors and those which will lead to growth and suggestions for improvement should be arrived at jointly by the cooperating teacher and student teacher. Both must work to develop a bond that will allow for mutual give-and-take dialogues.

Questions

1. What practices of collaborative relations are conducive to solving this type of problem?
2. What are some clues that a cooperating teacher might be treating a student teacher in a manner that causes her to be uncomfortable?
3. How could a mentor role as described in this chapter be helpful?

Creating Positive Relationships

The student teacher is becoming familiar with and adapting to a new environment, testing skills in new activities and examining beliefs about teaching. He is no longer a student but not yet a teacher, and this role confusion can lead to a great deal of uncertainty. It is apparent that pupils' growth and academic achievement are the responsibility of the cooperating teacher who ultimately will need to approve all actions undertaken by the student teacher.

The student teacher's personality may be quite different from that of the cooperating teacher and this may cause a need for adjustment in order for the two to work together effectively. Shaw-Baker (1995) reported a framework that is useful in helping maintain communicative competence with student teachers:

- **Extroversion and Introversion.** Student teachers, as well as cooperating teachers, may be extroverts or introverts. Extroverts are energized by all the events bombarding them throughout the day. In conflict situations, their preference is to talk it out. They have difficulty listening. Introverts are stimulated by their inner thoughts and reflections. They need periods of privacy to reflect upon their thoughts and experiences.
- **Information Gathering.** Some persons are literal in their interpretation of material. They want the facts and are not as concerned about the theory behind them. Student teachers of

this type will see lessons in isolation with little relationship to others before or after. Other individuals are more global in their approach to information. They prefer to see relationships between curricula and lessons. In conflict situations these individuals hear figuratively what the other person's word means or what they think was meant. These individuals see links between cause and effect and can put the symptoms of a problem into the bigger picture.

- **Making Decisions.** Some persons weigh the information and decide upon a plan of action based upon logical, objective consideration. Others make decisions about the information they gather to solve problems by analyzing the situation, considering cause and effect of various actions and then deciding their plan of action based upon their personal, subjective values. They are mediators and conciliators who can usually express the right feeling.
- **Lifestyle.** A fourth difference in the way supervisors and student teachers communicate is their preference for establishing their lifestyle. Some prefer to organize their lives in a planned and orderly manner. Others may prefer a more spontaneous, flexible lifestyle. Although they are more flexible, they have difficulty getting things done on time or seem less organized. In conflict situations, these individuals seek alternatives to the events that caused the conflict.

There are other ways to view how individuals interpret mutual experiences. Anthony Gregorc (1984) described physiological perspectives from which individuals could view identical situations and react to them differently. For example, a teacher who is highly "Abstract- Random" according to Gregorc's Style Delineator, might view a very prescriptive directive from the principal as being too confining and restrictive to her creative teaching style. On the other hand, her colleague, who is highly "Concrete - Sequential," interpreted the same directive as providing needed focus and direction.

Winter (1998) revealed how personal work styles impact the classroom environment. For example, a teacher who is characterized by a high "Dominance - Directness" profile will seek and initiate change while his "Submissive - Steadiness" peer will strive for stability and will hold on to tradition.

Having a student teacher in the room causes some teachers to feel so uncomfortable that it becomes a difficult task to share a class with a student teacher. If a cooperating teacher is aware of the different styles listed above, and realizes that one style is not superior to another, he may be better able to determine the most appropriate type of communication for the experience. Although conditions for tension will likely exist, this very association has the exciting potential for wholesome and enriching contacts between an experienced educator and a teaching candidate.

A cooperating teacher can encourage the development of more positive relationships by:

- Being available.
- Spelling out expectations early.
- Establishing and maintaining communication with the student teacher.
- Giving the student teacher some options and choices.
- Giving the student teacher the opportunity to develop her own style.
- Accepting the student teacher as a colleague.
- Including the student teacher in more than the immediate environment of the classroom.
- Seeking and using the student teacher's ideas whenever possible.
- Demonstrating confidence and trust in the student teacher.

A collaborative approach will make communication about substantive matters much easier and both parties will be more comfortable. This kind of environment obviously is more growth-producing.

Offering Suggestions in a Constructive Climate

Every cooperating teacher eventually will have to give criticism or offer advice to a student teacher. Grossman and Keller (1994) stated that the ability to give meaningful feedback to student teachers is of utmost importance. Many teachers wonder whether a direct approach can lead to a deterioration of relationships so that effective communication becomes more difficult. The research of Seiferth and her colleagues (1984) found that student teachers want and need constant and ongoing feedback given in a tactful and polite way. The findings suggest that cooperating teachers create pitfalls if they fail to offer critiques or feedback and if they do not develop friendly relationships with their student teachers.

Johnson (1977) points out that student teachers do not see the need for comments on things like teaching strategies but rather about themselves as teachers. They are concerned with self-centered questions such as "Who am I? What Do I Do? What Difference Do I Make?" The student teacher can be guided and assisted in identifying and developing desirable personal characteristics such as congruence, self confidence, and empathy. The cooperating teacher should give feedback relative to teacher behaviors central to the act of teaching.

Student teachers are all different and a cooperating teacher must be able to determine the best procedure for relating to each one. Too many directive strategies can lead to unacceptable reactions if the student teacher feels more comfortable with a collaborative or indirect approach. On the other hand, a student teacher who is struggling may appreciate direct behavior in order to have something concrete that can help to solve immediate problems. The alternative of giving no comments is undesirable because it may create greater concern on the part of a student teacher.

There is no single way to create an ideal personal relationship with a student teacher since personalities are involved and a variety of external factors influence the relationship. However, the following alternatives, suggested by Babkie (1998), should be helpful in establishing a trusting and low stress environment:

- Try to eliminate problems before they start.
- Provide specific feedback.
- Have a regular and frequent meeting time.
- Allow the student teacher to make mistakes.
- Support, encourage, and reward a student teacher's progress.
- Accept differences in the student teacher's approach.
- Evaluate yourself as well as the student teacher.

The cooperating teacher must not be too critical. Constant criticism is likely to cause a student teacher to become defensive or withdrawn. During each discussion with the student teacher, focus on professional growth and improvement. Share helpful hints with the student teacher based on your own experience. Give sound educational reasons for your suggestions and decisions. Above all, be a good listener. Personal relationships between a supervisor and a student teacher should focus on establishing a collegial relationship where the student teacher ultimately assumes more and more responsibility for his actions and becomes an effective decision-maker in the classroom.

Intense Personality Differences

A match or mismatch of cooperating teachers and student teachers on personality characteristics may have an important role in the overall effectiveness of the student teaching experience (Hughes, 1982). Among the different personality factors that may affect participant relationships are flexibility, empathy, and self-esteem. A cooperating teacher would be well advised to examine his own personality in relation to these variables and determine whether they may pose barriers to communication with a student teacher.

Differences in personality and style can add some zest and balance to a class, provided that not all energy is put into emphasizing the dissimilarities and conflicts.   Having a student teacher who may not be similar in style and personality with the cooperating teacher may be a way to help reach diverse learners. The cooperating teacher, being more experienced, normally will be the first to recognize the   situation and take the initiative in establishing a constructive emotional climate.

There can be instances where the differences are so extreme that two people become uncomfortable when they have to work with each other. When this happens, it is difficult to be objective because the problem rests with the feelings of the personnel involved. An atmosphere can develop where rigidity predominates, as hinted at in the introductory vignette to this chapter. Some people find certain types of personalities incompatible with their own and they have difficulty establishing effective communication with them. It can become very complicated when two such individuals are assigned to work together as student teacher and supervisor.

A little tension can be constructive provided it is acknowledged and accepted by both parties. There are certain moves that a cooperating teacher can initiate to improve tense situations and create a desirable climate for working together on a long-range basis.

- Recognize and accept the differences without trying to convince the other person that you are right.
- Try to view the variation in style as an asset rather than a liability.
- Attempt alternative methods of communication that will place less emphasis on personality conflict.
- Plan autonomous activities so that both have independent responsibility but the cooperating teacher can still observe performance.
- Arrange for the student teacher to have some time with other teachers with whom he can feel comfortable.

How can a supervisor know when personal relationships with a student teacher reach an acceptable level? Intuition can be deceptive and student teachers may conceal their true feelings. In order to provide some criteria for more objective self-analysis, Worksheet Number Four was devised and appended in this book. Supervisors who are interested in criteria for self-evaluation may wish to study it and adapt it for their use.

Case Study No. 13: Not Enough Room

The walls of the classroom seem to close in on you now that you have a student teacher. Since you are accustomed to working alone in a classroom, your student teacher is proving to be a distraction and this is leading to some frustration. She seems not to have anywhere to go in the room except close to you and you constantly feel compelled to explain what you are doing. You are not certain that she is as sensitive to these concerns as you, but you want to make some changes in order to feel more comfortable and to be able to communicate with her more effectively. What do you do?

1. Have a conversation with her and disclose your feelings.
2. Find some alternative activities that will give you more opportunity to follow your normal routine.
3. Plan to be out of the room more so that she can work with the class and you can have some time alone.
4. Find work space for her in the room that gives her ownership.
5. Examine your own views about collegiality.
6. _____

Comment

It might be well to do some searching to determine the basis of the frustration. Is it a reluctance to share a class with another person? Is it an irritation in dealing with a different type of personality? Is the difficulty caused by the fact that the student teacher seems to be needing more of your time? Once a teacher determines the basic problem, an acceptable alternative will be easier to select.

Questions

1. What practices of collaborative relationships are conducive to solving a problem of this type?
2. What should be the priorities in determining a method to reduce the tense feelings that the cooperating teacher is feeling?

Case Study No. 14: He Is Ruining My Students

Jan Smith has a reputation of being an excellent teacher. Last year she was recognized as "Teacher of the Year" in her district. Miss Smith is highly motivated and has extremely high expectations for herself and her students. She is often found working in her classroom early in the morning and well into the evening. Her lessons are fast paced, rigorous, and conducted in a business-like manner. She closely aligns her lessons to the district's curriculum guide which reflects the state-wide standards. Jan's relationship with her students is cordial and caring yet formal. Miss Smith has supervised student teachers before but has never found it to be a rewarding experience.

Bill Wilson, a non-traditional student teacher and father of two small children, has been assigned to Miss Smith's classroom. Bill's "laid back" manner is in direct contrast with Jan's teaching style. Bill does much of his planning and preparation at home as his family obligations prevent him from spending a lot of extended time at school. Bill's lessons are paced to ensure that no students are left behind and he gives very little homework. Students have a lot of latitude in deciding what topics they study and how they will be investigated.

Parents begin to complain. They are concerned about their children not bringing work home and the lack of material being covered by "Mr. Bill". Parents worry that their children will not be prepared for the state-wide competency tests that are scheduled for later in the year. How would you respond to this situation if your confronted by it?

1. Resume control of the class and ask the student teacher to observe and note the differences in technique.
2. Use the student teacher more as an additional teacher who can increase student learning.
3. Discuss the situation with him and present a list of specific improvements that need to be made.
4. Conduct regular informal assessments to ensure that students are learning important concepts.
5. _____

Comment

Student teachers often feel insecure when working in the presence of a veteran educator. This can be complicated when working in the shadow of a teacher who has been recognized for excellence. This problem can be minimized by the cooperating teacher recognizing that her unique approach is not the only way to be a successful and competent teacher. Yet the academic success of the pupils is the responsibility of the cooperating teacher. Therefore, she must ensure that strategies employed by the student teacher are effective.

Questions

1. Do complaints from parents necessarily indicate that there is a problem with the techniques employed by the student teacher?
2. What unique difficulties exist for a student teacher who is working with an exemplary instructor?

Case Study No. 15: Close Identification With Another Teacher

Your student teacher had appeared uncomfortable with you from the beginning, but he did develop a close relationship with one of the young teachers in the building. They have a lot in common and you are aware that he is avoiding you in order to be with the other teacher. There is also evidence that he has been talking with the other teacher about his problems. Since you feel that you need to develop closer communication with him, what course of action do you pursue?

1. Share your thoughts and feelings with the student teacher.
2. Arrange for specific times when the two of you can be together.
3. Ignore the situation.
4. Talk to the other teacher and express your concerns.
5. _____

Comment

There may be several reasons for the student teacher to be associating with another teacher, but it would appear that he is uncomfortable with the cooperating teacher. The younger teacher is more likely to share his interests, accept his values, and be less critical because he does not have to accept the responsibility for the student teacher's progress.

Questions

1. What are some other clues that a cooperating teacher might be treating a student teacher in a manner that causes him to be uncomfortable?
2. What could be done to ensure that the student teacher gets the support he needs?

Personal Adjustment
Up One Day: Down the Next

It is assumed that teachers' self-perceptions constitute an important variable in determining the nature of the teacher-pupil interaction. Manning and Payne (1984) found a number of personality descriptors that related to success in teaching. If teachers were rated as excellent, they perceived themselves more positively, e.g., achievement oriented, self-reliant, and comfortable. If they were rated as poor, they perceived themselves more negatively, e.g., fearful, inadequate, and dull. The excellent-rated group perceived themselves to be stronger and more assertive.

Knight and Rikard (1997) discovered that student teachers who had the ability to control constraints in their clinical experience had a heightened self-image. Such constraints included the ability to establish effective management systems, to develop good rapport with supervisors, and to "fit in" with other teachers in the building. Susan Harter (1990), found that the ability to develop competency in domains deemed important to the individual greatly impacts one's self-esteem. These studies affirm the notion that the ability to develop self-efficacy and be successful in student teaching strongly impacts the self-esteem of student teachers.

Student teaching can be anxiety producing when feelings of self-adequacy and security are threatened. Discussions with student teachers often reveal that they are concerned about issues such as the physical and emotional stamina required by teachers, the ability to answer all of their pupils' questions, the fear of failure, and not knowing how to handle unruly students. Even more mature non-traditional students often share many of the apprehensions of their younger peers. However, Butler (1998), found that non-traditional student teachers did find it less difficult to forge quality interpersonal relationships with their cooperating teachers and other professionals in the building.

The criterion of success frequently used by student teachers is the amount of personal satisfaction the experience provides rather than the achievement of instructional objectives. The nature of the relationship between cooperating teacher and student teacher has a direct bearing on the realization of that goal. If the student teacher is forced to expend energy maintaining, improving, or clarifying this relationship, there may be little enthusiasm or energy left for the larger task of teaching.

Self-concept is undoubtedly affected by the importance which is placed on success in student teaching. It may be complicated by the fact that student teaching is a new experience which calls for a series of adjustments. This newness can initiate an emotional cycle that runs from elation to dejection. This innovation cycle seems to be typical of any new experience and involves different reactions at various stages in the period of student teaching. A typical ten-week student teaching experience as described in the following graph may produce emotions ranging from enthusiasm to depression.

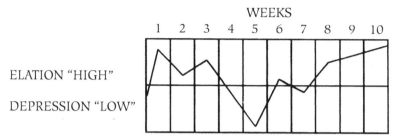

WEEKS

1   2   3   4   5   6   7   8   9   10

ELATION "HIGH"

DEPRESSION "LOW"

The student will most likely enter the experience with some feelings of insecurity and fear. These initial concerns are soon overcome as he is welcomed by the staff and finds that the pupils are more cordial than anticipated. The first peak of enthusiasm may be reached after only a few days as a student teacher. Typically a rather sharp emotional decline will occur around the fourth or fifth week. This may be caused by such factors as an altercation with a pupil, poor scores on the first test which the student teacher developed and administered, or a criticism by the cooperating teacher or university supervisor. There will then be a gradual building of confidence and satisfaction up to the end. The peak of enthusiasm may be partially caused by the anticipation of the conclusion of the experience.

Cooperating teachers frequently observe changes in feelings that result from some personal situation or from a recent experience. The above illustration may explain why. The cooperating teacher is in a position to modify behavior if there is an awareness of the student teacher's emotions. If a cooperating teacher is aware that elation and dejection are normal phenomena, he can better help the student teacher cope with such feelings.

Many worries are eliminated or diminished through student teaching and the cooperating teacher must be prepared to assist the student teacher in the process. It is important for the cooperating teacher to recognize that new surroundings are creating new problems and restructuring old ones.

Case Study No. 16: A Change In Personality

Your student teacher has had excellent rapport with his pupils and has adapted well to the added responsibilities of this new experience. During the fourth week, however, he starts to show personality changes. He has started yelling at pupils when something does not go exactly as planned or for such minor things as unconsciously shuffling papers. Your student teacher's responses to your questions about class presentations, unlike previous responses, are curt and disconnected. His personality seems to be completely different. What do you do to get him back on the right track?

1. Take no immediate action and hope that the behavior will disappear as quickly as it appeared.
2. Attempt to establish good communication once again by being a more empathetic supervisor.
3. Confront the student teacher about his change of behavior.
4. Observe the student teacher more closely for a few days and look for clues that might explain his actions.
5. _____

Comment

This vignette illustrates the classic profile of a student teacher experiencing frustration after a few weeks of student teaching. The obvious task is to determine the cause of the problem and then help the student teacher deal with it. The personality of the student teacher will have considerable influence on the technique used, but the establishment of empathy is likely the most reasonable alternative.

Questions

1. What factors in your classroom might prompt a student teacher to become frustrated?
2. How do you cope when you become frustrated with situations in your school or classroom?

Case Study No. 17: Too Well Adjusted

You have put much effort into making Jessica's student teaching experience happy and successful and you apparently succeeded too well. She has had no real difficulties and she is convinced that everything about teaching is marvelous. She is really anticipating next year and you have reason to believe that she thinks that it will be as simple and exciting as student teaching. At this point you begin to wonder if you have protected her to the point that you have been unfair to her. What course of action do you take now?

1. Do nothing, assuming that her enthusiasm and positive attitude will prevail over future adverse circumstances.
2. Arrange for some experiences that will confront her with some of the typical problems of teaching.
3. Arrange for her to observe some troublesome classes in the school.
4. Arrange for her to talk with or observe some first-year teachers.
5. _____

Comment

The student teacher has somehow managed to avoid any problems. This could indicate that she has a strong self-concept and can meet the challenges that confront her. It also could indicate that she has been protected or "riding the coat tails" of her cooperating teacher. Since problems are often the grist that produces growth, it would appear that the student teacher should be involved in a broader segment of the educational program.

Questions

1. What kinds of problems present the best learning opportunities?
2. Can student teaching realistically prepare a person for all the problems of teaching?

Personal Relationships With Pupils
The View From the Other Side of the Desk

The traditional undergraduate student teacher may find the transition from student to teacher to be complicated. Socially, a traditional student teacher may be only a few days away from college life. He may appear at the school looking like a teacher, but this appearance does not guarantee maturity. Initially, he is merely a college student who is dressed up, painfully aware that some of the pupils are not much younger than he, particularly if he is student teaching at the secondary level. But student teachers of all ages and maturity levels typically have some difficulty finding their identity during student teaching. The problem may be compounded by an unclear perception of the student teacher's role. The pupils may call him a teacher, the university personnel regard him as a student, and the cooperating teacher may consider him to be a teacher one moment and a student the next.

According to Bray (1995), there has been a marked increase in the number of non-traditional students (people over 25 years of age or who have changed careers) who have entered teacher education programs.   For the non-traditional students, moving into the classroom setting as a teacher may be a bit easier than for their younger colleagues.

The problem of adjusting to students can present a real dilemma for the inexperienced student teacher. Motivated by the desire to be accepted but admonished to get the respect of pupils, the student teacher may vacillate from one position to the other or waver just enough to be inconsistent. Perhaps the greatest error is in trying to role play a different personality. So the best advice to a student teacher in this area is to "be yourself".

Abebe and Shaughnessy (1997) found that dealing with disruptive and unmotivated pupils was near the top of the list of stress-producing factors that confronted student teachers.   Their survey found that student teachers desired more input into the suspension of incorrigible pupils and concluded that they needed better preparation for managing unmotivated and disruptive pupils. The reality of the classroom often causes student teachers to be more willing to use stronger methods of discipline than they had envisioned.   Classroom control usually is more difficult than anticipated. Abstract discussions about classroom discipline do not seem to prepare prospective teachers for the realities of teaching and controlling pupil behavior.

In order to cope with anxiety and to be effective in discipline, a student teacher may make decisions based on the need to survive rather than on concerns for producing student learning. In an attempt to become established, a student teacher may concentrate so much on safe subject matter and traditional instructional techniques that he becomes oblivious to students. If this occurs initially, the pupils may respond negatively and complain about dull classes. Very little will happen in the classroom until the student teacher makes some gesture that indicates a genuine concern for pupils.

Canter (1996) suggested developing a positive rapport with students while simultaneously creating a discipline plan. Seeking student input about issues that need to be incorporated into a discipline plan and then using appropriate suggestions is one way that student teachers can accomplish the task described by Canter.

The student teacher also may be tempted to assume a role which has been found to be effective in achieving acceptance in other situations. This is usually a predicament involving peer acceptance in which there is a completely different relationship than is appropriate in student teaching. The social techniques that have worked in college are often the ones that will cause problems with pupils. The result may be that there is a breakdown in respect for the student teacher as an adult. Often an intense desire to be accepted causes rejection.

As the student teacher becomes less idealistic in discipline, he may attempt the hard line approach, setting rules and suspending privileges when the rules are broken. Theoretically standards are relaxed when control is working and a more desirable relationship develops. Unfortunately this may never happen because the student teacher may be too insecure or fail to be convincing, resulting in a web of unrealistic demands and rules that cannot be enforced. This increases the frustration of both the student teacher and the pupils.

The task of the cooperating teacher is to help the student teacher develop a more comprehensive outlook in the area of pupil-teacher relationships in the school environment. The following procedures are worthy of consideration in assisting a student teacher:

- Arrange for the student teacher to assume total responsibility gradually.
- Try to identify any unusual behavioral patterns and counsel with the student teacher before any unfortunate moves are made.
- Caution the student teacher not to make threats or disciplinary sanctions that cannot be carried out.
- Point out that pupils want their teacher to act like an adult.
- Stress that genuine respect from a class is achieved from such factors as enthusiasm, respect for people, listening to their concerns, and designing interesting class sessions.
- Explain that respect takes time to earn but can be destroyed in an instant.
- Help the student teacher understand pupils and their life styles.
- Arrange case studies of two or three of the unique students in the class.
- Suggest some professional readings concerning establishing positive student-teacher relationships.

Out-of-class contacts can present difficulties. For example, a beginning student teacher may wonder if discipline will deteriorate by speaking to pupils when they meet in informal settings. Male student teachers in high schools may receive attention from teen-age girls and be tempted to see them socially. An insecure or immature student teacher may gravitate to the company of pupils, avoiding more uncomfortable contacts with teachers.

At times, a student teacher may become the target of a romantic gesture from a pupil in his charge through a number of innocent-appearing activities. An amorous relationship between a student teacher and pupil would be unprofessional, unethical and possibly illegal. If this happens a cooperating teacher must take immediate action.

It is sometimes difficult to convince student teachers that they can affect pupil behavior in the classroom. If such is the problem, Worksheet Number Five in the Appendix may be useful for a student teacher to use in analyzing teacher impact upon pupils. The form calls for the student teacher to provide evidence of having met acceptable criteria in establishing good personal relationships with pupils. It further challenges the student teacher to consider ways of improving personal behavior in the classroom.

In the classrooms of today, teachers often are expected to work in a collegial fashion. In response, many teacher preparation institutions stress to their undergraduate teacher candidates the importance of developing excellent collaborative and interpersonal skills. A *Student Teacher Readiness Assessment* (see Worksheet Number Six in the Appendix) stresses the importance of skills in personal responsibility and interpersonal relations. An awareness of these criteria by both the student teacher and cooperating teacher may minimize many of the problems discussed in this chapter.

Case Study No. 18: A First-Name Basis

Your student teacher believes that informality is a good way to build community and a positive classroom environment. He wants his pupils to call him by his first name. Against your advice, he is soon on a first name basis with his pupils. At first it is not a major issue but before long the informal atmosphere deteriorates into chaos. He has lost control of the class and it is difficult to tell who is in charge. What course of action do you take?

1. Talk with the pupils involved and request that they accord him the respect due a regular teacher.
2. Suggest that he ignore the students when they use his first name.
3. Tell him to firmly insist that they address him by his last name.
4. Inform him initially that using his last name is a good way to put some positive professional distance between him and his pupils.
5. _____

Comment

Student teachers often believe, and rightly so, that developing a positive rapport with their students is critical to their success. But novice teachers need to learn that there is a fine line between healthy interaction between teachers and pupils and a relationship that is too informal. The name is not really the issue. It is the respect that matters. The use of first names could be the first step toward an atmosphere of inappropriate familiarity. Respect has to be earned and once lost it is very difficult to reestablish. It is essential to prevent such problems before they start.

Questions

1. What are some methods of establishing rapport with pupils that can be used by student teachers?
2. What can a cooperating teacher do to prevent a situation such as this from occurring?

Case Study No. 19: You Are Only A Student Teacher

Your student teacher was in the room alone with the class when he made an assignment that a few of the students did not like. He explained that it was required and would be counted as part of the class grade. One student countered with, "I don't believe that. You are only a student teacher. Our teacher will give the grades." Your student teacher reaffirmed the requirements and continued with the class, but was upset by the challenge. He asks for your advice. What do you do?

1. Support him in what he did.
2. Talk to the class and define the student teacher's role clearly.
3. Indicate that he must prove that he is the teacher by his actions.
4. Talk privately with the pupils involved.
5. _____

Comment

Student teaching has been considered analogous to cooking in someone else's kitchen. Regardless of the autonomy given, there will be occasional instances of a student teacher's authority being challenged. Unfortunately the student teacher may feel that he is not totally in charge and may respond accordingly. The cooperating teacher should support the student teacher. She should also make certain that both parties understand the amount of responsibility that the student teacher can exercise. The discussion about roles and responsibilities needs to take place prior to the beginning of the student teaching experience and pupils need to be informed of the power delegated to the student teacher from the outset.

Questions

1. How can a cooperating teacher help a student teacher gain the confidence of the class?
2. Are there any responses which student teachers can be prepared to give to skeptics?

Case Study No. 20: Too Close For Comfort

Pam's student teaching had been going well, so the cooperating teacher was exercising only minimal supervision. After several weeks, the cooperating teacher observed that certain pupils were constantly surrounding her. When asked if the students were a nuisance, Pam responded negatively and then stated that the pupils had been to her apartment a few times and that she felt that she was really getting to learn about high school students. This was a surprise to the supervisor. What kind of response should she make?

1. Remind her that professional behavior is jeopardized when teachers and pupils fraternize too closely.
2. Explain the importance of maintaining rapport with pupils, but present some alternatives that would be more appropriate than the one she has chosen.
3. _____

Comment

As pointed out in this chapter, student teaching is a time of change in status, attitude, responsibilities, and perhaps in professional goals. It is a time when student teachers need guidance in order to create a successful experience. The student teacher is still a student, yet is on the verge of becoming a professional. During this time she may be attempting to play both roles, but it is important that she move toward the more mature one. Supervision of a successful student teacher does not mean backing away. An alert cooperating teacher will help a student teacher establish desirable student contacts without becoming involved in informal situations that might cause problems.

Questions

1. Should a cooperating teacher become involved in the after-school life of a student teacher and pupils?
2. What guidelines are useful in counseling student teachers about pupil-teacher relationships?
3. How does the cooperating teacher decide the correct balance between allowing autonomy for the student teacher and providing direct supervision?

Case Study No. 21: They Are Playing Games With Me

The students have learned how to frustrate your student teacher. She has been unable to establish any kind of working relationship with them in spite of the fact that she has tried a variety of approaches ranging from permissiveness to assertive discipline. The students often pretend they do not hear directions or complain that they did not understand the assignment, usually accompanied by knowing glances from the perpetrators. They often deliberately appear to be unable to comprehend what is being studied. In her frustration she turns to you and complains that the pupils are playing games with her. How do you respond?

1. Specify consequences to the pupils if such behavior continues.
2. Suggest additional alternatives to the student teacher.
3. Leave her alone at present to see if she can overcome the situation by herself.
4. Go over the situation together and devise a plan whereby both of you can approach the problem without it looking as if the student teacher is weak.
5. _____

Comment

Student teachers often unconsciously convey messages of insecurity which in turn can be exploited by students. Perhaps the alert supervisor should look for verbal and nonverbal behaviors that would contribute to the students' agitating the student teacher and then devise a plan to overcome them.

Questions

1. How far should a cooperating teacher allow the situation to deteriorate before intervening?
2. What are the behaviors that students will most likely notice?

Case Study No. 22: Conflict With The Class

Your student teacher had never liked the last hour class. The conflict between them had been developing for several days and it came to a climax with a test review. A defensive explanation of a questionable test item led to an angry response from several pupils. The student teacher failed in an attempt to shout them down. You pass by the door and observe that he is in trouble. What course of action do you take?

1. Enter the classroom quietly, but make your presence known.
2. Demand that the class get quiet immediately.
3. Take over the class and discuss the problem.
4. Walk on by and do nothing until you have had a chance to talk with the student teacher.
5. _____

Comment

The cooperating teacher must confront the fact that the student teacher has apparently lost control. A direct, forceful response will make the student teacher look inadequate. A more low-key approach may work better but the students must know that you do not approve of what is happening. The student teacher needs to understand that getting into a power struggle with pupils is fruitless. First there must be stability; then the causes of the problem can be determined.

Questions

1. What is the cooperating teacher's role in reconciling the differences?
2. What preventive alternatives could be considered?

Brian and Miss Bennett walked toward the lunch room and were stopped for a moment by a student who had a question about a homework assignment. Brian was still aware of the incident that they had witnessed earlier between Gordon Rogers and Sally Hawkins.

"Pardon me if I am making improper observations about another teacher," Brian began, "but I am glad that I have you as my cooperating teacher instead of some others I have seen."

"You are pleasant enough to work with almost anyone, Brian," countered Miss Bennett. "But this business of human relationships is frequently overlooked. There can be problems in student teaching

between a student teacher and supervisor as well as between a student teacher and pupil."

"We have not always agreed on everything, but I have felt that you had respect for and confidence in me. And even when I took exception to some of your ideas, you were tolerant," commented Brian, "and you certainly have made me aware of how important it is to demonstrate high standards of teacher behavior. That is one of the most valuable lessons I have learned."

As they turned into the cafeteria, Miss Bennett dismissed the praise by remarking, "One thing that we have always agreed on is the quality of food in the cafeteria. It has a way of creating consensus among people who generally disagree on most things." They picked up a wet tray and nodded toward the pizza in preference to the hot dogs supreme.

Remember:

- **Student teaching is a growth situation in personal relationships as well as other professional skills.**
- **A student teacher cannot make maximum development in a subordinate role.**
- **The student teacher is a colleague with less experience than you.**
- **Differences in personalities should be considered as an asset instead of treated as a problem.**
- **Honesty, thoughtfulness, and tact affirm and help to establish and maintain good personal relationships.**
- **Student teaching is generally considered to modify the personality of a student teacher toward a more positive self-concept.**
- **A student teacher will likely take a more conservative and less permissive attitude toward pupils as the experience progresses.**
- **In a successful experience, student teachers and cooperating teachers will have learned from one another.**

Useful References

Abebe, Solomon., and Michael F. Shaughnessy. 1997. Strengthening the Teaching Profession: Preparing Educators To Cope with Stress. ERIC ED 411239.

Babkie, Andrea. 1998. Twenty Ways to Work Successfully With a Student Teacher. *Intervention in School and Clinic* 34 (November): 115-117.

Bray, Jane. 1995. A Comparison of Teacher Concerns for the Nontraditional and Traditional Student Teacher. ERIC ED 390844.

Bunting, Carolyn. 1988. Cooperating Teachers and the Changing Views of Teacher Candidates. *Journal of Teacher Education* 39 (March-April): 42-46.

Butler, Judy D. 1998. The Student Teaching Experience: A Comparative Study. ERIC ED 417181.

Canter, Lee. 1996. Discipline Alternatives. First, the Rapport - Then, the Rules. *Learning* 24 (March - April): 12 - 14.

Coolican, M., C. Giebelhaus, and M. Sudzina. 1997. Mentor or Tormentor: The Role of the Cooperating Teacher in Student Teacher Success or Failure. *Action in Teacher Education 28* (Winter): 23-35.

Enz, Billie J., and Susan J. Cook. 1991. Student Teachers' and Cooperating Teachers' Perspectives of Mentoring Functions: Harmony or Dissonance? Paper presented at the annual meeting of the American Educational Research Association, San Francisco, CA, April 20-24. ERIC ED 350291.

Fuller, F., and O. Brown. 1975. Becoming a Teacher. In K. Ryan (Ed.) *Teacher Education* (Seventy-fourth yearbook of the National Society for the Study of Education) (pp. 25-52). Chicago. University of Chicago Press.

Gregorc, Anthony. 1984. Style as a Symptom: A Phenomenological Perspective. *Theory Into Practice* 23 (Winter): 51-55.

Grossman, John, A., and Daniel L. Keller. 1994. A Model for Improving the Preservice Teacher/Cooperating Teacher Diad. Paper presented at the Annual Meeting of the Mid-Western Educational Research Association, Chicago, IL. October 13, 1994. ERIC ED 377181.

Harter, Susan. 1990. *At the Threshold: The Developing Adolescent.* Cambridge, MA: Harvard University Press.

Head, F., A. Reiman, and L. Thies-Sprinthall. 1992. The Reality of Mentoring: Complexity in its Process and Function. In T. Bey & C. T. Holmes (Eds.), *Mentoring: Contemporary Principles and Issues* (pp. 5-24). Reston.

Hughes, Robert, Jr. 1982. Personality Factors in the Student Teaching Triad. Paper presented at the annual meeting of the American Educational Research Association, New York. March 19-23, 1982. ERIC ED 240097.

Johnson, James. 1977. The Student Teacher as Self: or How Am I Doing. *Kappa Delta Pi Record* 13 (February): 70-2, 94.

Kahn, Brian. 2001. Portrait of Success: Cooperating Teachers and the Student Teaching Experience. *Action in Teacher Education* 22:4 (Winter): 48-57.

Karmos, Ann, and Carol Jacko. 1977. The Role of Significant Others During the Student Teaching Experience. *Journal of Teacher Education* 28 (September-October): 51-55.

Knight, Sharon M. and G. Linda Rikard. 1997. Obstacles to Professional Development: Interns' Desire to Fit in, Get Along, and Be Real Teachers. *Journal of Teaching in Physical Education* 16 (July): 440-453.

Looper, Sandra. 1999. What Your Student Teacher Would Like to Tell You. *Teaching K-8* 30 (November-December): 58.

Mahan, James M. 1977. Influence of Supervising Teachers in a Cluster Program. *The Teacher Educator* 13 (Spring): 2-6.

Manning, Brenda H., and Beverly D. Payne. 1984. Student Teacher Personality As a Variable in Teacher Education. *The Teacher Educator* 20 (Autumn): 2-12.

Roe, Betty D., Elinor P. Ross, and Paul C. Burns. 1989. Human Relations. Chapter Two in *Student Teaching and Field Experiences Handbook*. Columbus, Ohio. Merrill Publishing Company.

Schwedel, Andrew I., Bernice L. Schwedel, Carol R. Schwedel, and Milton Schwedel. Relationships. Chapters 3-6 in *The Student Teacher's Handbook*, 2nd ed. Hillsdale, NJ. Lawrence Erllaum Associates.

Seiferth, Berniece B., and Marie Samuel. 1984. Cooperating Teachers: Why Not the Best? ERIC ED 264176.

Shaw-Baker, Margaret H. 1995. Communication: The Key to Successful Field Experiences. Chapter 4 in Slick (Ed.), *Making the Difference for Teachers: The Field Experience in Actual Practice*. Thousand Oaks, CA. Corwin Press, Inc.

Stahlhut, Richard G., and Richard R. Hawkes. 1990. Mentoring Student Teachers: A Conceptual Model. Paper presented at the annual meeting of the Association of Teacher Educators, Las Vegas, NV, February 5-8, 1990. ERIC ED 320864.

Tabachnick, B. R., and K. M. Zeichner. 1984. The Impact of the Student Teaching Experience on the Development of Teacher Perspectives. *Journal of Teacher Education* 35 (Nov-Dec): 28-36.

Winter, Jeffrey (National Louis University). 1998. Identifying and Supporting Diverse Styles of Interaction: A Guide for Supervisors. Paper presented at the annual meeting of the Association of Teacher Educators. Dallas, Texas, February 16.

Williams, Wayne, and Justyn Graham. 1992. The Relationship Between Cooperating Teachers' Personal Attributes and Professional Backgrounds and the Attitudes of Their Student Teachers. *The Teacher Educator* 28(Autumn): 34-44.

Woolley, Sandra, Anita Woolley, and Michele Hosey. 1999. Impact of Student Teaching on Student Teachers' Beliefs Related to Behaviorist and Constructivist Theories of Learning. Paper Presented at the Annual Meeting of the Association of Teacher Educators, Chicago, IL, February 12-16.

Zerr, Rita G. 1988. What Supervisors of Student Teaching and Student Teachers Tell Us About Student Teaching. Paper presented at the annual meeting of the American Association of Colleges for Teacher Education, New Orleans, LA, Feb. 20. ERIC ED 300362.

4

Working With College Supervisors

The class was just starting and Brian was beginning his introduction to a new unit of study. It had been difficult to find the right approach, and he was uncertain whether he had chosen the appropriate activities to achieve the new state curriculum standards he was trying to address. He looked up just in time to see the door open and a familiar figure move to a seat in the back of the room. He forced a smile and tried to conceal his apprehension. Not his college supervisor today! What will he think of this class? Why could he not have come yesterday when the lesson went so well?

Miss Bennett whispered a word of greeting to Dr. Douglas and handed him a copy of Brian's plan. She then excused herself from the class, assuming that Brian would be more comfortable with only one supervisor in the room. Dr. Douglas indicated that they would confer after the class observation had been completed.

Dr. Douglas met Miss Bennett in the conference room after the class was over. He talked informally for a few minutes and then opened his folder to his notes. He then began to inquire about Brian's progress. . .

The College Supervisor
Serving in Many Worlds

College (or university) supervisors assume a unique role among professional educators. They work primarily in public schools but are not on the staff. They may hold university rank but their role is not the one that is traditionally associated with a professor. They may be former teachers or school administrators working as adjunct faculty. They are members of the student teaching triad, but are not housed in the same school facility as the cooperating teacher and student teacher.

A perusal of the student teaching handbook of any teacher education institution will reveal that the college supervisor must assume a number of different roles. Authorities agree that the university supervisor should be both supportive and evaluative in nature (Miller, 1994). The supervisor is the watchdog for the completion of university requirements during student teaching, the facilitator of relationships between student teachers and cooperating teachers, and the personal confidant of anyone in the triad who chooses to engage him. The responsibility of the college supervisor constitutes the totality of the student teaching experience ranging from formal instruction, classroom observation and individual work with student teachers.

The impact of the university supervisor has been a subject of considerable discussion over the years (Guyton and McIntyre 1990). Some agree with Bowman (1979) and Ellenburg (1981) that the supervisor does not have a significant role in the development of student teachers. Their findings conflict with a study by Friebus (1977) who concluded that college supervisors supersede or rank a close second to cooperating teachers in some areas of influence. A more recent study by Borko and Mayfield (1995) added another perspective by concluding that most cooperating teachers and university supervisors played limited roles in helping their charges learn to teach effectively.

Although it is generally recognized that the cooperating teacher has greater impact on a student teacher's performance than the university supervisor, most would agree with the research of Zimpher (1980) that without the motivating presence of the university supervisor, student teaching would have a rather flat profile. She found that the supervisor filled roles that would have been otherwise overlooked. Supervisors were involved in defining and communicating the purposes and expectations to be fulfilled by the student teacher and the cooperating teacher, phasing the student teacher into the classroom's ongoing instructional activity, and evaluating the student teacher's performance. Her findings were supported by Giebelhaus (1995) who concluded that when the university supervisor made frequent contact with the student teacher and the cooperating teacher, and when more direct interaction among all members of the triad occurred, cooperating teachers felt less isolated and student teachers experienced less anxiety.

Student teachers want, need, and deserve support from a university representative. They are still enrolled as students earning credit toward a degree and paying tuition. Lack of support from the university would send the message that student teaching is not a high priority.

Metcalf (1991) conducted an extensive review of the research and discovered that some studies had pinpointed specific ways in which a college supervisor affects a student teaching program. According to her analysis, supervisors:

- Promote self- evaluation.
- Promote planning.
- Promote adjustment to the teaching role.
- Affect student teacher attitude.
- Offer coaching for mastery of specific instructional techniques.
- Foster greater communication between the university and schools.
- Offer suggestions to help with specific problems.
- Give feedback regarding performance.
- Manage the student teaching experience.
- Act as personal confidant to the cooperating teacher and student teacher.
- Evaluate and offer constructive criticism about the student teacher's performance.

Winter and Prokosch (1995) found that the field experience allows for many opportunities for assistance from the college supervisor:

- Student teachers were sometimes more willing to ask "basic" questions of their college supervisor so as to avoid losing "credibility" in the eyes of the cooperating teacher.
- When cooperating teachers have difficulties in providing critical feedback, the college supervisor was the main source of evaluation and guidance.
- The college supervisor facilitated learning about record keeping, conference preparation, grade books, text selection or inclusion when the cooperating teachers were unable or unwilling to take the time to explain procedures.
- College supervisors were able to assist the student teacher in reflecting on educational choices when cooperating teachers had difficulty.
- College supervisors provided knowledge of what other teachers and schools are doing.

Recent innovations in preservice teacher preparation reveal that the level of collaboration and collegiality that occurs between the university and the public school has a direct bearing on the quality of the clinical experience for all those involved. Many teacher education institutions have identified Professional Development Schools where most, if not all, of the clinical experiences for preservice teachers are conducted. Szuminski and Others (1999) described an Alternative Teacher Education (ATE) Program in the state of Georgia where the university supervisors, cooperating teachers, and student teachers collaboratively planned the teacher education program of the college. Another partnership outlined by Kroll and Others (1997) showed that close collaboration between universities and public schools resulted in many ways for faculty from both institutions to interact with one another. Wilson (1996) presented an example of the benefits of such close collaboration. She found that the most supportive cooperating teachers were those who were familiar with the program of the university's teacher education program, including the content of the student teacher's preservice course work. Zimmerman and Others (1998) advocated the expansion of the traditional triad to establish "clear communication among methods, foundations and subject matter faculty, clinical faculty, cooperating teachers, and prospective teachers." So the current trend in providing clinical experience for student teachers encourages universities and public schools to work cooperatively rather than in isolation.

In summary, research seems to indicate that the role of university supervision may be critical in the administrative, managerial, and interpersonal dimensions of the student teaching experience. The college supervisor also represents the education profession. He may have had recent experience as a teacher or been in contact with many public schools in his role with the university. Through this professional experience and knowledge of trends and innovations, he should possess a broad knowledge of educational developments. The college supervisor is a resource person who can enhance the student teaching experience and possibly other aspects of the school's program as well.

Roles and Responsibilities

The list below describes the numerous roles that college supervisors perform in fulfilling their responsibilities as representatives from higher education. Cooperating teachers who are aware of these complex roles will more likely come to accept, appreciate, and use the services of this unique individual.

- **Placement consultant.** The initial responsibility may be to place a student teacher in a setting that will have the possibility of providing growth. This will involve interviews with students and a knowledge of school settings so that appropriate placements can be made. Consideration will be given to geographical areas, grade levels desired, subject areas to be taught, and personal needs of the teaching candidate. He will make contact with university and public school personnel to implement the placement.

- **Orientation advisor.** The university supervisor is responsible for preparing the student to enter the classroom as a student teacher. A good orientation will substantially reduce the demands made on a cooperating teacher, especially in the initial days.
- **Instructor.** The teaching role of the college supervisor is manifest through individualized instruction. In some cases instruction is as simple as the presentation of ideas and concepts to a student teacher. In other instances, it becomes more complex and involves helping a student teacher develop through instructional analysis and feedback. His availability to work with student teachers in this manner should not be underestimated.
- **Seminar director.** Many student teaching programs include regular seminars which give student teachers opportunity to share experiences and to pursue ideas with their peers. One role of the university supervisor is to conduct the seminars. This involves preparing the agenda for the meeting and providing the resources necessary for success.
- **Counselor.** A university supervisor will be aware of and responsive to the problems existing with or anticipated by a student teacher. The problems may be both personal and professional. Through listening and sharing, a supervisor helps a student teacher overcome those barriers that might hinder her potential to be a teacher.
- **Liaison.** The college supervisor may frequently be a liaison person who interprets the university program to the cooperating school and explains the cooperating school's program to the appropriate personnel at the university. As an intermediary, the college supervisor attempts to eliminate misunderstandings or to resolve conflicts between the cooperating teacher and the student teacher. The position requires close contact with both public school and the university personnel.
- **Supervisor.** The most preferred role may be that of the classical concept of supervision where the college supervisor works with a student teacher to improve instruction. The university supervisor can work with the student teacher and cooperating teacher to obtain the maximum growth and development of a student teacher. He may use lesson plan analysis, classroom observation, and conferences to promote formative development. In this way he becomes involved with the student teacher in analyzing problems and developing solutions. The supervisor may be in the best position to provide assistance because of his experience as a teacher educator.
- **Consultant**. A supervisor can serve the public school by informally serving as a consultant. Supervisors' knowledge and

experience can be shared to provide new ideas and information to public school personnel. An informed supervisor should be able to provide information about a variety of topics, including methods, materials, resources, ideas, and available university resources.

- **Evaluator**. Evaluation of student teaching is significant and unavoidable. One of the greatest services performed by college supervisors is in the evaluative domain. Supervisors will be able to provide a concept of effective student teaching which the student teacher and cooperating teacher may use in evaluation. In addition, the college supervisor will help a student teacher and cooperating teacher develop formative evaluation procedures that will lead to effective growth. Finally, the supervisor will decide whether university requirements have been met and submit a final evaluation or grade.

Marrou (1989) asserts that public schools are looking for additional qualities in the university supervisor. They seek people who are highly knowledgeable in teacher education and who can articulate the processes of becoming an effective teacher. In response to a question about the kinds of problems that university supervisors deal with on a day-to-day basis, she identified four categories:

- **Communication**. The cooperating teacher's expectations are either not clearly communicated to the student teacher or are not realistic for preservice teachers.
- **Interpersonal**. The cooperating teacher or the student teacher may be going through certain emotional traumas that make working together as a team a difficult proposition.
- **Inability to Plan**. The student teacher may not understand the subject matter, may be unable to follow a correct sequence, may fail to show creativity, or may develop an abstract idea insufficiently.
- **Inability to Manage**. Student teachers may not demand total attention from the class before beginning a lesson. They may spend too much time on routine management items that need to be taken care of in a matter of minutes.

The impact of the college supervisor depends, to a considerable extent, on the perceptions of the members of the triad about the role he plays. In the ideal situation, a university supervisor will make contributions that would not otherwise be a part of the program. He does this in a variety of ways in a great number of different situations.

Case Study No. 23: Establishing Rapport With The College Supervisor

Your student teacher mentioned the name of her college supervisor when she arrived to begin student teaching, but you took little note of it. The first few days were busy and you and she did not discuss who the person was or what his role would be. You were taken by surprise when there was a knock on the door and you greeted a stranger who introduced himself as Sandra's supervisor. What are you supposed to do? What questions should you ask? What should you tell the person about the school, the program, and your impressions of Sandra?

1. Make no gesture but wait for him to take the initiative.
2. Indicate that you are busy at the moment and suggest that he and the student teacher talk.
3. Review what you have been doing and ask for suggestions.
4. Ask him questions about your responsibilities, ranging from initial orientation through supervision to evaluation.
5. _____

Comment

Since the college supervisor is not always visible, it is easy to forget about his involvement. The important point to remember is that he is a part of the triad and can be a resource person for you as well as a facilitator for the student teacher. Basically, this visit is an opportunity to establish a comfortable working relationship for the three of you and to secure additional information about the process. While you are the host or hostess, establishing good rapport is the responsibility of all parties involved.

Questions

1. What should a cooperating teacher attempt to know about the various roles of the college supervisor that were described above?
2. What procedures could be used to help a college supervisor become established as a valuable member of the student teaching team?

Assisting The Student Teacher
Support from the Outside

The first responsibility of the college supervisor is to assist the student teacher in developing competency sufficient to perform effectively as a beginning teacher. In the typical scenario, the supervisor will rely on observation and conference techniques to assist the student teacher. The number of visits may vary from three to six or more per semester, depending upon the program of the university. Some states mandate the number of supervisory visits by statute. Zahorik (1988) found that there were three types of university supervision. A cooperating teacher may wish to be aware of these types so that he can understand better his approach to supervision. These three styles are:

- **Behavior prescription**. Behavior prescription supervisors tell student teachers to use certain instructional and management acts and avoid others. Their procedures may include presenting research evidence, prescribing practices from the perspective of an experienced expert, offering advice, and sharing evidence from observation of the student teacher in action. The supervisor is direct and assertive in offering suggestions to improve teaching.
- **Idea interpretation**. This type of supervision consists of presenting beliefs to the student teacher that the supervisor has about what classrooms and schools ought to be like. Supervisors may identify what they consider to be perceived injustices and suggest ways that change can be made in classroom practices. They may have a more socially active agenda and will suggest that the student teacher should be a change agent.
- **Person support**. Person support focuses on facilitating student teacher decision-making by creating a climate that permits and encourages student teachers to think for themselves. The student teacher is encouraged to be reflective and to devise plans of action that will overcome teaching problems. The supervisor asks questions and prompts the student teacher to reflect on her behavior and how it can be modified to improve her teaching.

Although a cooperating teacher cannot select the supervisory style that the college supervisor will employ, he can assist by making certain that the college supervisor is acquainted with the teaching environment. This will include knowledge of the students, school policies, curriculum and community values. A cooperating teacher should view himself as one who is active in interpreting the school climate to the college supervisor in order to make the relationship more effective. This is less of an issue in Professional Development Schools where the university supervisor spends considerable time at the school.

In reality, the college supervisor should be a catalyst who causes the student teacher to formulate a broader perspective on teaching through reflection. The supervisor encourages the student teacher to go beyond the superficial to a more intellectual analysis of teaching, to think about what is happening, to see relationships, and to formulate plans of action for subsequent experiences. Any of the above styles may contribute to that objective. The cooperating teacher is involved in helping interpretations to be accurate and in following through on teaching analysis after the supervisor has gone.

The college supervisor may provide personal as well as instructional assistance, functioning as a counselor or liaison. The supervisor may assist with personal problems and help facilitate the student teacher's adjustment to a new role. When conflict situations arise, the college supervisor may be called upon to help to resolve them. The cooperating teacher may help by demonstrating confidence in the college supervisor and by pointing out how he can be helpful in solving personal problems.

In summary, a college supervisor renders assistance to the student teacher in a number of ways. The most frequent activities include the ones listed below:

- **Gives personal assistance.** Such support may range from answering questions concerning requirements and details to counseling with a student teacher when problems exist.
- **Helps a student teacher develop teaching skills.** Through observations and conferences, the supervisor helps the student teacher become more skilled in teaching and expand knowledge of resources and ideas.
- **Serves as an intermediary in misunderstandings.** In the event that there are disputes between a student teacher and cooperating teacher, the college supervisor should be involved in resolving the problem.
- **Helps the student teacher evaluate performance and set goals.** Through a series of supervisory strategies a supervisor will lead the student teacher to become aware of strengths and weaknesses and to consider strategies that will lead to more effective performance.
- **Serves as a teacher on a one-to-one basis.** A supervisor should assume the role of a teacher through interaction with the student teacher.

In the past a college supervisor has been viewed incorrectly as an evaluator or critic. The emerging trend is to present the supervisor in a more comprehensive role that gets away from "the person who checks up" notion to that of a professional supervisor who serves as a catalyst in the formative growth of a student teacher.

Case Study No. 24: Rejecting The College Supervisor's Suggestions

The college supervisor spent several hours visiting your student teacher's classes and conferring with each of you. Her primary concern appeared to be to help Bill improve in some of his weaker areas and her suggestions offered alternatives that could lead to better performance. Bill became upset and said that the college supervisor had been too critical of his work. His final comment was, "How can she make any valid judgments? She was not here long enough to know what this class is like." Since you recognize some validity in the supervisor's suggestions, what course of action do you take?

1. Remain noncommittal for a while.
2. Encourage the student teacher to follow up on the recommendations.
3. Analyze the suggestions categorically with the student teacher and assess their validity
4. _____

Comment

There will be little or no growth if the comments are summarily rejected. It is comfortable to remain with an established routine, but teaching is a dynamic process and must involve reflection and modification. In whatever way seems feasible, a student teacher should be encouraged to reflect on the recommendations and to either accept or have a sound reason for rejecting them. At the same time, most college supervisors realize that they witness only "snapshots" of the student teacher's experience. With this in mind, most supervisors will ask student teachers for an explanation of what was observed before making sweeping recommendations for change. If the supervisor does not ask the student teacher to provide some context for his actions, the host teacher can help provide the "big picture" for the college supervisor.

Questions

1. How valid is the comment that the supervisor's impressions may be incorrect because he only viewed a brief part of the class?
2. What can be done to help a student teacher overcome feelings of insecurity and be open to constructive suggestions?

Case Study No. 25: Disagreement About The Teaching Of Values

Ann's college supervisor could be classified as an "idea interpreter" because he believes that the school should improve or even reform society. He observed her on the day that she chose to show a videotape that focused on value conflicts. During the post teaching conference he complimented her on her technique and timing but suggested that she could have gone further in getting students involved in sharing what it was like to be in a conflict situation. When he mentioned that she might have students role play the conflicts and then discuss the basic issues, Ann resisted, saying that the students were too young for such intense situations. Her supervisor disagreed, and the conference ended without any reconciliation of the different points of view. Ann is concerned and consults with you about the difference of opinion. What do you do in this situation?

1. Suggest that she put the situation behind her and use her best judgment in the future.
2. Explain what you think should be done.
3. Talk with her and see if there is an acceptable compromise between her position and that of the supervisor.
4. Encourage her to try the supervisor's strategy.
5. Share your concern with the college supervisor about his proactive stand.
6. _____

Comment

The underlying difficulty in this incident may be that the student teacher is uncertain as to how to accept a role that makes her uncomfortable. She may perceive that she should please the supervisor, and when her practices are questioned, she may find it difficult to respond. The main problem may be that she fails to accurately perceive the role of the college supervisor.

Questions

1. How can a cooperating teacher help a student teacher overcome apprehension created by a college supervisor?
2. How much authority should a college supervisor have in suggesting topics and strategies for student teachers which might conflict with school practices?

Assisting The Cooperating Teacher
A Relationship of Peers

Both the cooperating teacher and college supervisor bring knowledge, insight, and perspective into the student teaching experience. The cooperating teacher possesses knowledge of the school and pupils as well as recent teaching experience. The college supervisor provides an increased understanding of the student teacher and a comprehensive view of the responsibilities and goals of teacher education in general and student teaching in particular. Both parties can complement each other when they work together and share their skills and perspectives.

One of the initial responsibilities of the college supervisor is to acquaint the cooperating teacher with the expectations of the university student teaching program and the role of the cooperating teacher in it. This may be accomplished through discussion of details and requirements, but it also should involve ideas regarding supervisory procedures and processes. Prior to, or early in, the student teaching experience the college supervisor and cooperating teacher need to consider the following topics:

*   **The basic rationale of the student teaching program.** Discussion should include the philosophy, principles, and objectives of the program as viewed from the perspective of the university.
*   **The university and state requirements.** Student teaching will be involved with rules and guidelines which originate both from state mandates and university programs. Such requirements will likely include a minimum number of weeks, observation requirements, evaluation procedures, and a variety of reports and activities.
*   **Information about the student teacher.** The college supervisor may be the cooperating teacher's best source of professional information about the student teacher. He should be able to outline the student teacher's academic record as well as reveal necessary individual information about the student teacher.

- **Basic concepts of supervision.** The supervisor should describe his role and outline the cooperating teacher's responsibilities. This is a good time for questions about the nature and extent of supervisory responsibilities.
- **Role of the teacher education institution.** The supervisor may describe the kind of support that can be expected from the university, what services will be provided, and where and how the university authority extends into student teaching in the public school.

It is helpful for a college supervisor to be informed of the general nature of the school so that he can be aware of the particular challenges and opportunities facing the student teacher. The following information can be helpful for a college supervisor:

- The general profile of the class or classes that the student teacher will be teaching.
- The academic content that the student teacher will teach.
- Established routines and procedures.
- Special projects or activities that will occur while the student teacher is there.
- General teaching styles and procedures used by the cooperating teacher.
- The amount of latitude the cooperating teacher feels comfortable granting the student teacher in trying new strategies or techniques.
- Available resource materials.

Subsequent contacts with the college supervisor will probably occur every few weeks. During this time he may want to observe the student teacher in an instructional setting and conduct a follow-up conference. If possible, he will seek the cooperating teacher's analysis through a private conference. After being informed of the current status, the college supervisor may assist the cooperating teacher by:

- Suggesting additional experiences for the student teacher.
- Summarizing the student teacher's progress from a different perspective.
- Suggesting alternative procedures in methods, planning, conferences and pupil contacts.
- Reviewing requirements and assuring that the university standards and state regulations are met.
- Counseling with student teachers who are having problems.

- Serving as a liaison between the student teacher and cooperating teacher.

Contacts with the college supervisor can present the opportunity to secure professional knowledge. Conversation with the college supervisor may provide information and assistance in such areas as:

- The latest developments in educational programs.
- Information concerning state standards, guidelines, and mandates.
- Knowledge about the broader educational scene and its implications for the schools.
- Teaching skills.
- Resource materials.
- Employment opportunities for new teachers.

The university supervisor's peer relationship will go beyond communication with the cooperating teacher. A supervisor should establish working relations with others in the building. A discussion with the principal about requirements and policies will help establish the necessary conditions for a good student teaching experience. They may want to explore the advantages of a student teacher being in the building and to agree on the new responsibilities of the parties involved.

Other teachers have an impact on student teachers and they should also get to know the college supervisor. Teaching aides and other auxiliary personnel should be introduced to the college supervisor as well. The mutual exchange of views and ideas from these contacts can be beneficial and informative for all concerned. Such communication can help provide more effective articulation between the higher education and public school sectors.

Case Study No. 26: Intruder

The university supervisor came at a time when both you and the student teacher were busy. Because she was on a tight schedule and you and the student teacher were involved in a team activity that consumed the time available, there was little opportunity for a conference. You did manage to get a few words with her in the department office while you were eating a quick lunch but the setting was anything but private. The dialogue was rushed and superficial. The supervisor left for another school as you left for your next class. You are concerned because you feel that the supervisor may have felt as if she were treated like an intruder. Since there was little communication, you, and possibly she, felt that the visit was not productive. How do you deal with this situation?

1. Ignore it because it probably will not happen again.
2. Make a special effort to be available when the supervisor next visits by having an alternative class procedure that will allow the two of you to converse.
3. Contact the supervisor with a list of times when you will be available to exchange information.
4. Contact the supervisor as soon as possible, perhaps by e-mail, and give a summary of your assessment of the student teacher.
5. _____

Comment

If there is one essential ingredient to a successful student teaching experience, it is clear and frequent communication among all parties involved. Busy supervisors, cooperating teachers, and student teachers frequently have difficulty finding time to get together. However, the fate of the student teacher may be affected by a lack of communication. All parties should make an effort to see that time is arranged for professional conversation. If face to face conferences are not always possible, staying connected via e-mail may be an alternative. Nabors (1999) suggested that important dialogue can be conducted electronically among the members of the triad. While it is not suggested that all communication be conducted electronically, technology can be used to keep communication channels open.

Questions

1. What are some ways that a cooperating teacher can make a university supervisor feel accepted when time is a factor?
2. What alternatives exist for preventing a tight time frame for conversation between a university supervisor and a cooperating teacher?

The conference with the college supervisor continued in a professional manner. Dr. Douglas asked questions that assessed the nature of the student teacher's progress in meeting requirements. He was particularly interested in the amount of responsibility the student teacher was assuming, and he suggested a few teaching procedures which might be tried. He answered Miss Bennett's questions and discussed a few ideas that might be used for more effective analysis of Brian's teaching.

Brian came by after he had completed some obligations. After a discussion of his progress, Brian and Dr. Douglas explored plans for future goals and tasks. Dr. Douglas suggested that planning should be more thorough and that Brian should spend a little more time observing other teachers and concentrating on the analysis of the strategies that seemed to make them successful. In response to one of Brian's questions, Dr. Douglas presented a rather detailed explanation of the technique of reflection through written records and analysis. Brian took out a pen and scribbled a few notes in the margin of his lesson plan and made a few entries in his portfolio journal. Miss Bennett silently mused over the change in Brian's reaction to his college supervisor.

Remember:

- Clear and frequent communication among all members of the triad is essential for a positive student teaching experience.
- The college supervisor possesses expertise that is helpful to both cooperating teacher and student teacher.
- The college supervisor is in a position to assist with problems and difficulties.
- The college supervisor is concerned with the improvement of educational practice.
- The cooperating teacher should consult with the college supervisor.
- The college supervisor facilitates and supplements good supervision.
- The college supervisor needs the confidence of both the cooperating teacher and the student teacher.
- The college supervisor is a guide, confidant, and troubleshooter.
- The college supervisor should be informed of the student teacher's activities in detail.
- The student teacher will perform better when the college supervisor takes an active role in her experiences.

Useful References

Bain, Catherine. 1991. Student Teaching Triads: Perceptions of Participant Roles. Paper presented at the Annual Meeting of the Northern Rocky Mountain Educational Association. ERIC ED 338620.

Borko, Hilda and Vicky Mayfield. 1995. The Roles of the Cooperating Teacher and the University Supervisor in Learning to Teach. *Teaching and Teacher Education* 11. 501-518.

Bowman, N. 1979. College Supervision of Student Teaching: A Time to Reconsider. *Journal of Teacher Education* 30 (May-June): 29-30.

Cole, Ardra L., and J. Gary Knowles. 1995. University Supervisors and Preservice Teachers: Clarifying Roles and Negotiating Relationships. *The Teacher Educator* 30 (Winter): 44-56.

Ellenberg, F.C. You Can Pay Me Now or You Can Pay Me Later. *Clearing House* 54 (Jan): 200-05

Ervay, Stuart. 1985. Campus-Field Compatibility in Student Teaching. *Action in Teacher Education* 7 (Fall): 37-40.

Friebus, R.J. 1977. Agents of Socialization Involved in Student Teaching. *Journal of Educational Research* 70 (March-April): 263-268.

Giebelhaus, Carmen R. 1995. Revisiting a Step-Child: Supervision in Teacher Education. ERIC ED 391785.

Guyton, Edith, and D. John McIntyre. 1990. Student Teaching and School Experiences. Chapter 29 in Houston (Ed.) *Handbook of Research on Teacher Education*. New York. Macmillan Publishing Company.

Koehler, Virginia. 1984. University Supervision of Student Teaching. Paper presented at the Annual Meeting of the American Educational Research Association, New Orleans, April. ERIC ED 270439.

Kroll, Linda and Others. 1997. The effect of a School-University Partnership on the Student Teaching Experience. *Teacher Education Quarterly* 24 (Winter): 37-51.

Kull, Judith A., and Others. 1991. Models of Collaborative Supervision Involving Teacher Educators and School Personnel in New Roles and Activities via Collaborative Supervisory Teams. ERIC ED 352350.

McIntyre, D. John. 1984. A Response to the Critics of Field Experience Supervision. *Journal of Teacher Education* 35 (May-June): 42-45.

McIntyre, D. John and William R. Morris. 1980. Research on the Student Teaching Triad. *Contemporary Education* 51 (Summer): 193-196.

Marrou, Judith R. 1989. The University Supervisor: A New Role in a Changing Workplace. *The Teacher Educator* 24 (Winter): 13-19.

Metcalf, Kim K. 1991. The Supervision of Student Teaching: A Review of Research. *The Teacher Educator* 26 (Spring): 28-42.

Miller, Susan Peterson. 1994. Self-Evaluation, Effective Feedback, and Goal Setting: An Integrated Approach to Clinical Supervision. *The Teacher Educator* 30 (Summer): 2-15.

Nabors, Martha L. 1999. New Functions for "Old Macs": Providing Immediate Feedback for Student Teachers through Technology. International *Journal of Instructional Media* 26: 105-107.

Neimeyer, Roger C., and R. Arden Moon. 1988. Supervisory Sense Making. *Action in Teacher Education* 10 (Spring): 17-23.

Richardson-Koehler, Virginia. 1988. Barriers to the Effective Supervision of Student Teaching: A Field Study. *Journal of Teacher Education* 39 (March-April): 28-34.

Rikard, G. Linda. 1990. Student Teaching Supervision--A Dyadic Approach. *Journal of Physical Education, Recreation and Dance* 61 (April): 85-87.

Shaver, Judy C., and Beth S. Wise. 1989. Evaluation of University Supervisors of Student Teaching. ERIC ED 313356.

Simmons, Joanne M. 1986. An Exploration of the Role Perspectives and Evaluative Judgment Criteria of Three University Student Teacher Supervisors. ERIC ED 285855.

Szuminski, Kathleen A. and Others. 1999. Sharing the Arena: Changing the Roles and Negotiating Power Among Teacher Education Participants. *The Teacher Educator* 34. (Spring): 291-308.

Wilson, Linda J. 1996. Mary and Ann: A Reciprocal Preservice Teacher and Cooperating Teacher Relationship. Paper presented at the Annual Meeting of the Association of Teacher Educators. St. Louis, MO. February 24-28. ERIC ED 395909.

Winter, Jeff, and Neil Prokosch.(National Louis University). 1995. Student Teachers and Field Experiences: What is the Role of College Supervisors? Paper presented at the Annual Meeting of the Association of Teacher Educators. Detroit., February 18-22.

Zahorik, John A. 1988. The Observing-Conferencing Role of University Supervisors. *Journal of Teacher Education* 39 (March-April): 9-16.

Zimmerman, Sara O. and Others.(Appalachian State University). 1998. Supervisory Observations: An Effective Practice or Necessary Hindrance? Paper presented at the annual meeting of the Association of Teacher Educators, Dallas, TX. Feb. 13-17.

Zimpher, Nancy L. 1980. A Closer Look at University Student Teacher Supervision. *Journal of Teacher Education* 31 (July-Aug): 11-15.

5

Supervising Observations

Brian entered Miss Bennett's room and happily announced that he had just completed his final required observation. Miss Bennett was somewhat surprised and quickly responded, "You have five weeks remaining in student teaching. Are you certain that you have completed the minimum number of required observations?"

"Oh yes, I have been keeping a record," explained Brian. "I started early and observed frequently so that I could get them over with. What a relief! The teachers I observed are all right, but I get bored just sitting in a classroom."

Miss Bennett protested mildly, "But there is value in observing. This may well be the only time in your career when you can see other teachers practice their skills. Are you certain that you want to finish just yet?"

Brian's answer was definite. "I learn more when I am teaching than when I am observing. I wish the university would eliminate these unrealistic observation requirements from student teaching. Now I can devote my time to teaching. If you want me to assume some additional work, let me know. I have time for it now that the observations are out of the way."

Miss Bennett was not prepared for this reaction and was thankful that class was to begin in a few minutes. Now she could try to find out more about observations before she had to give a response to Brian. . .

Observations
Learning by Looking

A colorful sports personality is credited with the nonsensical aphorism that you can observe a lot by looking. This whimsical statement says what professionals know: observation is a valid, efficient, and beneficial way of learning. It introduces students to the more experienced practitioner in a way that does not inflict any difficulty on the client. It is a way of broadening awareness and understanding of teaching styles and techniques. In many instances it is the only practical way to be aware of many techniques used by professionals.

The universality of requirements to view various teachers in student teaching programs attests to the support that the teaching profession gives to this activity. Any student teacher should expect to make frequent observations as part of the total experience of the professional semester. The cooperating teacher will be involved both as a person being viewed and as one who is instrumental in scheduling and following up on other observations.

Observation is a way of introducing student teachers to practitioners who possess differing skills and techniques. The learner's world is broadened through these contacts because so many different kinds of situations can be viewed in a relatively brief period of time. Through this process a future teacher can become aware of sophisticated teaching techniques without having to discover them through trial and error in the classroom.

One of the benefits of an observation is that it can be part of the process of discovery where a student teacher engages in self-analysis by comparing his skills with those of others. Observations should broaden a student teacher's perspective through increased awareness of teaching behaviors and techniques and assist the student teacher in developing his unique teaching style.

Observations should provide the opportunity for teaching candidates to see specific indicators of effective and ineffective teaching in action. A good role model can help a student teacher see how personality factors, subject matter knowledge, and teaching techniques work together to bring about pupil learning. Exposure to less effective teaching models can also contribute to the saturation of prospective teachers (Treiber, 1984). Through this process, student teachers can detect inadequate teaching behaviors and speculate about alternative strategies that might be more effective.

One of the most important reasons for requiring observations during student teaching is that it may be the last opportunity to see other teachers in action. While collegial efforts are common in some schools today, a substantial number of teachers still operate in isolation without professional contact or feedback from their peers. Cooperating teachers should use this fact as additional motivation to encourage observations.

Observations should be active and exciting experiences. A student teacher likely will have a more positive attitude toward them if they provide answers to some questions about teaching. The challenge to the cooperating teacher is to provide productive and relevant viewing experiences for student teachers.

The Cooperating Teacher's Role

The role of the cooperating teacher is to facilitate the continued professional growth of student teachers during this stage of their professional development. Cooperating teachers must plan an active role in monitoring and guiding student teachers' emerging perceptions of what it means to teach. A balance must be struck between the idealistic and theoretical influence of the college and the reality of the public school environment. Observations can help to broaden such perspectives.

A cooperating teacher will need to work with a student teacher in preparing for an observation by indicating what can be learned and by discussing procedures for coding and understanding what they see. A conference after an observation can help a student teacher understand what was seen and contextualize the information which was gathered. Mills (1980) suggested the following steps as a means of helping student teachers understand what they are to follow in the observation process. Basically, these steps are:

- Select an area of concern.
- Select one or more appropriate recording techniques.
- Observe and record.
- Share and analyze data.
- Discuss and question findings.
- Infer from findings one's own future behavior in similar situations.
- Determine goals and processes for the next observation.

The ultimate goal of the above procedures is to help the student teacher understand that watching and analyzing are not the same thing. Without systematic guidance, student teachers may end up investing considerable amounts of time in an essentially unrewarding activity. Student teachers must be trained to observe as well as teach (Treiber, 1984). The observations that are unappreciated are likely those where the student teacher has no idea of what to look for. A cooperating teacher can help structure observations so that they are considered to be meaningful and productive in the student teacher's development of his teaching style. This involves the following steps:

- **Set up the process for observations.** Arrange for a tentative pattern of observations and assist the student teacher in scheduling them.

- **Prepare the student teacher for the observation.** Describe what might be learned.
- **Arrange for observations that fit the student teacher's particular level of readiness.** Determine the student teacher's level of development and see that the observations conform to the needs of that stage.
- **Provide for observation of various types of teaching situations.** The range can be from academically talented classes to less able groups, from different types of educational programs to different styles of teaching.
- **Help the student teacher analyze and evaluate what was observed.** Discuss the significant activities and determine what was learned from the experience of observation.

Case Study No. 27: Little Interest

You are aware that it is beneficial for your student teacher to watch you as well as other teachers. Unfortunately, he seemed to become bored after only a few observations. He tends to spend more time in the teachers' work room instead of sitting in on a class. You become concerned when you talk with him about his lack of observation time and his answers are vague and evasive. What do you do to get him interested in viewing teachers in class settings?

1. Ask the student teacher to explain what he would do differently if he were the teacher in the class he observed.
2. Arrange for an observation with one of the best teachers in the building.
3. Ask the student teacher what specific questions or concerns he has about teaching and arrange observations in classrooms where his expressed concerns may arise.
4. Confront him with the university requirements for observations.
5. Discuss the problem with the university supervisor.
6. _____

Comment

The scenario in this case seems to present the all-too-typical process of looking at a class without any concern for analysis. Student teachers become bored very quickly when they are inactive. Though observations are passive, they can be exciting if they have a sense of purpose and direction.

Questions

1. What topics or ideas might most likely motivate a student teacher to want to observe?
2. How can other teachers be of help to you in structuring better observation experiences for a student teacher?

The Observation Sequence
One Step Leads to Another

Observations need to be sequenced throughout the entire period of student teaching in order for the student teacher to gain maximum benefit from this activity. Early observations will focus on much different ideas than later ones. The following suggestions reveal the kinds of learning that take place as a student teacher achieves more instructional maturity.

Initial Observations

In most cases the larger number of observations during the first few days of teaching will be in the classroom of the cooperating teacher. The teacher may use this occasion for modeling and for informing the student teacher about the nature of the class and her routine. These contacts should also allow the teaching candidate to get to know the pupils and become aware of the classroom routine. A student teacher will want to know what the pupils are like, how the teacher functions, how routine procedures are managed, and how a new person will fit into the whole classroom scheme. A cooperating teacher may want to ask a student teacher to observe the following procedures in order to become oriented:

- Classroom organization.
- Classroom management procedures.
- Pupil relationships.
- Teaching style.
- Lesson content.
- Instructional materials used.
- Problems.
- Nature of the students.
- The evaluation procedure.

The outcome of these structured observations should be an orientation to teaching with an understanding of the dynamics of the classroom and of the personnel who are involved in it. A cooperating teacher should be aware of her role of modeling and should be available for conferences where the classroom activities are discussed and questions are explored. A teacher also may find it beneficial in the initial days to provide an agenda of topics that the student teacher should review during observation. The topics above should give more purpose to the student teacher's observations. By focusing on the cooperating teacher's behaviors as well as the dynamics existing within a classroom, student teachers can gain significant insights into the roles they will be assuming.

The initial days are not too early for student teachers to have the opportunity to observe other teachers whose style and teaching situations may differ from those of the cooperating teacher. The early days also can provide the opportunity for student teachers to see their students in other settings so that they can compare behavior patterns in the cooperating teacher's classroom with actions in other areas of the school. In a broader context, observations during the first few weeks may help the student teacher become more aware of the complexity of the school setting. They may find it beneficial to observe other teachers in their subject areas or grade levels. This should provide a more complete picture of the school environment and can help alleviate boredom that might result from extensive observations of the cooperating teacher. The initial observations should raise the level of interest of student teachers by stimulating and challenging them to become involved. They should lead to familiarization with the classroom and a better concept of their roles.

Case Study No. 28: Confusing Practices

During your student teacher's first few weeks, she has spent time observing a number of veteran teachers. After a while, she questions you about the consistency with which school policy is followed throughout the building. Students are considered tardy in some classrooms if they are not seated in their designated spots in neatly arranged rows of desks when the bell rings. In other classrooms many students arrive with drinks and snacks and lounge on sofas and chairs arranged haphazardly around the room. She observed that in a few rooms students listen to music on their headphones or converse with others as they complete their tasks whereas teachers down the hall insist on complete concentration. In each of the classrooms teachers were teaching and students appeared to be learning. Your student teacher wants to know how students can be expected to adhere to school regulations if only some teachers follow them. What should you say to her?

1. Explain that the curriculum sometimes drives the appropriate procedure in various classes.
2. Tell her that most students are capable of adapting to their environments.
3. Explain that such diversity often exists when teachers work in isolation.
4. State that, ideally, all teachers should follow school policy, but that student learning is the primary objective.
5. _____

Comment

Your student teacher's reaction is a valid one. Sometimes students are confused when they go from one classroom where the atmosphere is casual to another where rules are rigidly enforced. However, teacher individuality and creativity promote interest and enthusiasm among students. Instructors will have different procedures due to the differing nature of the content they teach.

Student teachers should understand that diversity is a natural and necessary process within the school.

Questions

1. Should a cooperating teacher only schedule observations for his student teacher with those teachers who are considered conventional?
2. How much guidance should be provided in teacher contact?
3. _____

Formative Observations

After the objectives of the initial observations have been achieved and the student teacher experiences the role of teacher, new questions and opportunities will emerge. As indicated previously, a student teacher will be gradually increasing teaching activity from the first day in the school. A new set of teaching tasks will develop when this involvement becomes more extensive. These experiences may lead to questions about how to solve teaching problems and how to relate to pupils more effectively. Observations can provide assistance in both areas. After a few days of teaching, a student teacher may find it beneficial to visit other instructors in order to discover different styles and techniques. The following challenges may be addressed with some degree of effectiveness provided the student teacher is aware of what he is to look for:

- **More effective teaching techniques.** The student teacher may look for ways of arousing student interest, analyzing teaching behavior, and looking for ideas that would make his classroom more successful.
- **Better understanding of pupils.** Students may behave differently in other classrooms. What teacher behaviors seem to influence their conduct?
- **Identify teaching needs.** A student teacher may see his own deficiencies more accurately. By the same token, he may also better understand pupil needs and how to meet them.

Formative observations should encompass a considerable portion of a student teaching experience and expand knowledge of teaching skills. During this period, the teaching candidate will be analyzing and discovering areas of strength and weakness. A cooperating teacher will need to continue to review and discuss observations with the student teacher. This dialogue should cause a student to reconstruct the experience and gain insights that may have been overlooked previously.

Summative Observations

This series of observations will be conducted near the end of student teaching. By this time the student teacher should be almost ready to assume teaching responsibilities without a great amount of supervision. He should be viewing the teaching act in more abstract terms and be aware of its more subtle components. These final observations may be the most rewarding.

The student teacher should see teaching in more scientific and artistic terms and have an increased awareness of the critical role of the teacher in directing learning. This more sophisticated analysis of teaching through observation should allow the student teacher to become more evaluative with the ability to detect relationships that would have been overlooked earlier and to understand why a teacher is behaving in a particular way. In addition, the student teacher may be considering alternatives that would work in his situation or which could be adapted to a different setting.

An example of a sophisticated analysis of teaching was provided by a former student teacher of the author who deliberately observed both good and poor practices. His strength was that he converted all ideas into positive suggestions when he recorded them. This resulted in a list of constructive ideas that could be reviewed for his own benefit at a later time. In one such class, he made the following comments:

Great Idea

- Allow students to answer the questions posed without interrupting.
- Question the students in order to determine whether directions have been understood.
- If a threat is made, a teacher should be able to carry it out.
- Be patient and tolerant.
- Allow students to answer questions without cutting them short.
- Make visual aids large enough for all to see.

It did not matter whether a poor, average, or superior teacher was observed. The student teacher compiled a list of principles in a positive tone that will guide his teaching.

A student teacher should have formulated a more comprehensive outlook on teaching as the experience nears its completion. Education may be viewed in a more integrated way which means understanding better the critical role of a teacher. The student teacher should have a valid frame of reference for the evaluation of teaching and should have a more comprehensive picture of the function of the school.

If a student teacher fails to observe at any phase of the experience, a valuable learning opportunity will have been missed. On the other hand, if observations are crammed into any brief period of time, a student teacher will be denied an opportunity to learn as completely as possible. The student teacher's notion of what to look for may be vague at all three levels of the experience unless the cooperating teacher provides some direction.

Case Study No. 29: A Critical Reaction To A Class

Steve has just observed a teacher who is considered to be rather ineffective. When he returns, he repeats a list of criticisms of the class and is very negative about the teacher's procedures. You suspect that his comments are accurate, but you wonder how you can approach the discussion of the observation without appearing to be unethical. What do you choose to do?

1. Ask him to formulate some positive recommendations based on this negative experience.
2. Discuss the points that he mentions and determine alternative strategies rather than focus on the perceived shortcomings of the teacher.
3. Admonish him not to be too hasty in making judgments.
4. Ask him what he would have done if he had been the teacher in that situation.
5. _____

Comment

The analysis of this situation involves a matter of ethics as well as learning (See Chapter Ten). Poor teachers cannot be singled out just for illustrative purposes, but a future teacher has the right to know that the profession has to deal with ineffective teaching styles. An observation of this type may be summarized best by using the positive qualities described in this chapter, and focus should be on principles rather than personalities.

Questions

1. What can be learned from observation of poor teaching?
2. Are there ways that a cooperating teacher can professionally prepare a student teacher for an observation of a teacher who has marginal skills?

Alternative Procedures
Enriching Growth Opportunities

The focus of this chapter to this point has been on observations within the same school structure and in a conventional manner. There are also other types of observation activities that will contribute to helping future teachers gain a comprehensive picture of school practices. Diversified exposure can help shape expectations, attitudes, and beliefs about what constitutes good teaching and positive learning climates. It then seems logical that expanding the scope of student teachers' observations could result in a broader, more sophisticated, and refined understanding of teaching .

Observation of Other Levels of Instruction

One of the major purposes of observations is to expand student teacher awareness of the wide range of teaching styles. It is desirable to observe classes in fields other than the student teacher's major, other grade levels, and in other schools.

In recent years there has been a movement away from curricular isolation and teachers operating in the vacuum of their own classrooms. For example, *The Vermont Framework of Standards and Learning Opportunities* (1996), encourages teachers to collaborate with colleagues and make interdisciplinary connections among the disciplines that are taught. In order to operate in a more cooperative environment, educators must have some knowledge about what is occurring in other parts of the building.

Observations should serve to expand a student teacher's perspective of school curricula and examine how other activities mesh with those in his chosen field. Student teachers have the opportunity to view firsthand the operations of other educators whose style and teaching situations may differ dramatically from what they experience in their cooperating teachers' rooms.

Studying Other Schools

Significant results can be achieved through observations beyond the boundaries of the assigned school. Student teachers have the opportunity to see other educators whose style and classroom climates may differ from what they have been experiencing.

Observations in various settings can allow a look at teaching at different grade levels, as indicated above, and other types of school communities. A nearby school, for example, may operate on a different set of premises and serve a different type of student population. Knowledge of other settings may help prepare student teachers for placement in schools that may be unlike the ones where they are student teaching. If logistics permit, two student teachers could "swap" positions for a day with a peer in nearby school and then compare notes on their impressions of the learning environment in each other's placements.

Observing Other Student Teachers

Student teachers may be assigned to a school where there are other student teachers. If so, the cooperating teacher may consider having them observe each other. There is strong evidence supporting the use of peer observations as a learning activity for student teachers. Rauch and Whitaker (1999), found that pairs of student teachers improved their teaching by sitting in each other's classes and giving written feedback. Student teachers also reported that the experience of being an evaluator was enlightening. Peer critiques, in addition to the feedback received from the cooperating teacher and the college supervisor, enhanced the outcomes of the observation process (Giebelhaus, 1995).

Exposing student teachers to peer review is consistent with the expectations for licensed teachers. Some professional organizations have called for teachers to be more collaborative and collegial in their professional development and renewal (National Association for the Education of Young Children, 1996). Some states are requiring teachers to assist each other in professional development. Colleagueship is one of the five standards identified by the Vermont Department of Education (1999) and requires teachers to "observe, mentor and collaborate with colleagues to ensure best practice for improving student performance."

Student teachers may be able to communicate with each other in more comprehensible ways because of their similarities. Hawkey (1995) suggested that student teachers may learn from each other because the intimidation factor is lessened when receiving critique from a peer rather than a superior. Such peer assistance may contribute appreciably to their growth.

Self Observation

A final recommended evaluation procedure is for the student teachers to view themselves. The availability of videocassette recorders has made self analysis a practical reality. It is difficult to imagine a more striking way of illustrating and reinforcing concepts about teaching than by allowing prospective teachers to observe themselves as they are actively teaching. Video recordings permit student teachers to see both their weak and strong points and allow cooperating teachers to serve as resource persons in interpreting the teaching behaviors.

Because the VCR provides a vivid account of teaching events, the feedback assumes a more concrete character. Video recordings have the advantage of being able to be played more than once and at times more convenient to those who might observe them. Student teachers and cooperating teachers can view the tapes separately and talk with each other later about the major points.

There is one caution in using video tapes. A recording cannot completely capture the essence of a classroom, so the activity must be reviewed in context. Secondly, one must realize that a videotape is not a professional production. In these days of slick presentations on commercial television, the student teacher must be cautioned not to expect a perfect reproduction. Some of the sights and sounds on the monitor may be a distortion of what really happened in the classroom. In spite of these limitations, self-analysis through a videocassette is a technique worth considering.

It has been demonstrated that student teachers can increase their knowledge about their own teaching by conducting an audio tape analysis of their instruction (Anderson and Freiberg, 1995). A record of the pace of instruction, quality of questions, clarity of the information presented, and type of student responses can be captured on audio tape.

Scheduling And Analyzing Observations
Precision and Professionalization

An effective observation begins with good planning. This is a two-step process which involves both preparation for learning and appropriate scheduling arrangements. The preparation involves determining who is to be observed, what the student teacher is to look for, and how he will record and analyze the information secured from the experience.

The second step is to make the arrangements for the visit. It is a matter of professional courtesy to request an observation in advance. It gives the teacher the opportunity to structure the class so that it has more relevance to the observer.

Arrangements for observations may be made by the student teacher, cooperating teacher, department chairperson, or building administrator. The student teacher should learn the procedure that is practiced at his school and follow that policy. Some schools operate on an informal basis while others have very specific procedures. A useful student teacher visitation request form is included in the Appendix as Worksheet Number Seven. Teachers may wish to use this form or a modification of it for scheduling observations.

Developing a Context for Observation

Once the visitation is arranged, a frame of reference can be developed which will make the observation more meaningful. Student teachers seem to profit most from observations that have specific goals. A student teacher who realizes that it is important to note a teacher's questioning style, for example, will gain more from the experience than the one who is only instructed to "observe." If possible, a cooperating teacher should apprise a student teacher of the style of the teacher to be observed. Sometimes the cooperating teacher may simply want the student teacher to compare the performance of one or more pupils in a different class. There are numerous other possibilities for preparation based on the qualifications of the teacher to be observed and the needs of the student teacher.

Many student and cooperating teachers prefer to have a set of criteria that may be analyzed during an observation. Those who prefer such instructions will find two such forms as Worksheets Number Eight and Nine in the Appendix. Worksheet Number Eight is a form that encourages thinking about the elements of a typical lesson and Worksheet Number Nine is a checklist that forces the observer to note whether certain criteria exist.

The student teacher should arrive early enough for the observation to allow time for any preliminary discussion or orientation that the teacher would desire to make. A student teacher can take more meaningful note of the classroom procedure if he is aware of what is planned. Early arrival also insures that the normal flow of activity will not be interrupted.

The teacher undoubtedly will take note of the visitor's reactions from time to time. The student teacher should be prompted to display an active interest in the class and not appear to be bored or indifferent. The anecdotal records in many student teaching offices contain examples of student teachers who were seen to be sleeping or bored with the class, resulting in a teacher's refusing to allow visits from future student teachers. An alert cooperating teacher will see that a student teacher understands how to benefit from the visit.

Follow-up

An observation is not finished with the conclusion of a lesson. The observer should make a point to thank the teacher for allowing a visit to the class. The teacher may want to make a few comments about the lesson or even solicit reactions to what was seen. A few constructive comments by the student teacher are always in order. The teacher who watches a student teacher hastily making an exit following an observation may be aggravated or disappointed and not be receptive to further visits. Remind the student teacher that he is a guest in the school and should be courteous to the host or hostess.

The observation experience concludes with an analysis session between the cooperating teacher and the student teacher. This discussion can lead to a productive examination of teaching. Questions are good techniques for encouraging the student teacher to reflect on what was observed.

An effective observation should result in improved student teaching performance. Actual modification of teaching following a classroom visit will depend upon the attitude of the observer, timing, and application of what has been seen. An observation structured in a professional manner can be more beneficial than a similar period of teaching.

No student teacher ever became a skilled professional by simply watching masters apply the craft of teaching. But, during well designed observations, the student teacher should be mentally engaged in the events as they unfold. Thus, observations are as much a part of a rewarding teaching experience as the work within the classroom. The strategy for making observations work is to see how they are integrated with the total learning process of a student teacher.

Case Study No. 30: No Change

Since you were convinced that it would be productive for your student teacher to observe other classes, you scheduled visitations which you thought would be beneficial. Although he apparently was completing the suggested observations, there was no evidence that he was gaining any ideas. Your inquiries about the nature of his observations brought only vague responses. Furthermore, there has been no evidence of his having changed his teaching as a result of visitations. Since you are concerned about this lack of progress, what course of action do you take?

1. Suggest that he discontinue observations for a few days.
2. Provide more structure so that he will know what to look for.
3. Ask the student teacher to take notes on the observation.
4. Conduct a follow-up conference about the observation.
5. _____

Comment

The lack of response may result from the student teacher's not seeing any reason to complete the observation. It might be a good idea to think about what has occurred prior to the observation. If there was little or no orientation, it might be well to begin there. The follow-up inquiry also could be examined to see if the questions contribute to a student teacher's understanding or whether they may appear to be an oral examination. In any event, the observations should be continued.

Questions

1. Why would a student teacher be reluctant to talk about a class that he has observed?
2. What procedures from other professions might be adopted by teachers to demonstrate the value of observations?

Brian entered the teachers' work room with a list of notes and a look of enthusiasm on his face. He had just observed one of the more popular teachers in the building.

"The class of Mr. Lawton's is everything you said that it would be. I really enjoyed watching him teach. I picked up two or three ideas that I can use next week in my class. Time went by so quickly that I had

difficulty realizing I had been there for an hour. He even had me involved in the discussion."

Miss Bennett resisted the temptation to remind him of his previous negative attitude toward observations and simply commented, "I thought you would enjoy seeing him. Now, what did you notice about the way that he motivated the students?"

Remember:

- **The cooperating teacher should guide the student teacher in choosing observations.**
- **Observation is the most efficient method of learning about teaching in many situations.**
- **Observations will be more meaningful with adequate preparation.**
- **The value of an observation will be in proportion to the time spent in its analysis.**
- **Observations can provide opportunities for reflection on the nature of one's own teaching.**
- **The perceptive observer will improve professional skills.**
- **Peer and self-evaluation are valid ways to improve one's teaching.**
- **Student teaching may be one of the few times in the student teacher's career when observing colleagues at work is possible.**

Useful References

Anderson, Jeffery B. and Jerome H. Freiberg. 1995. Using Self-Assessment as a Reflective Tool to Enhance the Student Teaching Experience. *Teacher Education Quarterly* 22 (Winter): 77-91.

Balch, Pamela M., and Patrick E. Balch. 1987. Becoming an Effective Observer. Chapter 6 in *The Cooperating Teacher: A Practical Approach for the Supervision of Student Teachers.* Lanham, MD. University Press of America.

Beyer, L. E. 1984. Field Experience, Ideology, and the Development of Critical Reflectivity. *Journal of Teacher Education* 35 (May-June): 34-41.

Burstein, Nancy Davis. 1989. The Transition and Supervision of Student Teachers in Elementary Schools: A Comparative Analysis of Two Assignments. ERIC ED 324296

Garland, Colden. 1982. Providing Guidance Through Observation and Conferencing. Chapter 7 in *Guiding Clinical Experiences in Teacher Education.* New York. Longman, Inc.

Giebelhaus, Carman. 1995. Revisiting a Step-Child: Supervision in Teacher Education. A paper presented at the Annual Conference of the Association of Teacher Educators. Detroit, MI, February 18-22. ERIC ED 391785

Hawkey, K. 1995. Learning From Peers: The Experience of Student Teachers in School-Based Teacher Education. *Journal of Teacher Education 46*: 175-183.

Mills, Johnnie Ruth. 1980. A Guide for Teaching Systematic Observation to Student Teachers. *Journal of Teacher Education* 31 (Nov-Dec):5-9.

National Association for the Education of Young Children. (1996). *Guidelines for Preparation of Early Childhood Professionals: Washington, DC.*

Rauch, Kristin and Catherine R. Whitaker. 1999. Observation and Feedback During Student Teaching: Learning from Peers. *Action in Teacher Education 21* (Fall): 67-78.

Treiber, F. 1984. Ineffective Teaching: Can We Learn From It? *Journal of Teacher Education* 35 (Sept.-Oct): 45-46.

Vermont Department of Education (1996). *Vermont Framework of Standards and Learning Opportunities.* Montpelier, Vermont.

Vermont Department of Education (1999). *Standards for Vermont Educators: A Vision for Schooling.* Montpelier, Vermont.

6

Supervising Planning

Brian seemed to be gaining confidence daily as he became acquainted with the school routine and participated in more teaching activities. His work with the class had been satisfactory and he was scheduled to assume a full teaching load within a few days. He had been working diligently on lesson plans, poring over a variety of resources, aligning his instructional goals with the state and local standards, and consulting the planning section of his student teaching guide.

Miss Bennett assumed that Brian would consult with her about his teaching ideas for the new section, but he had not made any reference to his plans since she assigned the unit to him. She wanted to see his tentative plans to be certain that he was making progress, and she wondered if she should make any suggestions once she saw his notes.

Miss Bennett decided to approach the subject with her student teacher. At the beginning of a conference she casually stated, "Four more days and you will have full responsibility and a new section to teach. Do you have your plans developed yet?"

Brian shuffled some papers and looked at her in an uncertain manner and shook his head . . .

The Planning Process
More Than Notes on a Paper

Student teachers sometimes have difficulty understanding the importance and mechanics of planning. This may be especially true if the cooperating teacher carries out effective lessons without a formal written plan in sight. The beginning student teacher often fails to realize that planning skills of veteran teachers evolve over time. The formal written lesson plan provides a solid foundation for student teachers to think through a specific learning experience. Student teachers who may need some convincing that written lesson plans are important should consider the following:

- Good plans reduce stress and anxiety.
- Planning helps insure positive results from the lesson.
- Well-planned lessons can reduce pupil behavior problems.
- Planning lessens the amount of "ad lib" teaching.
- Well planned lessons have a clear instructional focus.
- Lesson plans can show intentional links to the local, state, and national standards.
- Written plans may be required and reviewed by the principal or other supervisor.

Probably all teacher education institutions require preservice teachers to write lesson plans prior to student teaching. In spite of their efforts to be realistic, student teachers may fail to realize the value of planning until they are actually confronted with the actuality of teaching a class.

According to O'Neal (1983), student teachers initially may not take planning seriously although cooperating teachers consider quality lesson plans to be essential to instruction. A cooperating teacher may be confronted with the task of explaining the effect of planning on teaching. Such a responsibility may range from the development of specific daily plans to a planning strategy for organizing large units of work or time blocks. Generally, a cooperating teacher may need to see that student teachers can:

- Generate plans that are in concert with the school's mission and goals.
- Develop a long-range plan.
- Develop daily plans that guide the individual lesson.
- Demonstrate alternative methods of planning.
- Plan far enough in advance to allow time for gathering resources and time for reflection.
- Devise a system of planning that can be used in the future.

It might be well to review the basic elements of a plan with the student teacher. Beginning with the premise that a plan is more than having something to do each minute of the class, a cooperating teacher may want to provide a simple analysis of the basic questions that must be answered in developing a viable structure. Consider discussion of the following questions in looking at the scope and sequence of planning:

- **Who will be taught?**
  Nature of the student group
- **What is to be taught?**
  Content

- **Why should it be taught?**
  Goals and objectives
- **When is it to be taught?**
  Timing
- **How will it be taught?**
  Methods and techniques
- **How will it be evaluated?**
  Determining progress

The above framework provides for considerable flexibility while showing how various components of planning are related regardless of whether they are for one hour or one semester. It should prevent the student teacher from feeling consumed by useless paper work and present planning as a viable tool instead of an abstract task.

The cooperating teacher has the right to expect a student teacher to prepare both long-range and daily plans, but he may need to help the student teacher learn to prepare, especially in the early phases of teaching. Planning should be required which will achieve the following results:

- The student teacher will be a partner in the teaching-learning process.
- The planning process will foster thinking about objectives and selecting the appropriate teaching techniques.
- The plan will offer the cooperating teacher an opportunity to make suggestions before a class is taught.
- The plan will be a guide that can be used in the analysis of a lesson.

The student teacher should learn that a well developed long-range plan will provide the context for more successful creation of daily plans and give continuity to lessons from day to day. The cooperating teacher should make certain that a student teacher sees the relationship between the two plans.

Teaching that is aligned with national, state and local standards is now expected in most localities. The student teacher who knows the requirements and focuses on what the results should be can select objectives and design learning activities that will likely yield the desired outcomes. Such plans also require designing assessment strategies to ascertain whether the targeted standard of learning was reached. The student teacher needs to understand that careful planning is essential to ensure a successful and meaningful learning experience.

A student teacher should be encouraged to develop her own style by formulating the type of planning procedure that works best for her. The cooperating teacher's role will be that of providing feedback and helping the student teacher see the strengths and weaknesses of her chosen alternatives.

In summary, a cooperating teacher can assist a student teacher by assuring that she understands the concept of planning, has the opportunity to write plans for different time periods, aligns specific objectives with state and local standards, and has the opportunity to develop her own style. If such assistance is effective and the above goals are reached, student teachers will recognize that good plans are the best tools which teachers can have for teaching effectively.

Case Study No. 31: No Allowance For Individuals

Rene's lesson plan was presented in advance and was well written. As you review it, you notice that she has made no provision for the fact that some of the more capable pupils will finish their assignments quickly while most of the other students will still be working. If the class is taught as proposed, some of her pupils will have nothing to do while the others are completing their work. This can lead to some confusion and may present some problems for Rene.

What do you do?

1. Nothing. She will soon discover the reason and correct it.
2. Inform her that the plan will not work and ask her to revise it.
3. Discuss the plan with her step by step and analyze what is likely to happen.
4. Share one of your plans for that lesson with her.
5. _____

Comment

One of the responsibilities of a cooperating teacher is that of helping a student teacher refine planning skills. The plans are submitted in advance so that the cooperating teacher can detect weaknesses or offer suggestions which would improve learning. In fairness to the student teacher and to the pupils who are involved, some sort of analysis and feedback before teaching would be more productive than a follow-up conversation about what went wrong.

Questions

1. How can a teacher discuss inadequate plans with a student teacher and avoid being too dominant?

2. What principles of planning need to be addressed in helping this student teacher be more effective?

Case Study No. 32: No Visible Plans

Reed is a confident student teacher. Despite your frequent requests, he has not produced any written plans. His teaching has been acceptable, but you are aware that it could be improved if you could talk with him in advance about his planned activities. On Monday morning you ask him if he has his plans for the week. He dismisses your question with the remark that he does not write anything down because it is all in his mind. Since you feel that prior analysis is important, what do you do to get something in writing?

1. Refuse to allow him to teach until he submits plans that you can approve.
2. Critique his lessons and show where he could have done better if he had planned more thoroughly.
3. Ask the college supervisor to clarify the university position about required lesson plans.
4. Verbally interrogate him about his proposed plans.
5. _____

Comment

Teachers plan in different ways. The possibility exists that this person is one who can mentally organize. Discussion and analysis would seem to be appropriate regardless of whether written plans exist. A cooperating teacher has the obligation and right to know what a student teacher is going to teach. It is also important for Reed to understand that a written lesson plan may not be essential for him to successfully carry out a given lesson but in his absence, it is a real necessity.

Questions

1. What causes resistance to written plans?
2. What are some key concepts about planning which a cooperating teacher could emphasize to a student teacher like this one?
3. How would you convince a student teacher to write formal lesson plans when he sees that such detailed plans are not always used by veteran teachers?

Case Study No. 33: Incomplete Plans

Rich is now doing a considerable amount of teaching. So far his performance has not been at the level that you had hoped. His presentations are not thorough and he shows no evidence of having given careful thought to lesson content. When you ask for lesson plans, you see just brief notes that serve as prompts at best. When you asked him to do more extensive planning, he responded that so many things he learned about planning at school seemed so irrelevant that he has not been doing them. What would you consider to be the next move on your part?

1. Ask Rich to complete a self-evaluation to see if he recognizes any deficiencies.
2. Give him a specific outline of the type of planning that you expect.
3. Ask to see plans at least a day in advance so you can review them.
4. Write an evaluation that shows concern on your part about the quality of his performance.
5. Work together with him in writing an acceptable plan.
6. _____

Comment

Plans serve as maps for a successful road trip through a class. The student teacher apparently has seen little linkage between lesson plans and classroom teaching. The basic task is for a cooperating teacher to convince him that planning is necessary.

Questions

1. What, in your estimation, is the relationship between written planning and effective teaching?
2. Is there the possibility that some variable other than planning might be involved?

Planning In Advance
One Week or One Hour?

How far in advance should plans be submitted? This is a frequent question and an arbitrary answer will not suffice because there are too many variables involved. Despite this, one must confront the fact that plans should be prepared far enough in advance for review by the cooperating teacher and possible modification by the student teacher.

It is frequently a problem for student teachers to submit plans very far in advance, especially in the early weeks of student teaching. Part of the difficulty comes from a lack of experience and resources to draw on, but problems may result from a student teacher's not being aware of what is needed and how it should be presented. Some student teachers may be accustomed to presenting papers at the last minute at college and this may continue into student teaching. Therefore, it is good practice for colleges and universities to implement interventions, such as the Student Teaching Readiness Assessment as shown in Worksheet Six, to help preservice teachers modify negative habits prior to student teaching. If the student teacher has been allowed to procrastinate during preservice training, the requirement to submit plans in advance will call for a change in procedure.

Planning in advance is especially necessary when outside resources are to be used. Media and library specialists, for example, often cannot respond immediately to requests for materials. A cooperating teacher should make certain that the student teacher understands the necessary protocol to secure help in planning from other professionals and support personnel.

The following suggestions may help a cooperating teacher secure the plans in time to analyze them and provide feedback to the student teacher.

- Provide a guideline for a lesson plan form.
- Give a specific time for submission of plans.
- Give feedback as quickly as possible.
- Make the requirements realistic.

Final decisions about some plans may have to be delayed until a previous lesson has been taught since most strategies need some last-minute revision in the wake of previous class activity. In spite of this, the basic operating procedure for planning in advance appears just as appropriate for student teachers as it is for experienced teachers. Plans should be ready far enough ahead so that effective organization for teaching is insured, but not so rigid that they cannot be modified when necessary. Certain factors determine the format of advance planning. These points should be considered in determining the nature and extent of advance preparation:

- The necessity of advance planning for a particular class or unit.
- The progress of the student teacher.
- The amount of preparation that would be involved.

- The ability of the student to think in long-range terms.
- Time available for preparation.
- Availability of resources for planning.

The same procedures should be applied both to long-range and daily planning. Preparing can often be enhanced if it is placed in context of the general goals of long-range organization. If a student teacher can develop unit plans, it should foster the ability to plan on a more specific basis. A cooperating teacher may want to emphasize this concept by requiring the student teacher to develop a unit plan.

Case Study No. 34: Last-Minute Plans

Your student teacher always has his plans but they come to you at the last minute. This results in your only having time to give them cursory review before the class begins. You would like to see his papers earlier in order to suggest occasional revisions. How do you go about telling him to submit the plans when you want them?

1. Give him specific deadlines for submission.
2. Confer with him and try to work out a system that will allow him to present the plans more ahead of time.
3. Review his schedule to determine whether he has enough time for adequate preparation.,
4. _____

Comment

This case raises questions about procedure. Has the teacher indicated that she wants the plans at a certain time? What kind of schedule does the student teacher have? Is the student teacher a person who tends to do things at the last minute? How familiar is the student teacher with the content that is being taught and the overall course of study for the class? What kind of communication exists between the two people? In many cases, the first step should be to look for the underlying factors before the specific incident is approached directly.

Questions

1. What factors probably cause lateness in planning?
2. Will it be effective if a teacher states specific deadlines and makes no other adjustments?

Case Study No. 35: A Question Of Time

Sharon is a creative person. She has great ideas for activities and projects, but either she does not get started early enough to develop them or she does not get started at all. The thoughts are good, but you are puzzled about how to get her to allow time to follow through on a project. What do you do?

1. Help her in developing ideas to completion.
2. Release some time from her teaching schedule so that she will have more hours for creative activity.
3. Talk with her to see if there is something that causes her to avoid completing a creative activity.
4. Ignore the ideas unless she can put them in practice and concentrate on what she is doing as a teacher.
5. _____

Comment

First of all, remember that creativity is a wonderful and valuable quality. This is a good example of how collegiality between the student teacher and cooperating teacher is important. If the ideas have merit, the cooperating teacher needs to help the student teacher focus her thoughts, identify the potential roadblocks, and provide feedback that will help bring creative thoughts to a finished product.

Questions

1. What are the problems that creative people can have with teaching?
2. What guidelines would you be comfortable with in balancing creativity with teaching requirements?

Case Study No. 36: Unprepared

Linda had volunteered to prepare materials for the children to use at the end of a unit, but she failed to produce them. When it came time to conclude the series, she substituted routine activities that needed little preparation, giving no explanation to you.

As the two of you walk to the parking lot at the end of the day, Linda casually comments that she had not been prepared to teach the section which she had chosen because a new person had entered her life and the relationship is accelerating. You now understand why the materials were not ready. What do you do in this situation?

1. Confer with Linda, review the requirements and develop a strategy which will prove to you that she meets her responsibilities.
2. Indicate that you will teach until you have seen proof that she is prepared.
3. Suggest that she find an appropriate balance in her personal life so that she can fulfill her responsibility during student teaching.
4. Dismiss the incident assuming she will make the necessary adjustments to get back on track.
5. _____

Comment

Distractions can come easily for some people and a romantic involvement can cause one to establish new priorities quickly. However, Linda has a career at stake and must stay on task. There needs to be an understanding very quickly about what Linda's responsibilities are and what she will do to meet them.

Questions

1. How much should a cooperating teacher become involved in making decisions that might affect a student teacher's personal life after school?
2. How can a cooperating teacher detect whether the explanation is valid or the student teacher is avoiding responsibilities she cannot meet?

Case Study No. 37: Good Class--Different Plan

Your student teacher has responsibility for two classes. His plans are well structured and complete. The problem is that he tends to deviate from his outline and fails to do what he has proposed to do. What do you do to reconcile this problem?

1. Discuss the situation with him and determine why this is happening.
2. Do not interfere as long as he is teaching successfully.
3. Review the plans in advance and help him adhere to them.
4. Watch for the results of the first test to determine whether he is deviating too much from what he intends to do.
5. _____

Comment

In some cases it is beneficial to deviate from a plan. All teachers have done that. Plans should be flexible and sometimes the teacher should change from the original intent. The critical questions are whether his teaching was effective, whether the content had value, and if the instructional objectives were met. If it is determined that his teaching had little instructional value, it would be worthwhile to call this fact to the attention of the student teacher and to encourage him to meet the intended objectives.

Questions

1. What might cause a constant deviation from lesson plans?
2. How essential is it to closely follow a pre-determined lesson plan?

Sharing Plans And Resources
With The Student Teacher
Opening the Confidential Files

One of the persistent questions that cooperating teachers have to deal with is that of whether to share plans with their student teachers. The positive position would be to advocate sharing them so the student teacher can become familiar with the teacher's style and possibly learn to develop effective plans more quickly. If a student teacher can review the plans of her supervisor, she may be more comfortable and, in all likelihood, it will save time and frustration.

On the other hand, it can be argued that a student teacher would be restricted by viewing a cooperating teacher's plans because of the implication that the student teacher should model the cooperating teacher. It also can be assumed that students came from their teacher education institutions with concepts of planning and some refreshing new ideas. This opportunity might be lost if they found that their ideas were in contrast with prevailing practices.

An eclectic position may be the best approach. A student teacher who is aware of a variety of alternative planning scenarios, including examples of her supervisor's plans, should be able to study them and then create plans that are of most benefit to her. Creativity is based on knowledge, and a cooperating teacher will improve a student teacher's skill in planning by seeing that a variety of alternatives are available for consideration.

In today's electronic age, there are scores of web sites for every subject area where sample lesson plans can be easily accessed.

Some states offer the potential for educators to develop a curriculum electronically. For example, the Vermont Department of Education (1999) has developed software that allows educators to design, share, and critique standards based plans on line. Student teachers can access this software to see examples of work done by professionals from all over the state and can even use the software to design their own lessons and units. By surveying a number of plans from multiple sources, the student teacher will understand that veteran teachers use a wide variety of planning strategies and formats.

The sharing of plans by the cooperating teacher can also include information about the facilities and resources available at the school that could be beneficial. Most likely, a student teacher could benefit from information about some or all of the following:

- Resources in the Media Center.
- Available technology resources.
- Available supplies and equipment.
- Community resources.
- Available funds.
- Pupil talents.
- Publications.
- Resources within the classroom.
- Expertise of faculty members.

Such materials and resources may have escaped the attention of a student teacher. If she realizes the value of these resources and learns of their availability, she may tend to plan more creatively.

A supervisor who wishes to analyze his procedures in working with planning may want to use Worksheet Number Ten in the Appendix. This guide contains seven recommendations for guiding planning, invites analysis of present activities and asks for possible improvements in helping student teachers plan more effectively.

Case Study No. 38: Imitating The Cooperating Teacher

Each teacher has to develop a style of teaching. A procedure that is ideal for one teacher may cause another not to succeed. You recognize this, but your student teacher has not been able to grasp this concept. Since you are an experienced teacher, she is certain that any procedure you use has to be superior to any of her techniques. Consequently, she observes you teach and then attempts to imitate your style. Instead of offering ideas for your approval, she asks for your suggestions and then tries to follow them. She is experiencing little success and is becoming concerned about her ability to teach. What changes do you make to improve this situation?

1. Switch classes and teach after the student teacher has taught.
2. Explain why your techniques may not be working for her.
3. Plan together and ask for her ideas instead of sharing yours.
4. Plan an activity that will prevent her from observing you teach.
5. _____

Comment

A student teacher should not try to be a carbon copy of her cooperating teacher. The description here seems to indicate that this student teacher is insecure and dependent. If the cooperating teacher suddenly withdraws all support, the student teacher may experience frustration and tension. Perhaps a gradual withdrawal would be less disturbing. The cooperating teacher should consistently seek to support the student teacher's ideas in as many ways as possible.

Questions

1. Do teachers sometimes unconsciously encourage student teachers to follow their procedures? If so, how is this done?
2. What steps can be taken to encourage greater independence in planning?

Case Study No. 39: Inadequate Videotape Preparation

Jason has decided to show an excerpt of a videotape to supplement his unit on the Civil War. Unfortunately, he did not pre-cue the tape to the appropriate place and spent several minutes trying to find the section he wished to use. In the meantime, students became unruly and it took several minutes to regain their attention. Once the desired section of the tape was located and the viewing began, the pupils were not attentive. What steps should the cooperating teacher take in this situation?

1. Analyze the class with Jason and get his perspective on what could have been done to make the video more effective.
2. Step in and control the pupils' behavior while Jason finds the correct segment of the video tape.
3. Reprimand the pupils for inappropriate behavior.
4. _____

Comment

This case emphasizes the need for attending to details. Using valuable class time to find the proper segment of the video is an open invitation for misbehavior. Pupils' attention could be improved by making sure the video is ready to be shown and has an instructional purpose.

Questions

1. How do you lead Jason to see that the pupil's misbehavior was due to poor planning on his part?
2. What can be done to help student teachers make use of appropriate supplementary material?

The class ended and Brian returned to the teachers' work room where Miss Bennett was reviewing some papers.

"How was the lesson?"

"Better than yesterday," Brian was quick to report. "I had several examples this time and there were no lapses of time because there was not enough for them to do."

"How was the timing?"

"The timing was much better than before. I did not stay with any one activity longer than fifteen minutes."

"I think that is best for this class," commented Miss Bennett.

Brian mentioned that one student had asked him in class why they had to study all that "stuff."

Miss Bennett inquired, "What did you tell him?"

Brian smiled and said, "I recalled that series of questions you asked me yesterday about objectives and explained why it was important and he seemed to accept it. And I thought you were putting me on when you were interrogating me regarding purposes."

"You cannot be too well prepared to teach that group," noted Miss Bennett. "I have always felt that it is better to prepare thoroughly than it is to adjust because of insufficient planning."

Brian responded instantly, "I completely agree. I would have been in trouble had I not planned carefully for this lesson "

Miss Bennett smiled as she closed her book. "You are making real progress, Brian. Continue to plan well and you will prevent many difficulties from occurring."

Remember:

- Good planning reduces anxiety.
- A student teacher needs to understand that good planning facilitates good teaching.
- A well-developed lesson plan may be a student teacher's best teaching aid.
- When planning, emphasis on results should prevail over emphasis on form.
- It is helpful for the student teacher to be familiar with the cooperating teacher's plans but not obligated to use them.
- Good planning depends on an adequate concept of purposes and a knowledge of the ability of the pupils.
- Plans should be viewed as a guide and not restrict the teacher's need to be flexible.

Useful References

Balch, Pamela M., and Patrick E. Balch. 1987. Planning with the Student Teacher. Chapter 5 in *The Cooperating Teacher: A Practical Approach for the Supervision of Student Teachers.* Lanham, MD. The University Press of America.

Berkey, Debra S., and Michelle Hamilton. 1987. Ranked Importance of Student Teacher Tasks as Perceived by Cooperating Teachers and University Supervisors. Paper presented at the National Convention of the American Alliance for Health, Physical Education, Recreation and Dance, Las Vegas, NV. ERIC ED 282864.

Garland, Colden. 1982. Providing Guidance in Planning and in Assuming Teaching Responsibility. Chapter 6 in *Guiding Clinical Experiences in Teacher Education.* New York. Longman, Inc.

Koeppen, Kim E. 1998. The Experiences of a Secondary Social Studies Student Teacher: Seeking Security by Planning for Self. *Teaching and Teacher Education* 14 (May): 401-411.

O'Neal, Sharon F. 1983. Developing Effective Instructional Planning and Decision-Making Skills: Are We Training Teachers or Technicians? ERIC ED 240105.

Vermont Department of Education (1999). Standards into Action. (Software). 120 State Street, Montpelier, Vermont 05620.

7

Observing, Analyzing And Guiding Student Teachers

Elaine Bennett strolled into the teachers' work room and surprised a group of teachers who were unaccustomed to seeing her in the middle of the morning.

"Not teaching today?" inquired Martha Wilson who normally has a break at this time.

"Mr. Sims is in charge of the class this morning," Elaine replied.

The critics were quick to go to work on her.

"Sure must be nice," volunteered Toni Bridges, a second-year teacher who had not yet acquired the knack of being well organized. "I wish I could have someone do my work and get extra pay for it."

"Best thing you ever did," roared Joe Hanley who had a reputation for neglecting his student teachers. "You should have left him alone with the class after the second day. They need to be by themselves because they cannot teach while you are in the room. I tell my student teachers that they can find me here if they need me. Otherwise, I will know they are getting along all right. Gives 'em confidence to be left alone."

"Perhaps I am from the old school, but I think we should not turn our classes over to an uncertified teacher education student." All eyes turned to Sylvia Rose, a teacher with inflexible standards and conservative values. "I want to know what goes on in my classes. Besides, you have to keep a close watch on some of these student teachers or they will be teaching our children a lot of liberal nonsense that they were exposed to at the university. A cooperating teacher should be in the room overseeing these young beginners."

Miss Bennett frowned. "I was following Brian's wishes and the guidelines of the university. He felt that he was ready to be left alone for a while. I think he needs to have this kind of responsibility occasionally."

"Sure he does," boomed Hanley.

"I do not think that you can help a student teacher if you are unaware of what is going on in the class," countered Miss Rose.

Toni Bridges interjected, "All I know is I wish I had the opportunity to use one in my class. I sure need the help."

Miss Bennett quickly finished her coffee, excused herself, and made a hasty exit to try to find a place in the building where she could have some possible solitude . . .

Supervising Instruction
Teaching From the Back of the Room

One of the most complex roles that a cooperating teacher can assume is that of instructional supervisor. The responsibilities must range from helping a student teacher achieve professional human relations skills to the development of teaching strategies. She must be willing and able to provide both latitude and support to a student teacher while still being accountable for the class. This delicate balance encompasses many phases of teaching and is most apparent when a student teacher is assigned to do most of the instruction.

Supervision involves a more passive role and requires a teacher to work on a one-to-one basis, using the tools of observation, conferences, and analysis to achieve positive results. In one sense, it is merely a different way of teaching.

The Supervisory Process

The part of supervision that involves analysis of instruction is important and complex. Because there is such a wide range of styles and procedures to choose from, a supervisor must first focus on principles that will guide the day to day process of analyzing student teaching. The first step in developing a supervisory process is identifying a set of principles that will guide the cooperating teacher in her interaction with student teachers. The principles should be developed for the following criteria:

- **The main objective of supervision is the improvement of instruction.** The focus is on the development of better skills of teaching through a formative rather than a summative process.
- **Objective feedback is essential for growth.** Student teachers generally will respond more positively to specific illustrations of teaching behavior rather than vague descriptions.
- **Teaching behaviors should be analyzed.** The objective data should not stand alone. The information gathered should be dealt with in context and analyzed. An effective analysis should lead to any necessary adjustments in teaching style.

- **Collaborative supervision is a desirable goal**. The process involves two professionals discussing teaching and learning. It is tempting to use direct communication, with the more experienced cooperating teacher telling a student teacher what to do, but the more collaborative approach involving sharing, problem solving, and negotiation should be more successful.
- **The research base should be stressed**. The profession, especially in the student teaching domain, has long been infested with the "it works for me" solution to problems. There is an emerging body of information from quality research that provides a basis for development of more effective teaching.

The set of procedures can be varied and complex, but the work of Cogan (1973) with clinical supervision and its more recent adaptations gives a frame of reference for supervision. The cycle of supervision involves three basic procedures: joint planning, teaching analysis, and conferences. Planning was the subject of Chapter Six, and conferences will be treated in Chapter Eight. This chapter will focus on several facets of instructional supervision and delineate some specific tasks involved in observing, describing and analyzing student teaching.

Determining The Best Approach For Supervision

Carl Glickman (1995) proposes that different supervisory approaches should be taken depending upon the developmental status of the person being supervised. This is determined by assessing the teacher's level of abstraction and level of commitment. The following represents Henry's (1995) application of Glickman's ideas specifically to the process of supervising student teachers.

The abstract, or conceptual, level ranges from low conceptual abilities to highly abstract skills. Persons with low levels of abstraction may be characterized by such factors as the inability to see more than one alternative to a problem or by tending to blame problems on external forces. Student teachers at low levels, for example, might be inclined to stereotype students or say that "everything" has been tried and nothing is working. When queried, they may admit to having tried only one or two approaches and may not recognize that there are alternative processes. In other words, student teachers with low abstraction think in concrete terms.

Persons with high abstraction are more able to discriminate, differentiate, and integrate. They are less rigid and see more alternatives to a question or teaching problem. Whereas persons at low levels of abstraction may resort to lecturing and asking low-level questions, persons who are higher in abstract ability will be more likely to take risks, explore ideas, encourage students to be creative and express themselves. Teachers at this level are more likely to see that differences exist among pupils and to use a variety of teaching models.

Persons also vary in their levels of commitment. Student teachers at low levels appear to be indifferent and perhaps even lazy. They see teaching as a job rather than as a profession, are inclined to be satisfied with minimum standards only and have little or no commitment to the profession.

At the other end of the continuum is a high level of commitment. These persons are committed to the students they teach and are eager to make their teaching more effective. They normally are high energy persons who plan to make a career in teaching.

The more effective supervisor will determine the developmental level of the student teacher in order to ascertain the most effective process for growth. Glickman identifies four quadrants for a frame of reference in making the decision:

- **Quadrant One -- Low Commitment and Low Abstraction.** This person has difficulty defining problems and knows fewer ways of responding to them. A student teacher in this quadrant is the one most likely not to go into teaching or to remain there for only a short period of time. The Quadrant One student teacher has little concern for students, sees teaching as a job to be performed, and usually thinks in concrete terms where there is only one solution or an easy answer to a problem. Students are categorized rather than considered to be unique. This person will likely be unimaginative or unconcerned about teaching. There is little variation in teaching technique which will probably be a conventional or traditional style. He is often one of the first persons leaving the school at the end of the day.
- **Quadrant Two -- High Commitment and Low Abstraction.** The Quadrant Two student teacher may be eager but lack a sense of direction. High on commitment, this person will devote an endless amount of energy to the job but this energy will likely not be coupled with a definable purpose. The problem is not desire; it is a lack of abstraction. This person may have a number of ideas but lacks the ability to bring them to fruition or to discriminate between those that work and those that will not.
- **Quadrant Three -- High Abstraction and Low Commitment.** The student teacher in this category will be highly intelligent but have a lack of concern for teaching. He may verbalize what can or should be done but does not follow through. Because of low motivation, progress toward acceptable levels of teacher

competency is slow to develop or is virtually non-existent. This individual is a thinker but not a doer.

- **Quadrant Four -- High Abstraction and High Commitment.** A student teacher at this level of development is a joy to supervise. This individual will demonstrate high intellectual capacity, see students as unique individuals, be aware of alternative teaching strategies, and be willing to try techniques that involve some risks. Furthermore, this person will be enthusiastic about and dedicated to the teaching profession. He likely will have been active in student professional activities and will try to take advantage of every opportunity that student teaching has to offer.

Determining Levels of Development

Student teachers cannot be neatly placed into one of the above quadrants. Most will be on a continuum from low to high but it is necessary to make some judgments in order to determine the best supervisory approach. In order to categorize the student teacher, a supervisor may want to employ one or more of the following options:

- **Gather information about the student teacher.** Many institutions require preservice teachers to maintain a portfolio which documents their educational experiences. A perusal of a student's portfolio would provide clues concerning that person's level of proficiency. Notice the academic level of the student and study the types of classes taken. Look at the type of activities in which the student has been involved. Are they numerous? Are they good training for becoming a professional? Finally, look at any written statements the student may have made. A review of this information should give an indication of commitment or abstraction.
- **Talk with the student teacher.** Initial conferences can often reveal a student's orientation. During the conversation look for the student teacher's ability to make abstract statements. Pose hypothetical questions and see what the responses are. Describe your expectations for the projected work load in order to observe the student teacher's response.
- **Observe the student teacher.** Note the pattern of behaviors and actions. How does he relate to pupils on an individual level? How is discretionary time spent? What kinds of questions are asked? What nonverbal cues do you get when you see the student teacher interact with pupils and adults?

Patterns should begin to emerge as the supervisor observes and analyzes the student teacher. From those patterns, a supervisor can identify the predominant level of development and then determine the best approach for supervision and evaluation.

Supervisory Styles for Different Quadrants

Once the developmental level has been determined, a decision can be made about the supervisory approach. The style chosen must match the developmental level of the individual being supervised in order to ensure maximum growth.

Supervising the Quadrant One Student Teacher

It could be argued that the Quadrant One student teacher is not ready to be placed in a public school for student teaching. Some teacher education institutions use strategies to determine a student's level of commitment and maturity. The previously cited Worksheet Number Six is an example of a form that may help in this endeavor.

In some cases the Quadrant One student teacher will be assigned to the classroom. This student teacher will need to be both motivated and informed. In this situation the supervisor can assume that the student teacher needs a structured environment. The procedure most likely to succeed would be a directive control model where the supervisor gives specific instructions and standardizes expectations. This model is characterized by the supervisor telling the student teacher what should be done and describing the indicators for success. For example, a supervisor might say, "John, I want you to spend a minimum of fifteen minutes in class tomorrow questioning students about their understanding of the assignment and having them draw conclusions about its relationship to the previous unit."

Supervising the Quadrant Two Student Teacher

The Quadrant Two student teacher may need a different type of directive supervision. Whereas the Quadrant One student teacher may benefit from directive control procedures, directive informational procedures may be used for the Quadrant Two student teacher. These differ from directive control in that the supervisor presents choices and allows the student teacher to make the decision from those choices. Control still rests with the supervisor because of the options presented, but the student teacher has some autonomy to make a selection. In a directive informational situation, a supervisor may say, "You can either have students demonstrate their ideas by creating a model on newsprint, work in groups to explore each other's ideas, or present case studies and ask them to relate them to their own experience. Which do you want to use?" In this case the supervisor would be filling in the vacuum of low abstraction ability by providing ideas. The highly motivated student teacher would then be willing to make a choice and spend the energy to see that the more complex activities are accomplished.

Supervising the Quadrant Three Student Teacher

Student teachers at this level can define a problem and think through possible solutions. A supervisor may want to present a collaborative style at this point. Collaborative supervision occurs when both parties present ideas and negotiate possible solutions. The suggestions will be examined in a collegial manner and the decision will be one that is mutually determined. The student teacher might present a thought or two followed by suggestions from the supervisor. The ideas will be examined and discussed and both parties will agree on a course of action.

Supervising The Quadrant Four Student Teacher

The best style of supervision for this unusual student is an indirect approach. Since the student teacher can think of problems from many perspectives and generate a variety of alternative plans, a supervisor's role is one of support and encouragement. Appropriate questions might be something like, "How are you going to introduce the unit or, "Have you thought about something really different and exciting for this class?" The supervisor takes on a supportive role and, through questions and interest, encourages the student teacher to be more creative.

Case Study No. 40: Determining How to Supervise

A request for you to supervise Steve came at the last minute. In fact, his approval for student teaching did not become final until the Friday before he was to begin on Monday because of a grade point problem. His papers were not neat and contained grammatical errors. There was a hint of some attendance problems in his classes at the university. His appearance and mannerisms are casual, but he does relate well to the students. He spends time with them in informal moments and they seem to genuinely like each other. Things went fairly well until he became frustrated one day and uttered a profane word at one of the students. Word got around school quickly. You now need to deal with this issue. What do you do?

1. Be very direct and tell him specifically what he must do to make amends with the student.
2. Give him two or three choices which you think will work and then let him determine the course that he will pursue.
3. Share some options with him and ask him to present some ideas of how he will deal with the situation. Then agree on a course of action.
4. Ask him how he plans to solve the problem.
5. _____

Comment

Probably the first task of the cooperating teacher is to determine the student teacher's level of development. Is he a Quadrant One who needs to be directed specifically or is he more motivated or abstract than a person with low ability? Then a decision on procedure is made. But regardless of the approach taken the student teacher must be made aware that swearing at students is not to be tolerated.

Questions

1. What clues are in the above vignette that will facilitate making a proper diagnosis?
2. What will be the consequences if the wrong diagnosis is made and an inappropriate recommendation is made?

Case Study No. 41: The More Mature Student Teacher

Your student teacher is about 20 years older than most student teachers. She completed her academic work a number of years ago, had a successful career in a field other than teaching and ultimately decided that she wanted to become a teacher. Her early field experience participation record was good and she had a high grade point average. She has worked with youth in situations outside school which may account for her mature presence. She also has several community contacts which should be helpful in student teaching. Her initial lessons seem to be going well and she is aware of the latest developments in her academic area. Students like her and so do you. What type of supervisory stance do you take?

1. Be directive.
2. Give her the choice of several alternatives.
3. Discuss plans and ideas collaboratively and negotiate together what your role will be in supervising her.
4. Encourage her to think in new dimensions and come up with creative activities.
5. _____

Comment

Although student teaching supervision is always interesting and usually exciting, one can only wish that all student teachers would show up with this kind of experience and attitude. However, the cooperating teacher may find this kind of role as challenging, or even more intimidating, than supervising a more typical student teacher. The responsibilities call for high level thinking and creativity. It can also be disconcerting to share the classroom with someone so competent. In this case the supervisor must not take offense if the pupils express partiality toward the student teacher.

Questions

1. Would you be collaborative or non-directive with this student teacher? Why?
2. What can you do to make this a more enriched classroom for the students?

Observing The Student Teacher

The necessity of observation as a process in the supervision of student teachers is obvious. Analysis and evaluation cannot be reliable unless the cooperating teacher is aware of the student teacher's behaviors with a class. This has to come through direct observation. The presence of an observer can be uncomfortable and intimidating, but it is a necessary process in supervision. The cooperating teacher is confronted with the challenge of creating an environment which permits the student teacher to feel comfortable while being observed. A logical beginning is to recognize the conditions that cause a student teacher to feel uncomfortable. The following situations are more likely to contribute to uneasiness on the part of the student teacher who is being observed:

• A lack of thorough planning.
• A perception of inadequacy.
• A feeling that the observation is an evaluation.

- Too much writing by the observer.
- Non-verbal behaviors that convey disagreement, confusion, or boredom.
- Uncertainty about the purpose of the observation.
- Infrequent observations.
- Lack of follow-up.

Specific suggestions for making observations less stressful can be inferred from the above list of causes. The procedures summarized below may be useful in helping a student teacher feel more comfortable with an observer present:

- Invite the student teacher to observe your work.
- Use discretion in writing.
- Be involved with other activity, such as grading papers.
- Show positive reinforcement through facial expressions.
- Observe regularly.
- Give compliments.
- Follow up with suggestions for growth.

Professional growth depends upon the ability of a teacher to perform an act, study it, and plan a future course of action which benefits from the prior experience. Independent teaching is a necessary condition in this process in that it provides an encounter with the classroom environment and creates the basis for concerns or judgments. The cooperating teacher's role is to help the student teacher reflect upon the act, provide information, and guide in the formulation of a more comprehensive plan of action. The predominant goal in this process is for the student teacher to become competent in performing and analyzing the teaching act. In order to accomplish this aim, an amount of discretion is necessary in providing the proper amount of experience at the correct time--a desirable portion of observed teaching and an adequate amount of independent practice.

The amount of observation time has to be carefully determined. Unfortunately two patterns can develop which work to the detriment of a student teacher. The first, and perhaps the most damaging one, is when a teacher chooses to allow a student teacher to be alone with the class most of the time (Joe Hanley in the opening vignette). This prevents the opportunity to observe difficulties or to reinforce good teaching behaviors. In essence, this places a student teacher in a trial and error predicament, a questionable practice in any profession.

The other pattern is one in which a teacher almost never leaves the room while a student is teaching (Sylvia Rose in the opening vignette). In this case the student teacher does not have a chance to establish a teacher-pupil relationship because the cooperating teacher will be the dominant person. It may cause a student teacher to be uneasy and to feel that the cooperating teacher wants to monitor every move. It simply smothers growth.

A student teacher needs to be in the class alone often enough to feel a personal responsibility for what happens and to develop confidence in working with the pupils. The cooperating teacher must be in the room enough to observe the teaching style of the student teacher for analytical and evaluative purposes. The ratio is most likely to be achieved when the cooperating teacher is in the room approximately one-half of the time.

The cooperating teacher will likely be more effective when the trend of supervisory observations cannot be detected. There are a number of alternatives that a teacher can choose, but the authors suggest that teachers consider the following practices:

- Observe for an entire period one day and be absent the next.
- Observe the first part of a class and then leave.
- Enter during the last half of a class.
- Be in and out of the classroom during the lesson.

The cooperating teacher normally is needed in the room a greater percentage of the time during the first few weeks of student teaching. It is a good practice to occasionally leave the student teacher alone for the entire day, but this should be done only when the cooperating teacher is convinced that the student teacher has matured to the point of being able to assume full responsibility for the class. The student teacher should know at all times where the cooperating teacher can be reached or where a responsible school official will be available in case of problems.

Case Study No. 42: A Request To Teach Alone

Your student teacher has had the responsibility of teaching one group of pupils for three days. His performance has been marginal, but you have refrained from criticizing in order to give him an opportunity to develop confidence. He asks you on the fourth day if he might teach the class without your presence because he is self-conscious with you in the room. He indicates that he feels he could teach better if he were alone. What decision do you make?

1. Grant his wishes and leave while he is teaching.
2. Decide to stay but look for ways to be unobtrusive.
3. Consent to leave but plan the next lesson jointly.

4. Agree to leave part of the hour.
5. _____

Comment

The student teacher apparently is becoming more uncomfortable with the supervisor present. Before a decision is made, it might be beneficial to determine why the student teacher wants to be alone. The cooperating teacher may learn that the student teacher feels that he is being evaluated, but the discussion may also reveal that he needs some help in specific areas. The problem may be further compounded if the cooperating teacher leaves the student teacher alone without discussing the reasons for his being uncomfortable with the supervisor present.

Questions

1. What are some acceptable guidelines for determining whether to leave the classroom during the first few days?
2. What messages could the teacher be unconsciously sending to the student teacher?

The Temptation to Interrupt

The passive position of the cooperating teacher can present tension on the part of both parties. A teaching candidate realizes that a competent teacher is watching him and making decisions about his potential to become a teacher. The cooperating teacher who is responsible for the class is placed in a passive role watching an inexperienced teaching candidate work with her pupils. The student teacher will probably make mistakes and it is tempting to break into class with comments that are intended to clarify confusion or to correct errors. Some common temptations that might cause a cooperating teacher to interrupt the flow of the class are:

• The student teacher makes an error in subject matter.
• The cooperating teacher wishes to add supplementary knowledge.
• The cooperating teacher wants to control the behavior of one or more pupils.
• The student teacher gets into difficulty and does not know how to overcome it.
• The students look to the cooperating teacher for answers or information.

Cooperating teacher interventions may be disconcerting for a student teacher. Regardless of the teacher's good intentions, the student teacher may find it difficult to regain composure after a cooperating teacher has interrupted. The cooperating teacher's presence as a participant may correct an immediate difficulty but it can initiate more serious problems. Such an intervention could produce a deterioration of pupil respect and convey the idea that the student teacher is merely responding to directions. Interruptions should occur only when irreversible damage is being done to the class.

Student teachers may continue to use faulty methods or dispense inaccurate information if their errors are not brought to their attention. Post (2000) recommended the following "Teacher's I'S" when dealing with student teachers' mistakes. She recommended that cooperating teachers should not:

- **Interfere** - jump in unnecessarily, which destroys the chance for the student teacher to resolve the situation.
- **Interrogate** - jump all over the student teacher afterwards to ask what he was thinking.
- **Impeach** - make fun of the student teacher for the errors made.
- **Impugn** - question, attack or contradict the student teacher in front of others, especially students.
- **Impede** - prevent professional growth by not discussing the problem.
- **Insult** - tell the student teacher she should "have known better."

A good planning conference between the cooperating teacher and student teacher should alert both parties to any potential problems. Most concerns can be discussed after class and then the student teacher can make the necessary adjustments in an ensuing session. A mistake in content, for example, can usually be explained by the student teacher the following day with no real problems as far as the pupils are concerned.

Case Study No. 43: SOS!

Jill has planned a lesson containing a component requiring students to construct a device that will serve as a learning aid for the lesson, but she did not complete the plans in time for you to provide her with feedback. The directions were unclear and the materials used for construction were insufficient and poorly organized. The confused students bombarded Jill with questions about how to proceed. She soon became frustrated and said to you from across the room, "They obviously can't do what I planned! Will you take over?" What do you do?

1. Sit quietly and let her cope with the students during the remainder of the period.
2. Take over the class and try to save the project.
3. Become involved in the class but try to make it look like a team project.
4. Insist that the students remain quiet even though there is nothing for them to do.
5. _____

Comment

The student teacher is placing blame on her pupils for the failure of the lesson. She did not realize the importance of thinking through the logistics of the activity and consulting with the cooperating teacher. The student teacher must be made to realize the problems that arose were not the fault of the pupils. Their response was in reaction to her lack of planning and consultation with her cooperating teacher. Perhaps the most important lesson from this case is that a more thorough planning conference would have been beneficial.

Questions

1. Is it advisable to deliberately permit a student teacher to experience difficulty?
2. Under what conditions should you "rescue" your student teacher?

Case Study No. 44: New Strategies

The University School of Education where your student teacher was educated is known as an innovative school in touch with the latest developments. The result is apparent as your student teacher comes with a number of ideas that are different from your practices. She believes that students learn from each other and the teacher's role is that of a facilitator. Additionally, she has indicated that she wants to evaluate her students by the use of portfolios rather than by giving conventional tests. One day in class she has the students in groups and they obviously are not on task. This concerns you because you think the student teacher should intervene and be more directive. Yet you are aware of the consequences resulting from interruptions. What do you do?

1. Get the student teacher's attention and quietly ask her to become more involved in directing the students.
2. Get involved in the activities yourself and make the rounds of each group attempting to get them on task.
3. Ignore the situation and make a note to discuss with her whether or not any learning was occurring.
4. Quietly leave the room in order to avoid further frustration.
5. _____

Comment

Many practices are changing so rapidly in education that it is difficult to determine what is and what is not worthwhile. It is sometimes comfortable just to remain with the procedure that works and to resist any changes. In this case, the cooperating teacher has to make a judgment as to whether the new technique is working.

Questions

1. How do you determine whether a new idea is working?
2. What strategies can be employed to prevent a confusing situation such as this one from happening?

Case Study No. 45: Going The Wrong Direction

Your student teacher is an advocate of pupil competition, but you have oriented your class more toward cooperation. As the student teacher assumes more responsibility for the class, he begins to set up competitive activities. Increasing pressures and rivalries are beginning to develop. The personality of the class seems to be changing and cooperation seems to be disappearing. You suspect that the quality of work is deteriorating. The student teacher is pleased with the level of competition, but you want to intervene and move more to the supportive rather than competitive mode. Should you do it and, if so, how?

1. Discuss your feelings with the student teacher outside of class and try to reach some agreement.
2. Compare hard data, such as test results, and then decide whether you should opt for a change of direction for the class.
3. Interject yourself more assertively into the class and present the alternative approach.
4. _____

Comment

Although competition is widely advocated as a desirable process, one must examine the nature of the competition in this class and the impact that it will have upon all the pupils. Competition produces winners, but it also creates losers. If a student teacher is oriented toward competition, a cooperating teacher must help the student teacher analyze the total impact of such a procedure.

Questions

1. Should a student teacher be permitted to engage in an activity that is inconsistent with the cooperating teacher's beliefs?
2. What kinds of intervention strategies should be considered in reconciling this dilemma?

Case Study No. 46: Management Difficulty

Your student teacher has difficulty demanding respect. Pupils just do not listen to her while she is talking. In addition, she is remiss in reminding pupils that they are not doing what is asked of them. Basically she just seems deficient in classroom management overall. You want to help her so that the learning climate improves. What do you do?

1. Be patient and wait for a logical opportunity to intervene.
2. Discuss the matter with the student teacher at the first opportunity.
3. Make a video recording of a portion of the class for the student teacher to see.
4. Meet with the class and explain that their behavior is not appropriate.
5. _____

Comment

There is the possibility that the student teacher may be aware of the situation but reluctant to discuss it because of the implication that she is unable to control the class. Direct interruption may not help but a frank discussion of the matter could be beneficial. A video recording might be used at a later time to identify particular problems.

Questions

1. What is necessary to secure respect from pupils?
2. What might have prevented this case from happening?

Supervision Through Cooperative Teaching

Cooperative teaching can be a helpful procedure for supervising instruction. According to Cogan (1973) a collegial relationship needs to be established in order for clinical supervision to occur. This professional relationship that stresses a collaborative approach can create an opportunity for educators to learn from each other as they work together. Team teaching provides an opportunity for both teachers to use their skills more effectively. The cooperative plan creates an opportunity for more creative activities as teachers working together pool their knowledge, ideas, and skills.

A cooperative arrangement has long been accepted as a procedure for induction into a profession or trade. The combination of mutual goals, shared responsibility, and contact with more experienced and more knowledgeable persons creates a climate for learning. The team situation provides an easier method for an individual to assume important responsibility. In the field of education, cooperation in more complex teaching situations is particularly desirable. Role definition is important in this type of arrangement. Each participant should understand his own sphere of operation and perceive that role as important to the accomplishment of the team task.

This team approach is especially recommended when the class can logically be taught in settings such as reading groups, physical education classes, and laboratory sessions. This method has the advantage of providing the opportunity for a cooperating teacher to assist a student teacher who may be having problems without the pupils perceiving that difficulties exist.

Case Study No. 47: A Nontraditional Situation

Your student teacher is in a situation where teachers work together. The classroom consists of individual and cooperative work with each teacher working on a one-to-one basis with pupils. She likes the class and seems to adjust nicely to the routine and quickly begins enhancing the classroom environment. The problem is that there is little opportunity for independent responsibility and the organization of a more traditional learning situation. Since the student teacher may interview for positions which stress the more conventional approach to learning, you wonder if this experience is meeting her needs. What do you do to deal with this concern?

1. Do nothing on the assumption that an alternative classroom will be an enrichment experience.
2. See that her observations include a number of classes that are taught more traditionally.
3. Adjust one or more of your classes so she can teach by the more traditional method.
4. Talk with her about how the units you are teaching could be taught in a more traditional fashion.
5. _____

Comment

The basic question here is whether a student teacher will only be able to teach by the way that she has experienced or whether she will be better prepared if she knows a variety of styles. Generally, one would assume that the more knowledge a person has regarding instructional methodology, the better she will be able to adjust. Certainly she will have been exposed to more conventional styles throughout her educational experience. The new approach may cause her to be better prepared to teach in spite of a lack of experience in more conventional classrooms.

Questions

1. How important is it to have experienced teaching a particular way before it can be used successfully?
2. What do the current trends in educational methodology reveal about the type of teaching that is encouraged?

Case Study No. 48: Resisting Difficult Groups

You have the pupils divided into ability groups and have been rotating with the student teacher enabling her to work with students who function at different levels. After a period of time, she begins to avoid working with the section that poses academic challenges. She comments that she prefers to work with the regular and advanced groups because she does not intend to teach students with learning problems. She further states that she is unable to accomplish anything with pupils who have difficulty learning. What is your response?

1. Agree to let her work with the groups that she chooses.

2. Explain that she should be prepared for all levels of students regardless of her present intentions.
3. Help her find more creative ways of working with the students who have learning difficulties.
4. Work together as a team with all groups for a while.
5. _____

Comment

Most teachers enjoy classes that are made up of bright students; fewer want to work with those who have learning problems. It seems that it ultimately would be a disservice to the student teacher if she is removed from the situations that demand a different approach. However, the student teacher may need help, and this may be a good opportunity for the cooperating teacher to suggest alternative techniques for successfully teaching problem students.

Questions

1. How can a cooperating teacher better prepare a student teacher to work with pupils who have learning difficulties?
2. What are the pros and cons of granting her request?

Analyzing Teaching
More Than Looking

Teaching analysis is based on the idea that observation and feedback will improve the instructional ability of a student teacher. In order to observe effectively, a cooperating teacher needs a frame of reference. Student teaching should be thought of as a time to study as well as to practice teaching. It is a time to put untried ideas to the test in a variety of real situations and to study the results.

Teaching requires specialized skills. Prospective teachers can learn these skills and supervisors can help preservice teachers acquire them provided they have an awareness of effective teaching and the ability to use feedback techniques which will aid in analysis. The purpose of this section is to present a brief summary of some of the prevailing concepts of effective teaching practices and to introduce some analysis forms which are relatively easy to learn and to use.

Concepts of Effective Teaching

Many different descriptions of effective teaching exist and most of them have merit. For the sake of presenting models that a cooperating teacher can use for reference, two descriptions are presented, each of which approach the idea of effective teaching differently. Cooperating teachers may find at least one of these helpful.

Sharpe (1969) identified eight basic skills of teaching in an extensive study of characteristics of student teachers. These behaviors were validated through observations of hundreds of student teachers. The criteria represent the behaviors as developed in theory and research and demonstrated by student teachers. They were classified under the title of the Student Teaching Performance Profile. The specific behaviors and a partial list of descriptors are as follows:

- **Understanding and friendly.**
  Friendly, understanding, tactful, good-natured.
  Shows concern for a pupil's personal needs.
  Tolerant of errors on the part of pupils.
  Finds good things in pupils and calls attention to them.
  Listens encouragingly to pupils' viewpoints.
- **Planned and organized**
  Businesslike, systematic, consistent, thorough.
  Presents evidence of thorough planning.
  Objectives are clearly discernible.
  Tells class what to expect during the period.
  Has needed materials ready.
  Keeps good records.
- **Stimulating and imaginative**
  Original, encourages pupil initiative.
  Presentations hold student interest.
  Animated and enthusiastic.
  Capitalizes on student interest.
- **Possesses self-confidence**
  Sees self as liked, worthy, and able to do a good job.
  Speaks confidently.
  Poised in relations with students.
  Takes mistakes and criticisms in stride.
  Accepts new tasks readily.
- **Mastery of subject matter**
  Recognizes important concepts and generalizations.
  Focuses class presentations on basic concepts.
  Relates to other fields.
  Traces implications of knowledge.
- **Communicates well and empathetically**
  Shows sensitivity to student perceptions.
  Makes presentations at level of understanding.

Draws examples from interests of students.
Makes effective use of media.
Has no distracting mannerisms.
Speaks well.

- **Uses reasoning and creative thinking**
Helps students understand information.
Seeks definition of problems.
Leads students to consider solutions.
Asks open-ended questions.
Frequently asks "why?".
Encourages application of knowledge.
Encourages students to see the relationships among facts.
- **Directs attention to the logical operations in teaching**
Seeks definition of terms.
Encourages students to make inferences from information.
Demands examination of evidence.
Leads students to state assumptions.
Examines beliefs and opinions.

A second way of looking at teaching is to observe what occurs within the framework of a particular lesson. One popular model is to follow a rather specific and sequential process. The steps in that model are:

- Establish an orderly climate for learning.
- Review previous learning.
- Preview the day's activity and define its goals.
- Present the new material, ideas, or skills.
- Allow time for pupil practice and drill.
- Check for pupil understanding.
- Assign new learning activities.

A cooperating teacher may find it helpful to use one of the above models to focus on growth in teaching skills. An observant teacher can determine which behaviors are at an acceptable level and which ones need to be improved. A student teacher may be more receptive when such techniques are described as part of a model of effective teaching rather than merely presented as the opinion of the supervisor. In many cases, it is beneficial to have tangible information that depicts the teaching act more graphically. The next section will focus on some promising ways of recording teaching behavior so that it is more discernible for the student teacher.

Reconstructing Teacher Activity

The reconstruction of teacher behavior should not be confused with the evaluation of teaching. Reconstruction is a data gathering procedure that will provide objective response to a student teacher for the purposes of analysis, modification, and improvement of teaching. A cooperating teacher using this process can provide information that can be used to determine more specifically what is happening in the classroom. It is naive to assume that such behaviors are not also related to evaluation, but at this stage, the focus is on development rather than appraisal.

There are endless forms and devices that can be used to provide feedback to student teachers. The ones described below are representative of what is available and the authors believe that these procedures are worthy of consideration because they describe teaching behavior in several ways and can easily be learned or used by an observer who has had little or no training.

Teacher Classroom Activity Profile

The Teacher Classroom Activity Profile is an analysis form that was developed in Sharpe's research on student teaching (1969) and is connected to the previously described Student Teaching Performance Profile. This form subsumes classroom activities into seven categories. These are:

- **Management--Non Learning**
  Management of the classroom when the teacher is not attempting to teach, e.g., reading announcements, taking roll, distributing materials, organizing equipment, idle time, disciplining pupils, waiting for the bell to ring.
- **Management—Learning**
  Management of the classroom so that learning may occur but the teacher is not involved except in a managerial role, e.g., showing a sound film or videotape, administering a written examination, supervising study time, student reports, lab activities, computer activity, etc.
- **Presentation**
  The presentation of subject matter by the teacher in some organized fashion, e.g., lectures, demonstrations, illustrated talks, blackboard presentation, reading.
- **Recitation/Drill**
  The solicitation of student responses that call for terse memorized data, oral testing to determine if assignments have been read, review questions, drill, and practice time.

- **Random Discussion**
  Random discussion involving student-teacher interaction but without analysis or synthesis. "Stream of consciousness" discussion without any apparent focus or purpose except to consume time until the class period is over.
- **Logical Thinking**
  Discussion that involves analysis and synthesis. The teacher is deliberately encouraging or permitting reasoning to occur. This category is more than reciting or repeating something that has been learned or memorized.
- **Thinking Process**
  Deliberate, conscious attention on the part of the teacher to the intellectual process, e.g., pointing out to the students the factual and/or logical basis of their thinking, pointing out errors in reasoning, examining the reliability and validity of evidence, defining terms, checking assumptions, examining the scientific method, examining values, seeking reason for conflicting opinions, or examining the method of inquiry.

The observer records a continuous line moving among the seven activities in three-minute intervals. If there is just a momentary shift in categories, a vertical line going up or down to the proper category should be made without interruption of the continuous line describing the prevailing activity. It has been found helpful to indicate the time at the top of the three-minute interval columns, starting in Column 1 with the minute the class starts and then recording the time at three-minute intervals after that in the numbered squares. Explanatory notes are keyed to the column number which indicates that sequence of three-minute instructional periods. Evaluative and other comments may be recorded in the section designated as "Anecdotal Records." Worksheet Number Eleven in the Appendix provides an example of a completed form.

Some teachers have found that they are more comfortable identifying teaching every minute instead of over a three-minute period. This can be done by simply identifying each column as a one-minute activity and proceeding accordingly. In the event that this is the choice, the form could be used for a maximum of 20 minutes, but this is sufficient in many instances.

The Teacher Classroom Activity Profile describes the way that a teacher spends time in the classroom, the types of intellectual activity stressed, and the number of activities that occur. It gives clues to whether objectives are being met, to organizational patterns and to possible teaching problems. Constant lines to the top of the form, for example, may describe interruptions caused by classroom discipline problems. Finally, the form enables a student teacher to reconstruct his own experience for reflection and possible modification of procedure.

The Teacher Classroom Activity Profile was developed under the auspices of a federal grant and is in the public domain. Cooperating Teachers who wish to use this form should feel free to make copies for their own use.

Scripting

Scripting is the recording of every person, event, or material that attracts the attention of the observer. The assumption is that the recording of all activity will provide a statement about what is happening in the classroom. Since the intent is to be descriptive and not evaluative, the narrative should contain an objective summary of the student teacher's class activity. A typical paragraph might read:

> The students filed into the classroom talking among themselves. The teacher entered as the bell sounded and asked the class to get quiet. Three boys in the back continued talking and two girls were making hand signals to each other across the room. The teacher checked attendance and walked outside the classroom to place the attendance record in the slot by the door. The level of noise in the class increased. When the teacher returned, he told the students to open their books to page 132 and to be prepared to give answers to the homework assignment. One boy indicated that he forgot his book and three students asked to sharpen their pencils. The requests to sharpen pencils were denied. The teacher asked a boy next to the boy without a book to share his book with another student during the period. The school intercom interrupted at this time to remind students of the track meet that afternoon.

With practice the observer can write quickly enough to keep up with the flow of events. It is impossible to record all that occurs in a classroom, but scripting can give a profile. The advantage of scripting is that it gives a written description of all practices in the classroom. The disadvantages are that it is subject to judgment on the part of the observer, it requires the observer to concentrate on writing at the expense of overall observation, and it presents a lot of material which may be difficult to reduce to specific descriptors.

Categorical Frequency Instruments

A categorical frequency instrument is a form that defines certain behaviors that can be checked off at specified intervals and then tabulated. They can be used to isolate almost any aspect of a classroom procedure. Focus can be on such classroom activities as verbal behaviors, questioning, instructional strategies, and pupil activity.

A cooperating teacher can determine the objectives for a student teacher's lesson and then record behaviors that would indicate whether they are being achieved. If a student teacher were to concentrate on asking questions, the supervisor may devise a form which records the number and the types of questions. Categorical frequency instruments are easy to construct, use, and tabulate. They can give immediate reports of activity.

Visual Diagramming

Visual diagramming is a method of capturing classroom behavior through the construction of a diagram that visually illustrates a pattern of activity. A typical use is to determine who is answering the student teacher's questions.

Classroom verbal actions can be done by drawing arrows on a paper that has symbols representing the teacher and students. A diagram might have a square at the top of the page representing the teacher and circles to represent all the students in the classroom. The observer would draw a line from the teacher to a pupil each time that pupil is called on. The result would be a profile of interaction and will generally indicate who is participating and who is not. The graph can be a dramatic picture of what is happening and apprise a student teacher of oversights in not involving all the students in the class. A variation of visual diagramming is to record interaction among the students.

Videotape Recordings

In Chapter Five, videotape recordings were described as observational tools. In a sense it is difficult to separate observation from analysis. In the analysis procedure, a student teacher would have cues as to what to look for and could view the teaching vignette using specific criteria. A cooperating teacher and student teacher might view the tape together, focusing on specific criteria and perhaps using the appropriate analysis instrument to make the classroom reconstruction more productive.

Written Communication and Analysis

The process of communication is essential in supervisory practice. Effective communication is a problem in nearly any situation, but student teaching can sometimes make it more difficult. Since accurate exchanges of ideas are essential for a good student teaching experience, every possible procedure should be practiced to increase understanding and to share information.

Written communication is a widely used and professionally acceptable supervisory tool (Bolin, 1988) and supplements the more traditional oral method. Written communication often extends beyond mere description of activity and becomes a technique for communication and reflection about teaching. This interplay of ideas can become a dialogue that serves as a record of past performance and a file of suggestions that could be applicable in future teaching activities.

A cooperating teacher and student teacher can exchange views and information in writing when conversation is not possible. A teacher observing a student teacher may want to communicate several ideas while watching. Since conversation is impossible at this point and since thoughts that are not recorded may be forgotten, writing becomes a valuable procedure. Written comments can be useful in developing clarity of thinking because both cooperating teacher and student teacher have the opportunity to consider precisely what they want to say. Some universities require their student teachers to keep a journal for this purpose. This running commentary has the advantage of describing the continuous progress of the student teacher.

Written communication can achieve the following functions:

- **Provides a record of progress.**
  Provides immediate reaction to performance.
  Offers suggestions for improvements.
  Indicates why a lesson was well taught.
  Gives encouragement to the student teacher.
- **Compiles a number of useful teaching ideas.**
  How to manage specific teaching problems.
  How to cope with difficult students.
  Ideas for providing variety in the classroom.
  Sources of instructional materials and aids.
- **Gives written confirmation of agreements.**
  Defines responsibilities.
  Clarifies verbal agreements.
- **Encourages reflection.**

Helps the student teacher to think about teaching.
Examines ideas and practices.
- **Provides a record of professional information.**
  School procedures and regulations.
  Professional information about students.

Written comments enhance interaction between a student teacher and cooperating teacher. Such communication is even more beneficial when one realizes that the comments may be retained for further reference.

A wire notebook makes a durable form for written conversation. A middle line may be drawn to serve as a dividing line for the responses of the two participants. An example of a bit of written communication is illustrated in Worksheet Number Twelve in the Appendix. Note that inquiries may be initiated by either party.

In summary, feedback techniques when used correctly will provide specific information which can be used to determine the effectiveness of teaching. The models above are excellent, but a creative teacher can devise other means of analysis by reviewing other books on supervision or by using her own creativity.

Case Study No. 49: What Does It Mean?

You have been in your student teacher's class for an hour carefully recording her behavior on an analysis scale. You are enthused about the possibility of its providing accurate feedback to her. She has been quite aware during the class that you are making more notes than usual. After the class is over, you give her the form and tell her that you have done an analysis of her teaching. She glances at it and then asks, "Was the class any good, or not?" What do you say to her?

1. "What do you think?"
2. "It depends on your objectives."
3. "This form does not attempt to evaluate your class."
4. "The form would indicate that..."
5. _____

Comment

It is not easy to separate the role of supervisor from that of evaluator. Since the supervisor is more experienced and in a position of authority over the student teacher, thoughts of evaluation are inevitable. In order to show that formative growth is separate from evaluation, a supervisor will have to prepare a student teacher for the context of an analytical observation such as this one. This will involve a pre-conference explaining how the supervisor is going to analyze, and then a follow-up discussion that focuses on growth rather than appraisal.

Questions

1. What is the difference between analysis and evaluation?
2. Can a person be both an effective supervisor and an evaluator?

Case Study No. 50: Reluctant To Write

As a cooperating teacher you feel that systematic written communication is essential, but your student teacher hesitates to put anything down on paper. He constantly "forgets" his journal and does not respond to your written comments. Since you feel that this type of communication is necessary, what do you do?

1. Inform him that the journal is to be in the room at all times and you are requiring him to make entries in it.
2. Continue writing and request a response.
3. Ask the university supervisor to reinforce the request.
4. Have a discussion with the student teacher and try to determine how written communication can be helpful.
5. _____

Comment

It is not unusual for written communication to be resisted. A perceptive supervisor will want to determine whether this condition also applies to oral communication. It would be well to ascertain whether the student teacher understands the purpose of written communication. This could be the essence of the problem.

Questions

1. What kinds of written comments might encourage a student teacher to want to participate in written exchange?
2. What are some positive responses to negative reactions about the value of writing in a journal?

Supervising Participation In Pupil Evaluation
The Curve Becomes a Question Mark

One of the most exciting activities for the student teacher is participation in the evaluation of pupil achievement. The student teacher who is allowed to share in this process should feel that he has earned his teacher's confidence. A student teacher's self-confidence can be quickly shattered, though, when the complications of evaluation begin to emerge. The first test results can be more effective in criticizing a student teacher than all the exhortations of a supervisor. Low test scores may indicate that the material was covered too rapidly or too abstractly. If the grades are too high, it may be an indication that the test was too easy or that pupils were not being challenged. A student teacher may discover that the terminology or phrasing of a test was so obscure that the results cannot be considered to be valid.

The evaluation procedure provides the opportunity for a student teacher to gain a different concept of student capabilities. The pupil who was vocal in class may have produced a rather unimpressive test response, and the pupil whose name cannot be recalled may have achieved the highest score in the group. Other visible cues of writing and expression may present an understanding of pupils that had previously evaded the student teacher.

The student teacher may possess a limited notion about evaluation. A test may be considered to be the objective for teaching and quizzes may be presented as punitive devices for coercing students into completing assignments. Perhaps of more concern is the notion that a student teacher may tend to view evaluation as an end instead of a growth process. The origin of this limited concept of evaluation may have arisen from a lack of experience or from poor example. In either case, the cooperating teacher should help him learn more about the process.

The joint approach to evaluation is usually preferable because it enables the supervisor to be in a position to help the student teacher develop a more adequate perspective regarding appraisal. The objectives of this shared approach should lead to a student teacher's having a more comprehensive understanding of evaluation. Consider the following as desirable goals to be achieved through the joint approach:

- It should help the student teacher understand the role of pupil evaluation.
- It should help the student teacher understand the total process of evaluation.

- It should help the student teacher understand what a student is capable of achieving.
- It should ensure that the student teacher understands the criteria that can be considered in determining a grade.

After the student teacher gains some understanding of the evaluation process, this knowledge should be applied through participation in the determination of grades. The cooperating teacher will want to review and approve the assigned grades before they are announced to the pupils. The student teacher can gain in confidence if his evaluation roughly corresponds to that of the cooperating teacher.

Case Study No. 51: Different Grades

You have decided to allow John to determine grades for the current grading period since he has done most of the instruction. When you check his report, you find that he has given three B's, fifteen C's, eight D's, and two F's. Since the class has traditionally scored better than this, you question him about the lower grades. He explained that he felt that this would motivate them to improve next time. You disagree but feel frustrated because he has already reported the grades to the students. What do you do?

1. Consult with the student teacher and try to reach an agreement that will permit him to make realistic adjustments without being embarrassed.
2. Support the student teacher.
3. Adjust the grades but keep the change a secret until he completes his student teaching assignment.
4. Ignore the situation and let him deal with the questions the students will inevitably ask.
5. _____

Comment

It seems as if a philosophy of evaluation is in order. The case has a clear message for supervisors: discuss grades and grading policies with student teachers before they report their grades to the pupils.

Questions

1. What criteria should be used to determine the correct standards for grades?

2. What is a possible compromise that the student teacher and cooperating teacher can reach?

Brian had been teaching about fifteen minutes when Miss Bennett returned to the room. As he continued, she cast a few knowing glances when he successfully made an explanation about a difficult topic. After a while she reached for the journal and entered a few comments.

When the class ended, they discussed the development of the lesson. Miss Bennett began by inquiring about the introduction and then asked for Brian's reaction to the lesson. After his comments she added, "I think that you showed considerable improvement in your development of student thinking today. The questions caused the pupils to relate the material we have been working with to the previous unit. I think they will do better in their future work because of this series of lessons."

Brian agreed and then glanced at the journal. Miss Bennett caught the cue and handed the book to him. "I recorded a few thoughts about your teaching style as you had requested. A little attention to the details which I have mentioned can help you with a few of your concerns. I also wrote down some ideas for teaching the next unit which you might like to consider as you prepare for it."

While Brian was reading the comments, Miss Bennett continued organizing some materials which Brian had planned to use with the next group. During this time Joe Hanley walked by, looked in the room and a puzzled look formed on his face. He shrugged his shoulders and sauntered on toward the teachers' work room.

Remember:

- **It is necessary for the supervisor to observe a student teacher but it is equally important to provide times when he can be alone with the class.**
- **Student teachers tend to become concerned when they are interrupted by their cooperating teachers.**
- **Feedback and analysis should be given in a variety of ways.**
- **Written and electronic communication are valuable supplements to oral dialogue.**
- **Written and electronic communication could include the university supervisor.**
- **Student teachers should participate in evaluation as well as instruction.**

- Cooperating teachers must recognize a student teacher's level of development and then apply the appropriate supervisory technique

Useful References

Anglin, Jacqueline M. and Diane E. Piland. 1993. It is Only a Stage They are Going Through: The Development of Student Teachers. *Action in Teacher Education* 15(Fall): 19-26.

Balch, Pamela M., and Patrick E. Balch. 1987. The Clinical Supervision Model. Chapter 2 in *The Cooperating Teacher: A Practical Approach for the Supervision of Student Teachers.* Lanham, MD. University Press of America.

Blank, Mary Ann, and Betty S. Heathington. 1987. The Supervisory Process: A Consistent Approach to Help Student Teachers Improve. *The Teacher Educator* 22(Spring): 2-13.

Bolin, Frances S. 1988. Helping Student Teachers Think About Teaching. *Journal of Teacher Education* 39 (March-April): 48-54.

Buttery, Thomas J., and David L. Weller. 1988. Group Clinical Supervision: A Paradigm for Preservice Instructional Enhancement. *Action in Teacher Education* 10 (Spring): 61-73.

Cogan, M. 1973. *Clinical Supervision.* Boston. Houghton-Mifflin.

Fishman, Andrea, and Elizabeth J Raver. 1989. "Maybe I'm Just NOT Teacher Education Material": Dialogue Journals in the Student Teaching Experience. *English Education* 21 (May): 92-109.

Freiberg, H. Jerome, et. al. 1987. Improving the Quality of Student Teaching. Paper presented at the National Meeting of the Association of Teacher Educators, Houston, TX, February 15-18. ERIC ED 288233.

Freiberg, H. Jerome, and Herscholt C. Waxman. 1988. Alternative Feedback Approaches for Improving Student Teachers' Classroom Instruction. *Journal of Teacher Education* 39 (July-August): 8-14.

Gangstead, Sandy K. 1983. Clinical Supervision of the Student Teacher: An Applied Behavior Analysis Approach to the Evaluation of Teacher Behavior. Paper presented at the Northern Rocky Mountain Educational Research Association, Jackson Hole, WY. ERIC ED 241476.

Glickman, Carl. 1995. Chapters 4 and 14 in *Supervision of Instruction: A Developmental Approach.* Newton, MA. Allyn & Bacon.

Henry, Marvin A. 1995. Supervising Student Teachers: A New Paradigm. Chapter 2 in Slick (Ed.), *Making the Difference for*

Teachers: The Field Experience in Actual Practice. Thousand Oaks, CA. Corwin Press, Inc.

Joyce, Bruce. 1988. Training Research and Preservice Teacher Education: A Reconsideration. *Journal of Teacher Education* 39 (September- October): 32-36.

Melnick, Steven A. 1989. Cooperating Teachers: What Do They See in the Classroom? Paper presented at the Annual Meeting of the American Educational Research Association, March 27-31, San Francisco, CA. ERIC ED 307724.

Meltzer, Myton Trang, and Betty Bailey. 1994. Clinical Cycles: A Productive Tool for Teacher Education. *Phi Delta Kappan 75* (April): 612-619.

Moore, Sheldon. 1988. Seeing is Believing: Supervision of Teaching by Means of Video Tape. *Action in Teacher Education* 10: (Summer): 47-49.

Ocansey, Reginald. 1988. An Effective Supervision Guide for Supervisors: A Systematic Approach to Organizing Data Generated During Monitoring Sessions in Student Teaching. *Physical Educator* 45 (Winter): 24-29.

Paesse, Paul C. 1989. Systematic Observation Techniques to Improve Teaching. ERIC ED 311007.

Paesse, Paul C., and Jack P. Flatau. 1990. Improving Criterion Process Teaching Skills During Student Teaching. ERIC ED 322145

Pallitotet, Ann W. 1995. I Never Saw That Before: A Deeper View of Video Analysis in Teacher Education. *Teacher Educator* 31 (February): 138-156.

Post, Donna. 2000. The Cooperating Teacher's I's: What to do When the Student Teacher's Lesson is Going Down the Drain. Paper presented at the National Meeting of the Association of Teacher Educators, Orlando, FL. February 12 - 16.

Shapiro, Phyllis P., and Agnes Teresa Sheehan. 1986. The Supervision of Student Teachers: A New Diagnostic Tool. *Journal of Teacher Education* 37 (Nov-Dec): 35-39.

Sharpe, Donald M. 1969. *Isolating Relevant Variables in Student Teacher Assessment.* Washington, DC. U. S. Office of Education. Contract No. OEC-3-7---061321-0342.

Silva, Diane. 2000. Triad Journaling as a Tool for Reconceptualizing Supervision in the Professional Development School. Paper presented at the Annual Meeting of the American Educational Research Association. New Orleans, LA. April 24-28. ERIC ED 442765.

Smith, Doug J. 1992. Intern Perspectives on the Quality of Cooperating Teacher Supervision. ERIC ED 347149.

Tannehill, Deborah., and Dorothy Zakrajsek. 1988. What's Happening in Supervision of Student Teachers in Secondary Physical Education. *Journal of Teaching in Physical Education* 8(October): 1-12.

Thomson, W. Scott. 1992. Using Videotape As a Supplement to Traditional Student Teacher Supervision. ERIC ED 357014.

Westerman, Delores A., and Shirley A. Smith. 1993. A Research-Based Model for the Clinical Supervision of Student Teachers. Paper Presented at the Annual Meeting of the American Association of Colleges for Teacher Education, February 24-27, San Diego, CA. ERIC ED 361282.

Wright, June L., and Barbara J. Kasten. 1992. New Lenses for Self Discovery. ERIC ED 346068.

8

Supervisory Conferences

The university student teaching handbook suggested that a student teacher and cooperating teacher conduct an extensive analysis of professional progress after a few weeks of student teaching. In compliance with this, Brian and Miss Bennett were discussing the details suggested in the university handbook to see that all requirements were being met. Brian turned a page and said, "Look at this!" He began to read aloud.

"Conferences are as essential to the student teaching experience as teaching if maximum professional growth is to occur. This continuing dialogue is a necessary procedure in providing complete analysis of the complex nature of teaching. A conference can help the student teacher solve immediate and long-range problems through the verbal input of the cooperating teacher. Substantive conferences should be regular experiences in a student teaching program."

Miss Bennett seemed mildly concerned. "Since you have been doing well, it has not seemed necessary to spend so much time in formal conferences. Do you think we should allow more time with this type of activity?" . . .

The Supervisory Conference
A Professional Mirror

Much of the formal supervision of student teaching occurs in a conference setting. A conference between a cooperating teacher and a student teacher can be defined as verbal interaction which focuses on growth of the student teacher. In essence, a conference is teaching on a one-to-one basis, involving analysis, information sharing, planning, and evaluation. Studies reveal that reflection is a worthwhile learning experience (Grant and Drafall, 1996).

Student teachers and cooperating teachers must successfully interact if they are to achieve significant growth. Pitton (1998) emphasized the importance of open communication and building a positive relationship with the cooperating teacher in order for a successful student teaching experience to develop. A supervisory conference must be more than talking about details; it must be substantive interaction which includes:

- Analysis.
- Information sharing.
- Discussion of ideas
- Evaluation.

In one sense a conference is a professional mirror where a supervisor reflects a student teacher's performance by providing accurate feedback. A conference should help a student teacher perceive teaching more accurately and provide direction for future activities. It is a method of providing information about progress, but more importantly, it helps the student teacher become more aware of her skills and how she can make improvements.

Conferences are part of the previously mentioned triad of activities focusing on the improvement of instruction. Planning sets the goals and procedures and observations provide information for analysis. The conference interprets what happened and the participants begin the process of developing future courses of action. Topics covered range from orientation to evaluation, and the procedures involve a variety of verbal and non-verbal behaviors.

Roles and Responsibilities of Participants

Each participant has a role to perform in order to make a conference successful, but it is the cooperating teacher who is in the best position to set the agenda. The cooperating teacher has the responsibility and the opportunity to:

- Structure the conference environment so that it is conducive for effective dialogue.
- Determine the content of the conference.
- Establish the affective climate for the conference.
- Determine the amount of input the student teacher will have.

Jin and Cox (2000) found that most cooperating teachers, especially those who have received no training in supervision, provided feedback to their student teachers through informal conversations. Informal conversations are desirable, but they should not be confused with formal conferences. Conversations help to establish rapport, relieve tension and communicate general information. Formal conferences, on the other hand, have specific purposes and focus on the development of the student teacher.

Researchers have found that cooperating teachers who do hold formal conferences with their charges dominate the conversations. Guyton and McIntyre (1990), reported that conferences were dominated by cooperating teachers and involved low levels of discourse such as descriptions and direction-giving. Previously, Tabachnick (1979) reported that directions, procedural issues, and classroom management were the predominant cooperating teacher topics. According to O'Neal (1983), cooperating teachers talk 72 percent of the time when conferences are in progress. The most frequent type of conversation was "review" (37 percent), involving such things as commenting on classroom events or student teaching activities. This was followed by direction-giving (24 percent).

The most frequent student teacher talk was to acknowledge the supervisor's comments. This usually involved remarks such as "yes, I understand, OK, etc." It appears from the research that teachers are directive, focus on specific activities and prone to spend little time in evaluation. Most of the conversation is in the cognitive domain with only three percent found to be in the affective domain.

The tenor of the conferences described above might be appropriate for Quadrant One student teachers (low commitment and low abstraction) outlined in Chapter Seven, but for other student teachers at more advanced levels of development, the conference should take on a different tone.

Quadrant Two student teachers (high commitment and low abstraction) should prepare a list of questions or concerns to be discussed at the conference. The student teacher should be prepared to justify the instructional decisions made. The cooperating teacher suggests options and the student teacher chooses one for further action.

The conference with a Quadrant Three student teacher (high abstraction and low commitment) can be more collaborative in nature where ideas are exchanged and solutions are negotiated. With Quadrant Four student teachers (high abstraction and high commitment) the relationship between the cooperating teacher and student teacher is more collegial. The conference might be dominated by the student teacher with the cooperating teacher affirming the positive actions of the student teacher and serving as a coach for fine tuning instructional skills and strategies.

Regardless of the student teacher's level of development, he should be an active participant and an attentive listener. He should plan to discuss ideas, ask questions, and take action on the recommendations made as a result of the interaction. If O'Neal's research is a guide, one can assume that a student teacher will not become too involved without encouragement from the cooperating teacher.

Sequencing Conferences
The Right Words at the Right Time

Conferences range from the informal to the formal and from information sharing through evaluation. One of the components of effective conferences is to match the type of conference with the student teacher's level of development. The number, length, type, time, and location of each will depend upon the needs of the participants.

A complete conference program will involve informal as well as formal interaction. Informal conferences are held as needed. The brief, casual conference keeps the lines of communication open and allows for immediate sharing and feedback. The practice of meeting informally on a daily basis is conducive to the development of collegial relationships. If the cooperating teacher and student teacher are accustomed to continuous interaction, they will find themselves discussing relevant topics in a casual environment which is less threatening than in a formal atmosphere.

Spontaneous interaction should be supplemented by more structured situations. These sessions should be scheduled for a specific time and place and include a planned agenda of topics which relate to the development of teaching competence. A typical agenda might include:

- A discussion of strengths and concerns.
- Planning.
- Information about the school and students.
- Specific analysis of teaching behaviors.

Both informal and formal conferences should encompass the totality of the student teaching experience. The content will vary depending on when the conference occurs. The early conferences will not resemble the later ones, but all are necessary because they focus on different purposes and growth levels.

Initial Conferences

The agenda for the initial conferences may be rather extensive. Student teachers need direct support during the first week. Student teacher questions and topics require about 42 percent of the conference time during the first week but decline to 8 percent by the seventh week (Johnson, Cox, and Wood, 1982). Initial conferences likely will focus on logistical details such as appropriate lesson plan format, deadlines, methods for receiving feedback, and transition of teaching responsibilities (NMSA, 2000). These needs require a considerable amount of information sharing during the early days.

Initial conferences also provide opportunities for a student teacher and cooperating teacher to become better acquainted. This is no small matter in that the quality of the interpersonal relationship between the student teacher and her supervisors is a major factor in having a successful clinical experience (NMSA, 2000). Conferences during the first few days can help relieve tensions caused by the new experience and establish a comfortable working relationship between the two persons. Part of the agenda will be concerned with helping the student teacher make the transition from university life to that of classroom teacher. If such assistance is to be effective, it will be necessary for the cooperating teacher to learn as much as possible about the student teacher.

In order to meet the concerns expressed above, a variety of specific topics must be included in early conference days. Consider the following as a reference point in developing an inclusive orientation for a student teacher:

- Orientation to the school.
- Philosophy of the school program.
- School rules.
- Class schedules.
- Explanation of the student teacher's role.
- Student teacher activities during the initial days.
- Information about supplies and equipment.
- Information about the classes.
- Roles of support staff and instructional assistants.
- Information about the school and community.
- Personal considerations which could affect student teaching.
- Extracurricular activities.
- Expectations.

In addition to the above suggestions, it would be well to review the first two chapters of this book at this time to become aware of the various kinds of activities that will be expected both from the cooperating teacher and student teacher and how conferences fit into those activities.

Conferences at this period most likely will be directive, with the cooperating teacher specifically telling the student teacher what he wants her to do. This is necessary at this time but the roles should move into less domination by the cooperating teacher as the weeks pass.

Case Study No. 52: The Conference Falters

You felt that the conference was important, but you perceive that your student teacher left believing that he was wasting his time. You had much to say about a variety of topics. You presented your ideas about what the student teacher should do in preparation for the first two weeks of student teaching. Then you mentioned a few activities and requirements that you want him to complete before student teaching ends. The student teacher seems frustrated and gives little response. What is wrong with the conference?

1. Nothing.
2. There is too much talk on the part of the cooperating teacher.
3. The topics are not relevant.
4. Preparation for the conference was not thorough enough.
5. _____

Comment

The above may look like a multiple choice question with the answer being very obvious. The topics are important but there has to be the appropriate climate for the conference to be effective. One would infer that there is a disproportionate amount of supervisor talk and not enough time for the student teacher to communicate.

Questions

1. What kind of preparation should be made to insure that both parties understand what is to occur during the conference?
2. How does the developmental level of the student teacher dictate each person's role?

Developmental Conferences

Developmental conferences are those ongoing contacts that occur after completion of the initial concerns and encompass the major part of the program. They include both informal and formal contacts. The conference agenda usually will be determined by the cooperating teacher although the student teacher may provide input as needs develop. The content of the conferences will depend on the student teacher's developmental rate and experience level. It generally can be assumed that a student teacher will be receptive to a performance analysis after a lesson. She may be more than ready for a discussion of teaching technique or classroom management after a frustrating experience with a class or a pupil. The needs of the moment frequently serve as the agenda for productive conferences.

The agenda for developmental conferences will be extensive because it will focus on all aspects of teaching. A cooperating teacher can expect to be involved in discussing the following topics:

- **Analysis of teaching skills**
  Development of subject matter.
  Affective behaviors.
  Teaching techniques.
  Academic achievement of pupils.
- **Evaluation of the student teacher's performance**
  Identify specific teaching skills.
  Discuss problems.
  Review the evaluation form.
- **Information about students**
  Official information such as IEP's.
  Personal observations and insights.
  Unique pupil behavior and possible causes.
- **Professional ideas and knowledge**
  Philosophy of teaching.
  Meeting the needs of diverse learners.
  Beliefs about pupil evaluation.
  Classroom management procedures.
  Discipline strategies.
  Organization techniques.
  The teaching profession in general.
- **Planning**
  Pre-teaching analysis.
  Post-teaching appraisal.
  Long-range planning.
- **Personal Concerns**
  Relationships with other faculty members.
  Personal problems.
  Pupil relationships.
  Value conflicts.
- **Enriching the teaching experience**
  Observations.
  Extraclass activities.

Although there is a wide range, the central core of conferences will relate to the daily teaching activities of the student teacher. Conferences may focus on discussions prior to teaching followed by analysis after the lesson has been taught. Many of the topics above will directly or indirectly relate to the activity involved with making the daily lesson satisfactory.

As was suggested earlier, a supervisor should move from the directive mode to a more collegial model as the student teacher matures. A collaborative approach will allow a student teacher more freedom to be in control and will permit a more open exchange of ideas. This style of conferencing permits discussion focused on joint problem solving and the negotiation of solutions.

Case Study No. 53: Ineffective Communication

You explained a number of details to the student teacher, ranging from procedures for checking attendance through a description of the social structure of the school community. She seemed interested and even made notes during the conference. The concern came near the end of the session when she appeared to be more confused than informed and asked you several questions about information you had just covered. What do you do?

1. Answer the questions as if they were routine.
2. Suggest that you talk about these matters later.
3. Question her about what she may have remembered.
4. _____

Comment

Two factors seem to be operating in this instance. First, there could be the implication that the teacher is giving too much information at one time. The second would indicate that the student teacher is disorganized. A carefully planned and well-organized system of conferences at this time might be helpful.

Questions

1. What are some ways to help a student teacher assimilate necessary information?
2. What types of alternative procedures could be employed by the cooperating teacher to try to enhance retention?

Case Study No. 54: No Concept Of Progress

Lori's student teaching performance had been lackluster. To date you have identified several problem areas in her teaching and suggested ways to remedy the difficulties. At mid-term you asked her to teach a lesson which you would observe. She was to complete a self-analysis and the next day you would jointly critique the lesson.

At the conference you asked Lori to describe how the lesson went. She gave only brief and vague responses with no elaboration. Her unresponsiveness revealed a lack of understanding about the dynamics of teaching and learning and an immature perspective about the conference objectives. What is your next step?

1. Ask her to read selected articles about self-analysis and professional reflection.
2. Have Lori observe skilled teachers in your building and talk with them about their educational practices and philosophies.
3. Modify your conference system so that you confer regularly, focusing on skills that are expected of teachers.
4. _____

Comment

It may be difficult for some student teachers to critique their own performance as this is a task that many college students have never had to confront. The teacher's goal should be to focus more on reflection, hoping that the student teacher can learn to evaluate herself more accurately and can articulate the dynamics of the learning environment.

Questions

1. How would you describe Lori's level of development? Why?
2. What conference techniques would help to achieve more accurate communication between these two persons?

Summary Conferences

The final conferences provide opportunities to review the experience, evaluate the present condition, and project future directions. These conferences should point to positive perceptions of skills and improved teacher behaviors. Conferences of this nature logically occur near the conclusion of the experience. These can be the most satisfying, especially when they are built on a successful experience and point to the future with the student teacher looking at the profession with confidence.

During the final conference experiences the topics for discussion should include:

• Review of the university's final evaluation form.

- Review of whether the goals established were met.
- Discussion of the growth that has occurred.
- Discussion of areas needing refinement.
- The student teacher's reflection about teaching.
- Future plans and educational goals.

The conference at this juncture will move more to an indirect approach on the part of the cooperating teacher. This style will recognize that the student teacher has competence in her own right and the supervisor's role is to help her clarify her thinking, to be aware of her potential, and to challenge her to seize other growth opportunities. The supervisor's role will be that of listener, clarifier, and encourager. It shows a strong collegial relationship, with the supervisor recognizing that the student teacher has a strong commitment to teaching and the desire and skills to succeed.

Case Study No. 55: The "Textbook" Conference

It was near the end of the experience and you and your student teacher are involved in a thoughtful conversation about the impact of a teacher on pupil behavior. Upon reflection, you realize that this student teacher is high in motivation and in abstraction and that you have taken a rather indirect approach in your recent conferences. You have focused your questions so that he could refine his own thinking and extend himself in new directions. You truly felt that you were colleagues and found that this conference was an enjoyable climax to a good student teaching assignment. Finally, he asks you what you think that he should do to improve himself as a teacher. How do you respond?

1. Ask him to think about his own skills and offer some ideas.
2. Give him a number of ideas.
3. Tell him that you think that he is where he should be and that anything else needed will come with experience.
4. _____

Comment

More often than not, things go well in student teaching. The previous case studies have all focused on problems. This one emphasizes the positive and implies that all the right things are happening. Fortunately many of these do happen and we take them for granted. This one may cause you to think of how you can work with a student teacher who is displaying maturity and probably needs more indirect coaching than direct supervision.

Questions

1. What oral strategies should a cooperating teacher use in a conference of this type?
2. What are some indicators that a conference is a "textbook" conference?

Effective Communication In Conferences
More Than Just Talk

A successful conference depends on the ability to communicate. Hours of talking can be futile if there is no comprehension or acceptance by the other participant. Southall and King (1979) observed that the most common critical incident perceived by student teachers was a lack of communication between the cooperating teacher and the student teacher. O'Shea, Hoover, and Carroll (1988) as well as Talvitie et al. (2000) believe that a lack of communication accounts for many of the problems associated with traditional student teaching programs. In a survey of over 300 student teachers, Connor and Killmer (1995) found that cooperating teachers were judged effective if they could communicate and provide appropriate feedback to their charges. So it is clear that the cooperating teacher will need to develop and refine several skills in order to make conferences successful vehicles for communication.

Establish Rapport

Good interpersonal relationships must be established between a cooperating teacher and student teacher. We have already observed that a conference is dominated by cognitive matters, but the success of a conference depends upon the affective climate of the discussion as well. A good conference models good human relations. An attitude of mutual trust and respect must prevail. If either party is uncomfortable, a strained relationship may develop which diminishes the productivity of a conference. The supervisor should set a positive tone and must be conscious of those factors that help to create rapport. The possibilities are numerous and may require practice before they are perfected. The following are helpful in establishing rapport:

- **Be an empathetic person.** You may not accept or change what a student teacher believes, but a good start toward creating a more positive climate for trying is to show empathy. Through verbal and non-verbal behaviors, respond to the student teacher so that you convince her that you understand how she feels. This is the beginning of communication.

- **Choose words carefully.** A poor choice of words or an ill-chosen expression can create unnecessary tension or alienation. Highly emotional words or phrases can be a detriment to the establishment of rapport.
- **Be a good listener.** Show that you are aware of what is being said through verbal and non-verbal responses. Do not get so preoccupied formulating responses that you fail to listen to what is being said.
- **Concentrate on supportive non-verbal behavior.** Body language is more believable than oral statements. Facial expressions, gestures, tone of voice, and other kinesic behavior, project a supportive climate.
- **Respond to the needs voiced by the student teacher.** When needs are expressed, problems need to be addressed. Work with the student teacher in a collegial manner to solve the problems or to satisfy concerns.
- **Maintain objectivity.** Emphasis should be placed on what was said and done rather than on opinions of what occurred. Look for the facts and try not to be influenced emotionally.

Encourage Reflection

A successful conference may be the one in which the supervisor has caused the student teacher to give careful consideration to a problem and to consider alternatives that were not apparent previously. The approach is where a supervisor leads a student teacher to the threshold of her own mind. Self-analysis should be encouraged throughout conferences because it is one of the most effective ways to produce change. This allows a student teacher to solve problems through discovery instead of listening. One of the best ways of encouraging self appraisal is through the questioning technique. Pultorak (1993) presented a taxonomy of questions that are purported to lead to reflective analysis. Consider how each of them might help a student teacher to be more reflective.

- What were essential strengths of the lesson?
- What, if anything, would you change about the lesson?
- Do you think the lesson was successful? Why?
- Which conditions were important to the outcome?
- What, if any, unanticipated learning outcomes resulted from the lesson?
- Can you think of another way you might have taught this lesson?

- Can you think of other alternative pedagogical approaches to teaching this lesson that might improve the learning process?
- Do you think the content covered was important to students? Why?
- Did any moral or ethical concerns occur as a result of the lesson?

The goal of such a taxonomy as the one above is to encourage a student teacher to think seriously about teaching. Teachers have often been accused of being reactionary and not determining decisions on informed practice. The movement to have preservice teachers develop professional portfolios has placed a greater emphasis on reflection and self-analysis. Verkler (2000) observed that the portfolio requirements help students make connections between theory and practice and have served as a catalyst for dialog with professors and classroom teachers. Peters (2000) discovered that preservice teachers who have engaged in portfolio development have a growing capacity to be more reflective and analytical.

Use the Right Technique

Communication can be ineffective if there is a mismatch between the perceptions of the student teacher and cooperating teacher. A mismatch occurs when the message received is not the one that was intended by the sender. One frequent cause of mismatching is that body language and voice tones do not correspond to verbal utterances. The recipient tends to believe the sender's nonverbal behaviors. Goleman (1995) stated that 90% of an emotional message is communicated non-verbally.

As indicated, student teachers need different types of supervisory approaches depending upon their levels of development. For example, the use of a directive behavior with a student teacher who is high in abstraction and motivation would not be productive. On the other hand, indirect procedures would not be effective for student teachers who are low in abstraction and commitment because they need help from a more knowledgeable and experienced professional.

Study the Results

Finally, determine whether the conference was successful. The following questions may serve to guide the supervisor's analysis:

- Does the student teacher show evidence of having new ideas?
- Does the student teacher bring up problems?
- Do we communicate freely and clearly?

- Are suggestions carried out?
- Is the student teacher learning to evaluate herself objectively?
- Is the growth of the student teacher steady and observable?

An effective conference contains interaction and serious dialogue in a supportive environment. Each participant should feel comfortable and secure enough to make the conference an individualized learning experience.

Case Study No. 56: A Lack of Reflection

Chad has been performing adequately but he has trouble identifying areas that need to be improved. Your objective is to encourage him to be more reflective. However, in your conferences, your reflective questions seem to get only brief, defensive responses. For example when you ask what he would change in the lesson, the response is, "Just about everything, I guess." When you ask if he thought the lesson was successful, he says, "Probably not." You are frustrated because you want him to think through questions, but your impression is that he thinks your questions are criticisms of his teaching. What do you do?

1. Examine your technique of asking questions to determine whether they are stated in a threatening or non-threatening manner.
2. Suggest that he write down his self analysis and then discuss it.
3. Attempt to be more positive and indicate that you are looking for the strengths of his lesson and not necessarily the negatives.
4. _____

Comment

As indicated in this chapter, questions are good ways of encouraging self appraisal. However, the questions must be presented so that they do not communicate criticism. A cooperating teacher should examine his nonverbal behaviors as well as verbal utterances in order to establish a climate where a student teacher can be open and not threatened.

Questions

1. What is most difficult in being reflective about your own work?
2. What preparation could you make which would cause a student teacher to be more receptive to the reflective process?

Case Study No. 57: No Empathy

The student teacher is trying to explain how he feels about his slow progress in the class. Whenever he makes a statement, the cooperating teacher is quick to offer a possible solution. The student teacher seems puzzled or frustrated at this approach and tries again. The cooperating teacher may say something like, "I know how you feel," but the student teacher is not convinced of that. Finally, the student teacher politely tries to end the conference, but the teacher says, "Go ahead and discuss anything you want. I want to help you." What is wrong here?

1. The student teacher is not a good listener.
2. The cooperating teacher is not a good listener.
3. The purpose of the conference has not been established.
4. The cooperating teacher is not prepared to respond in an empathetic manner.
5. _____

Comment

Communication begins when the conferee is convinced that the supervisor understands his feelings. This understanding has to be communicated through empathetic body and verbal language. Until this happens, solutions will not be accepted and the communications gap between them will be broadened. In this case, the reader can infer that the supervisor is not really communicating empathy to the student teacher.

Questions

1. What would be some appropriate behaviors on the part of the cooperating teacher?
2. What should be done to prevent this from happening again?

The class concluded and Brian had some time available to confer with Miss Bennett. He was eager to know what she thought of his technique, especially since he planned to use the same procedure in subsequent lessons.

Brian began, "They sat down at their tables and showed more interest than usual and seemed to handle the discussion questions with more insight than I had expected."

Miss Bennett agreed, "I felt that they were able to comprehend the reasons behind the questions and they had some supportive facts. What did you think of your introduction?"

Brian thought and slowly responded, "I guess it was not too good."

Miss Bennett responded, "But it was not all bad. Why did you think it was not so good?"

Brian quickly replied, "They did not pay close attention and it could have been difficult for them to see how it related to the later activities."

She inquired, "How could it have been made better?"

Brian considered the question and then speculated that a more animated procedure might have caused better response.

Miss Bennett accepted his evaluation and further stated, "You might list the important ideas for them to see. One other point, did you notice that you directed most of the questions to four students: Jo, Tom, Carla, and Rex?"

"Did I?" exclaimed a surprised Brian. "Now that I think of it, I believe that is right. They want to talk all the time but I should involve more pupils next time. I think that Kirsten, J. D., Megan, Justin, and Lindsey can hold their own with them. I will get them involved in tomorrow's discussion."

"Miss Bennett responded, "Don't overlook Casey."

"There is no way he could be overlooked," replied Brian.

Miss Bennett smiled and then gave an endorsement to Brian's technique that he had tried for the first time. The conference drifted into conversation, and they left feeling that the session had been productive.

Remember:

- A conference should involve the free flow of ideas that will foster an objective analysis of the student teacher's ability.
- The dialog should not be dominated by the cooperating teacher. Each participant has a contribution to make.
- A conference should be problem centered instead of person centered.
- Body language speaks loudly.
- A conference should be constructive with the student teacher feeling that it has been helpful.
- A conference should be private.
- A good conference should lead to concrete plans of action that are useful in guiding future activities.
- Frequent conferences are less stressful than infrequent ones.
- Conferences should be concerned with matters considered to be important by both participants.

- The supervisor who is an empathetic listener will be in a better position to help a student teacher analyze her teaching behaviors.
- The effectiveness of a conference is directly related to the quality of the preparation for it.
- Reflection is a valuable component of a successful conference.

Useful References

Balch, Pamela M., and Patrick E. Balch. 1987. Conferencing Techniques. Chapter 7 in *The Cooperating Teacher: A Practical Approach for the Supervision of Student Teachers*. Lanham, MD. The University Press of America.

Blank, Mary Ann, and Betty S. Heathington. 1987. The Supervisory Process: A Consistent Approach to Help Student Teachers Improve. *The Teacher Educator* 22 (Spring): 2-14.

Conner, Kathy and Nadine Killmer. 1995. Evaluation of Cooperating Teacher Effectiveness. Paper presented at the Annual Meeting of the Midwest Educational Research Association, October 11- 14. Chicago, IL. ERIC ED 394950.

Flickinger, Gayle Glidden, and Marilyn Ruddy. 1992. Off-Site/Reflective Conferences: University Supervisors and Student Teachers. *The Teacher Educator* 28 (Autumn): 2-9.

Glickman, Carl. 1995. *Supervision of Instruction: A Developmental Approach*. Boston, MA. Allyn and Bacon.

Goleman, Daniel. 1995 The Roots of Empathy. Chapter Seven in *Emotional Intelligence: Why It Matters More that IQ*. New York, NY. Bantam Books.

Grant, Joe W., and Lynn E. Drafall. 1996. *Developmental Thinking in the Student Teaching Experience*. Paper Presented at the Annual Meeting of the American Educational Research Association, April 8 - 12, 1996, New York, NY. ERIC ED 397031.

Guyton, Edith, and John McIntyre. 1990. Student Teaching and School Experiences. Chapter 29 in Houston (Ed), *Handbook of Research on Teacher Education*. New York. Macmillan Publishing Co.

Hanhan, Sara Fritzell. 1988. A Qualitative and Qualitatively Different Format for the Evaluation of Student Teachers. *Action in Teacher Education* 10 (Summer): 51-55.

Jin, Lijun, and Jackie L. Cox. 2000. Inquiring Minds Want to Know: Does the Clinical Supervision Course Improve Cooperating Teachers' Supervisory Performance? Paper presented at the

Annual Meeting of the Association of Teacher Educators, Orlando, FL. February 13-16. ERIC ED 439105

Johnson, William, C., Benjamin Cox, and George Wood. 1982. Communication Patterns and Topics of Single and Paired Student Teachers. *Action in Teacher Education* 4 (Spring/Summer): 56-60.

Kleinsasser, Audrey M. 1991. Perpetuating Teaching Myths or Debunking Them? An Analysis of the Debriefings Between a Student Teacher and a Cooperating Teacher. ERIC ED 335347.

NMSA 2000. Student Teaching at the Middle Level. FAX on DEMAND Service. Document No. 5009. National Middle School Association. Westerville, OH.

O'Neal, Sharon. 1983. An Analysis of Student Teaching-Cooperating Teacher Conferences as Related to the Self-Concept, Flexibility, and Teaching Concerns of Each Participant. Austin, TX. Research and Development Center for Teacher Education. ERIC ED 234030.

O'Shea, Lawrence J., Nora L. Hoover, and Robert G. Carroll. 1988. Effective Intern Conferencing. *Journal of Teacher Education* 39 (March- April): 17-21.

Peters, William H. 2000. Through the Looking Glass: The Journey of Preservice Teachers in Becoming Reflective Practitioners. Paper presented at the Annual Meeting of the American Educational Research Association, April 24-28. New Orleans, LA. ERIC ED 444950.

Pitton, Debra E. 1998. First Impressions. Chapter 15 In *Case Studies of Student Teaching: A Case Studies Approach to the Student Teaching Experience.* Upper Saddle River, New Jersey. Prentice Hall , Inc.

Pultorak, Edward G. 1993. Facilitating Reflective Thought in Novice Teachers. *Journal of Teacher Education* 44 (Sep-Oct): 288-295.

Southall, Carey, and Dorothy King. 1979. Critical Incidents in Student Teaching. *The Teacher Educator* 15 (Autumn): 34-36.

Tabachnick, B. R., T. S. Popkewitz, and K. M. Zeichner. 1979. Teacher Education and the Professional Perspectives of Student Teachers. *Interchange* 10 (4): 12-29.

Talvitie, Ulla. Lisa Peltokallio, and Paivi Mannisto. 2000. Student Teachers' Views About Their Relationships With University Supervisors, Cooperating Teachers, and Peer Student Teachers. *Scandanivan Journal of Educational Research.* 44 (1): 79-88.

Verkler, Karen Wolz. 2000. Let's Reflect: The Professional Portfolio as a Prerequisite for Internship. *Action in Teacher Education.* 22(2): (Summer). 116-120.

9

Supervising Participation In The Total School Program

It had been one of those long, dreary days when everything seemed to go wrong. A fire alarm interrupted a timed examination, the copy machine was down, and materials that were needed for a major class activity did not get delivered as promised. Linda and Cristie had a big argument in class, and it had now started to rain. As dismissal time approached, a voice sounded on the intercom, "Teachers are reminded of the open house this evening. Faculty should be in their rooms by seven o'clock."

"The end of a perfect day," commented Miss Bennett. "Did they tell you about this in methods class?" Brian forced a smile. The last thing he wanted to do was to return for the open house. He had papers to grade and had planned to relax a bit after that.

Turning toward the window, Brian inquired, "Do you think it would be all right if I did not attend tonight? I forgot about this and I have plans to get together with some friends later this evening after I finish grading papers. Since I already know several parents, I would like to be excused from attending the open house."

Miss Bennett considered the dilemma and could appreciate his feelings. He had been working hard and she knew the relaxation was well deserved, especially after this trying day. She also was aware that the school administration had assured the parents that their teachers would be available to meet with them this evening. Brian probably should be there to talk with some of them.

Miss Bennett made a quick check of the gray skies outside and softly inquired, "What did they tell you at the university? Do they expect you to attend?"

"I do not remember that it was ever discussed," was Brian's instant response . . .

Participation In The Total School Program
School Does Not End at 3:30

Teacher education programs made significant progress when they began to require a full-time student teaching experience that enabled a teaching candidate to devote all of his school time to living the life of a teacher. This development has allowed a student teacher to participate in the total program of activities before, during, and after the school day. The result has been a more comprehensive overview of the responsibilities of a teacher and experience beyond classroom teaching.

Participation can be defined as that period of time when a student teacher is involved in out-of-class activities which focus on the growth of students, involve management of the school or professional activity. It encompasses required as well as elective activities. Many, perhaps most, participation activities are more informal than classroom situations and provide opportunity for closer interaction with students, other school personnel and persons in the community.

The significance of participation activities was highlighted by two studies in the 1980's. Johnson and Yates (1982) queried persons in 902 teacher education institutions about their student teaching programs and found that overall student teachers spent 26 percent of their time in some type of participation activity. Richardson (1987) studied 300 student teaching teams and reported that 71 percent of student teachers participated in extracurricular activities. Since 1992, many states have embraced the principles identified by the Interstate New Teacher Assessment and Support Consortium (INTASC) as competencies that beginning teachers should possess before a teaching license is issued. Principle Ten of that document states the following performance criteria:

> The teacher fosters relationships with school colleagues, parents, and agencies in the larger community to support students' learning and well-being.

These studies and initiatives provide evidence for the fact that a cooperating teacher must give serious time and effort in overseeing the participation activities of a student teacher.

Value of the Extracurricular Program

Student teachers need to learn the vital role that the extracurricular and cocurricular programs play for many students. An opportunity to have a major role in a school play, perform in the marching band, or be involved with an athletic team may be a major reason for some students to attend school. The stage, concert hall, or athletic facility can also be an extension of the classroom and a place where certain components of the curriculum are best learned.

The extracurricular program is also a major public relations agent for the school. Not many people will visit classrooms to see classes being taught, but they will attend plays, concerts, and athletic contests. Ultimately, they may form an impression of the quality of the school based on what they experience at such events. It is important for student teachers to recognize that community perception and support of public schools is critical.

Benefits from Participation

Student teachers can learn from and contribute to out-of-class activities. Participation gives the opportunity for total involvement in school affairs. It is here that much of the formality of school vanishes and people reveal their true personalities. This hidden curriculum is that part of school life where students pursue their own interests. Student teachers need to participate in the extracurricular program in order to better understand the kind of contribution that activities make to the development of a pupil.

Participation experiences permit a different type of interaction with teachers. Student teachers can gain a more comprehensive understanding of a teacher's responsibilities as they work together with members of the host school's faculty. Teachers today are expected to be "team players" rather than isolates. For example, the state of Vermont (1999) designated *colleagueship* as one of the five standards for professional educators in that state. Participation provides the student teachers with opportunities to establish collegial relationships with practicing teachers and models the type of associations they are expected to maintain as licensed teachers.

Participation should help a student teacher develop greater awareness of what is involved in being a teacher. There may be a real learning vacuum if a student teacher does not have the opportunity to work with teachers in their extracurricular and professional activities. Implicit in this activity as well, is the implication that participation realistically acquaints student teachers with the great number of demands that are made on a teacher's time and energy.

Participation activities afford student teachers the opportunity to know pupils better. Informal interaction with youth allows student teachers to see a side of learners that may not otherwise be apparent. It is not unusual for student teachers to comment that they really became acquainted with their students when they worked with them in an extracurricular activity. This enriching opportunity can cause pupils to perceive that the student teacher has a genuine interest in them.

The participation experience can be an "elective" curriculum that presents the opportunity for student teachers to contribute their talents and pursue their interests for the benefit of the school. For example, a student teacher with musical talent may be able to assist a student with practice and an athlete may be able to contribute to coaching.

Student teachers may come to the school aware of some of the more recent educational developments and skilled in new technology. They may have had more experience with computers, for example, and be eager to share their knowledge with both teachers and students. In addition, they may be able to enrich the school program by sharing their understanding of such ideas as alternative assessment techniques, cooperative learning, and portfolio development.

Nearly every student teacher has a talent or skill that can make a contribution to the school's extracurricular program. It would be to a cooperating teacher's benefit to discover what unique talents and interests a student teacher possesses and give the opportunity to display those skills .

Participation activities offer the opportunity for the student teacher to achieve visibility in the school and in the community. Administrators, particularly, may have little opportunity to observe student teachers except through professional and extracurricular activities. Other teachers and school personnel will have their best opportunities to know student teachers in these situations as well. Most of the people from the community will only see a student teacher at a school function. Such visibility can be helpful and create a more positive image of who the student teacher is.

Participation reveals the comprehensive role and scope of school activities. Attendance at faculty meetings and participation in school activities may give student teachers a glimpse of teaching that had never occurred to them. A student teacher may have a limited concept of the scope and contribution of the total school program unless he participates in a range of activities.

A cooperating teacher can use the participation experience to view the student teacher from a different perspective. The informal moments will allow a cooperating teacher to assess additional qualities and be able to make a more comprehensive appraisal of the student teacher.

Finally, participation serves to acquaint a student teacher with the demands that are made on a teacher. School does not end with the final afternoon bell. There is a plethora of important activities that consume a teacher's time. From the scenario that opened this chapter, Miss Bennett is obligated to return for the open house on a rainy night, tired or not, and Brian should be there, too.

The time and energy spent in participation is a good investment for a student teacher. Worthwhile participation activity will make some important contributions to the overall development of a student teacher. In summary, it will help a student teacher:

- Get to know and understand pupils better.
- Understand the types of learning that occur outside the classroom.
- Be more aware of the demands that are made on a teacher.
- Meet and interact with parents and other adults in the community.
- Work with other teachers.
- Enhance his visibility overall.
- Learn about the purposes and functions of the school.
- Understand how forces work together for the education of pupils.
- Make a significant and real contribution to the students and school.

Case Study No. 58: Reluctant To Participate

Jim, your student teacher, commutes from campus, a distance of twenty-five miles one way. As a result, he has seen very little of school life after hours because of his reluctance to return in the evening. When you suggest that he participate in some evening functions, he says that he would like to but that the expense of a second trip makes it nearly impossible. You appreciate his problem but also realize that he is missing some valuable experiences and is failing to contribute as he could. What course of action do you take?

1. Accept Jim's explanation.
2. Tell him that he must make some adjustments because his assignment includes total involvement in the school.
3. Try to get him involved in such a way that he will want to participate in spite of the inconvenience.
4. Suggest an arrangement which would allow him to remain at the school when evening participation is required.
5. Most likely some faculty members find themselves in the same predicament. Encourage Jim to talk with them about how they handle such a situation.
6. _____

Comment

Since it is the cooperating teacher's responsibility to prepare the student teacher for the total teaching environment, she must be concerned with providing participation experiences. The student teacher may have financial difficulties or may not realize what the opportunities are from participation. It appears that a logical alternative would be some sort of arrangement for him to remain after school in the evening when necessary without having to make an extra trip. If he then resists, he probably is sharing his teaching time with campus life. Reluctance to participate speaks volumes about a student's level of maturity, professional development, and dedication to the profession. A discussion with the university supervisor would be appropriate.

Questions

1. What effects can there be on a student teacher who misses participation activities?
2. How can a teacher convince a student teacher that participation activities are necessary?

Case Study No. 59: Too Much Extracurricular Activity

Todd is a college athlete. When he started to student teach, he was asked to help coach one of the junior varsity teams. He was excited about it and welcomed the experience. The problem is that since he began coaching, he has not been as well prepared for teaching. You express this concern in a conference and he admits that he has been somewhat lax in preparing for his classes. He explains that he wants to coach and feels that this is an excellent opportunity to gain valuable experience. You are faced with the eternal question of the role of coaches in teaching. What response do you give to this future coach--and teacher?

1. Tell him that he is a teacher first and you want to see better teaching performance before you approve his involvement in coaching.
2. Talk with him about how to manage his schedule so that he can coach and spend the time necessary to be an effective teacher.
3. Suggest that he share the problem with the coach.
4. Adjust his teaching load to fewer hours so that he can have more time for coaching.
5. _____

Comment

Todd's involvement in after-school activities should be encouraged because it will enhance his learning and help to prepare him for his goal of becoming a coach. However, it is also the cooperating teacher's responsibility to see that the welfare of her pupils is not jeopardized. If Todd's inadequate preparation is affecting the students, then it is the obligation of the cooperating teacher to inform him to make the necessary adjustments in his schedule.

Questions

1. What is a good guideline for establishing balance between teaching responsibilities and extracurricular participation?
2. If coaching is the student teacher's major goal, should a cooperating teacher attempt to limit the coaching experience in any way?

Participation Activities
Educational Smorgasbord

The range of activities is usually extensive in any school where student teachers are assigned. Obviously a student teacher will not be able to see and do everything in the few weeks of supervised teaching, so priorities will need to be determined. Those activities that will be of most benefit in helping the student teacher learn about teaching should be of primary concern and responsibilities should be provided which are normally expected of a teacher.

Although there is no one pattern of specific activities that is appropriate to all situations, the following list represents those experiences where student teachers can usually be involved:

- **Faculty duties**
  Faculty meetings
  Attendance at school board meetings
  Hall and cafeteria supervision
  Supervisory responsibilities
  Reports and other required information
  Parent conferences
  Attendance at school functions
  After-school assistance to pupils
  Rehearsals and practices
  Conferences and meetings

- **Professional activities**
  Professional organization activity
  Inservice programs
  Professional conferences
  Committee assignments
- **Extracurricular functions**
  Athletic contests
  Student social activities
  Faculty functions
  Drama activities
  Musical events
  Community functions
  Fund raisers
  Academic competitions
  Student clubs
  Student government
  Field trips

Participation in faculty affairs gives the student teacher the impression of being accepted and allows direct involvement in essential activities. These kinds of experiences illustrate what is involved in carrying out extracurricular activities as well as demonstrate how teachers interact with staff and other persons associated with the school.

Professional activities are becoming more significant in teaching. Student teaching can provide a chance for a student teacher to see what the objectives of professional organizations are and how they achieve their goals. Such contact should increase understanding and allow the future teacher to make more intelligent choices in regard to future involvement.

The college background of a student teacher may help him to be a real contributor to extracurricular programs because special talents can be displayed at the more informal functions. School officials and pupils alike appreciate the fact that student teachers volunteer to participate in extracurricular activities. They perceive that it is an indicator of interest in and dedication to teaching. Pupils feel they get to know the student teacher better because of the personal interest that has been shown to them.

Some cooperating teachers may be interested in either preparing a detailed list of specific activities for their student teachers or keep a record of what they have experienced. Those teachers will find Worksheet Number Thirteen in the Appendix to be helpful. It lists several of the most typical participation categories and provides space for note taking.

Case Study No. 60: Looking For A Teaching Position

Your student teacher lives in an adjacent community and has strong ties to the area. He comes to you as a student teacher at a time when two teachers in his area of certification will be retiring. Both you and he know that there will be vacancies. He indicates during the first few days of student teaching that he would be interested in being employed here and asks your advice about how he should make his wishes known. He had been told at the university that student teachers who had a good teaching evaluation accompanied by participation in various aspects of the extracurricular program, were often asked to remain as teachers. He said he wants to get involved in "everything" so that he can enhance his chances of being viewed favorably and, consequently, employed. What is your response?

1. Tell him to concentrate on being the best student teacher that he can be and wait to see if the principal or personnel officer comes forward to discuss the position with him.
2. Sit down with him and devise a reasonable plan of action that will give him experience but not make it look as if he is blatantly becoming a candidate for the open positions.
3. Suggest a "wait and see" approach until he is certain that this is the type of school where he would want to teach.
4. Ignore the remark until you have had an opportunity to determine whether or not you would support him.
5. _____

Comment

A possible position can be quite appealing to a student teacher. The task of the teacher is to have him focus on his student teaching instead of campaigning for a position. A word of caution should be shared with eager student teachers about becoming over-committed to so many extracurricular obligations that their teaching performance suffers. Schools are sometimes reluctant to make a commitment to a student teacher early because they may have different thoughts after a few weeks. The message should go out that the student teacher and cooperating teacher are working hard to make it a good experience, and this includes seeing that he spends a portion of time participating in important extraclass activities. The cooperating teacher may be able to initiate the process of serious inquiry into the possibility of retaining the student teacher at the appropriate time.

Questions

1. What are activities in the extracurricular domain that a student teacher can include to help secure a favorable recommendation for the position?
2. What other recommendations would you make in order for the student teacher to become a viable candidate?

Case Study No. 61: Request For Time Away From Class

Your student teacher brings in a registration brochure advertising the national conference of a major educational organization to be held in a nearby city. She is excited about attending the conference and asks your permission to miss two days of class so she can participate in the convention. How do you respond to her request?

1. Defer the request to the college supervisor.
2. Tell her that her responsibilities are restricted to the school.
3. Leave the decision up to her.
4. Allow her to attend.
5. _____

Comment

Conference attendance can be a profitable learning experience for educators. New ideas are shared in sessions. Novice teachers will be exposed to seasoned veterans. Abundant networking opportunities exist for student teachers who are looking for future employment. Exposure to a major education conference would be a legitimate learning experience for a teacher at any career stage.

Questions

1. What concerns might you have about a student teacher attending such a conference?
2. What suggestions would you give your student teacher to help her learn the most from the experience?

Case Study No. 62: Critic Of The Profession

You and your student teacher have just left a rather unexciting meeting of your local teachers' association. After a bit of idle conversation, she asks why you bother to participate in the union. Her impression was that teachers have enough to do without attending boring meetings of organizations who charge high membership dues and spend considerable time talking about contracts and negotiations. She wants to know what the organization ever did for young teachers. How do you react to her questions?

1. Cite some significant accomplishments of a professional organization.
2. Arrange for her to get some information about the organization that will allow her to make an informed judgment .
3. Explain that the organization may not be perfect but that it does make a positive contribution to teaching.
4. _____

Comment

Professional organizations are important in the lives of teachers. The student teacher's comment reflects a lack of knowledge of what an organization does. She should have an opportunity to become more familiar with the goals and activities of a professional organization.

At the same time, such criticism may have some merit. If this is the case in your school, point out that a professional organization includes opportunities for professional development as well as advocating improved compensation and working conditions.

Questions

1. What should a student teacher know about professional organizations?
2. What are some means for involving a student teacher in the activities of teachers organizations?

Directing Participation Experiences
Interpreting the Menu

The world beyond the classroom may not be as readily apparent to the student teacher as the classroom. Since most of the participation activities are non-credit for pupils and constitute additional demands on teachers, the student teacher may need to be made aware of the obligations in the extracurricular domain. There also may be few or no guidelines regarding the kind of priorities that should be given to participation. The cooperating teacher may need to explain and interpret what the role of participation is and how teachers are involved as part of the educational mission. The guidelines below may be of assistance for this task:

- Explain what is expected from a student teacher in the extracurricular domain.
- Invite your student teacher to accompany you in your duties.
- Determine a student teacher's interests and see if they can be incorporated into the existing extracurricular program.
- Describe what a typical pattern of teacher obligations for out-of-class activities is like.
- See that student teachers come in contact with a broad spectrum of activities.
- Explain what students and student teachers can learn from participation.
- Inform the student teacher about policies relating to extracurricular activities.

The supervisor's responsibility is one of informing and guiding. This involves the necessity of making certain that the student teacher is aware of the number of extracurricular duties that consume a teacher's out-of-class time and arranging for participation in appropriate activities.

Case Study No. 63: Party Time

Your student teacher has agreed to help you chaperone a school social event. The activity had hardly started when it became apparent that you had one more person to supervise. A few of the pupils gathered around him for a while and he was obviously enjoying the attention. The situation became of real concern when he began to dance with one of the girls. You are aware of the problems that can be caused by too much association, but he shows no evidence of having any reservations about such contacts. How do you react to this situation?

1. Get him involved in an activity which will take him away from the small group.
2. Call him aside and explain the possible consequences of his becoming too closely involved with pupils.
3. Ignore the present situation but explain the consequences of such behavior at your first opportunity.
4. Order the students to stay away from him.
5. _____

Comment

The immediate task of the cooperating teacher is to transform the student teacher's role from that of a participant to that of a supervisor. If not, the situation may become more difficult and the student teacher may find himself with a complex social entanglement. It would be very difficult for the student teacher to behave as a peer on Friday night and then expect his pupils to respond to him as a teacher on Monday morning.

Questions

1. What could cause a student teacher to act immaturely at a social function?
2. What type of briefing should be given to a student teacher prior to his assuming a supervisory role in an informal setting?

Dr. Douglas met with the principal prior to his supervisory visit to Brian's class. After some informal conversation, he inquired about Brian's progress as a student teacher. The principal stated he was doing well and was a good representative of the university. He explained that Brian was one of the few student teachers who attended the open house recently. Furthermore, he is always looking for ways to make a contribution. He thought it was a good indication of interest that Brian stayed around after school instead of rushing to the parking lot to get away as soon as he could. He further stated that he feels teaching skill is highly correlated with success in directing extracurricular activities. He concluded his comments by mentioning he would be interested in considering Brian for a position if a vacancy should occur.

Dr. Douglas expressed his appreciation for the report as he scribbled a few notes for his records and then headed down the hall for a supervisory visit.

Remember:

- **The student teacher should be involved in the same kinds of activities as the cooperating teacher.**
- **Participation helps give a student teacher the feeling of being accepted and needed.**
- **Student teachers are exposed to a wider audience in participation activity than in a classroom activity.**
- **Participation should be accompanied by reflection and discussion if the activity is to be more significant.**

- **Student teachers have skills that they can contribute through participation in school activities outside the classroom.**
- **Willingness to participate in extracurricular activities is an indication of the student teacher's level of commitment to the profession.**

Useful References

Guyton, Edith, and D. John McIntyre. 1990. Student Teaching and Field Experiences. Chapter 29 in Houston (Ed.), *Handbook of Research on Teacher Education*. New York. Macmillan Publishing Co.

Johnson, J., and J. Yates. 1982. A National Survey of Student Teaching Programs. ERIC ED 232963.

McAteer, John F. 1976. Student Teaching Supervision Roles and Routines. *The Clearing House* 50 (December): 161-165.

Needham, Dorothy. 1977. The Learning Connection: Teacher, Student Teacher, Child. *Teacher* 94 (September): 80-83.

Quimby, Donald E. 1985. Student Teaching--A Principal's Perspective. *NASSP Bulletin* 69 (Oct): 14-18.

Richardson, R. C. 1987. What Really Transpires During the Supervision of Student Teachers: A Role Function Analysis. Paper presented at the annual meeting of the Association of Teacher Educators. Houston. February.

Vermont Department of Education 1999. *Five Standards for Vermont Educators: A Vision for Schooling*. Montpelier, Vermont 05620.

10

Legal And Ethical Aspects Of Student Teaching

On Monday morning Brian was at school early, impatiently waiting to talk with Miss Bennett. When she arrived, he shared a story he had heard during the weekend while back on campus. It was reported that one of last semester's student teachers had been named as a defendant in a court case. Co-defendants were his cooperating teacher and the school principal. While Brian did not know all the facts of the case, the suit was initiated by the parents of a student who had been injured during a class which the student teacher had been conducting. The parents, on behalf of their child, were seeking a huge cash settlement.

After relating this to Miss Bennett, Brian asked, "Can they do this? Can parents sue a student teacher and his cooperating teacher?"

Miss Bennett replied, "I don't know, but why don't we find out?". . .

The Law And Student Teaching
What Are the Rules?

We live in a society which is becoming more prone to turn to legal action to solve problems. Teachers and school corporations are increasingly becoming the targets of litigation. Gullatt and Tollett (1995) found that most states were crafting between fifteen and twenty new laws each year that impact teachers and their practice. With increased attention being placed on legal aspects of education, many teachers find themselves making decisions with one eye focused on what is best for their students and the other one on what the law says. Unfortunately, preservice teachers often have little, if any, formal instruction in educational law.

The nature of student teaching places student teachers in situations similar to that of regular teachers (Hall, 1989). This chapter will attempt to define some of the issues and note some of the prevailing trends regarding the legal status of student teachers and cooperating teachers. The authors have attempted to provide current information related to legal issues, but the changing scene, especially when 50 separate states are involved, makes it impossible to be completely up to date. ***The reader should check the latest regulations in his or her state when in question, using the information in this chapter as a guide.***

Common Issues and Legal Status of Student Teaching

Morris and Curtis (1983) reviewed state statutes and found a rather high level of commonalty in the issues addressed. The following areas were generally given attention:

- Definition of student teacher and student teaching.
- Definition of the legal status of student teachers.
- Provision for prescribing the duties and responsibilities of student teachers.
- Provision for immunity of student teachers equal to that of the cooperating teachers.
- Provision for student teachers to have equal status and authority with cooperating teachers.
- Provision for contractual arrangements, including payment by institutions, between the institution and school districts for conduct of student teaching programs.
- Provisions for tort liability insurance for student teachers.

All fifty states have provisions or implied authority for student teaching, but these provisions are not always documented. Individual states were found to vary greatly in their legal treatment of student teachers (Wood, 1976) and the same situation exists today. Several states were found to have clear statutes, while others had neither statutes, attorney generals' opinions, nor judicial decisions to follow.

Even though several states have not provided for student teaching by statute, the authority of the student teacher to teach in the absence of such laws has not been a subject of much controversy. Many believe that any state which requires student teaching as a prerequisite for teacher certification legalizes it in public school by implication. This appears to be a valid argument. Nevertheless, a clear statute is still needed in those states that have not granted legal authority for student teaching.

Because there is so much variation among states, the authors recommend that it would be well to determine the provisions in your individual state. The university office of student teaching should be able to provide that information.

Selection of Cooperating Teachers

The requirements vary for the selection of cooperating teachers. The following criteria are the most common, depending upon which state is involved:

- Joint selection of cooperating teachers by the university and public school district.
- Meets minimum qualifications for the employment of public school teachers.
- Cooperating teachers selected on the basis of training, experience, leadership qualities and positions in the school.
- Teachers who hold a master's degree and at least three years of experience.
- Criteria agreed upon by the university and cooperating school.

Selection criteria generally focus on degrees earned, teaching experience and special courses in supervising student teachers. States or individual institutions within states often require some sort of inservice training either prior to or during the time that a teacher is selected to be a cooperating teacher.

Case Study No. 64: Who Decides?

One of your students has very protective parents. On the day that your student teacher begins teaching the class, you receive a call from the girl's parents. They demand that you continue teaching the class because they do not want their daughter "practiced on." They state that they are paying taxes for their child to learn from certified teachers and threaten to contact their attorney if the student teacher continues to teach their daughter. What should you do?

1. Reassign your student teacher to another section.
2. Inform the principal about the telephone call.
3. Invite the parents to come to school, meet the student teacher and observe some class sessions.
4. _____

Comment

In most cases the persons selected to be cooperating teachers are judged to be among the most competent in the building. In order to supervise and provide appropriate learning experiences for the student teacher, they must relinquish their classes to someone who is less experienced and who does not have a teaching certificate.

The question is, "Who selects the teacher?" One can assume that an agent of the state has that authority, but a determined parent may have considerable influence on the decision. The parents are somehow going to need to be convinced that their daughter is going to get quality instruction while the student teacher is assigned to her class.

This becomes a critical issue for schools that typically host several student teachers each term or serve as a Professional Development School. Administrators must assure concerned parents that their child's education is not being compromised, and may be enhanced, by the presence of a student teacher in the classroom.

Questions

1. Are the parents within their rights to refuse to have their daughter in a class taught by a student teacher?
2. How can a school that regularly serves student teachers take a proactive stance for providing that experience?

Compensation for Cooperating Teachers

It is common for teacher education institutions to offer incentives to school districts and cooperating teachers for participating in their student teaching programs. These incentives are usually in the form of monetary compensation, tuition waivers or complimentary dinners coupled with an inservice program.

In those states in which teacher education institutions make payments to cooperating teachers, the question arises as to the authority to make payments which are in addition to the contracted salary of the teacher. Rulings differ among the states. The affirmative point of view is that the payment is legal because of the extra duties of the cooperating teacher and the fact that funds come from outside the school district. The negative opinion holds that teachers would be receiving compensation in excess of what is specified in the district's salary schedule.

Since few states neither authorize incentive payments by statute nor state board of education administrative regulation, on what authority are these payments made? The primary answer seems to be that since teacher education institutions are empowered to finance their teacher training programs, they have authority to pay these incentives. They will probably continue to regularly make such payments unless prohibited by specific statutes, judicial decisions, or contract agreements.

Duties And Responsibilities Of Student Teachers
What Is Legal?

There is a great deal of diversity from state to state regarding student teachers' legal responsibilities. Most states fail to provide any legal status to student teachers, and eight states fail to recognize student teachers or student teaching experiences at all (Hall, 1989). A survey of the laws and attorney general opinions on the responsibilities and authority of student teachers shows great variation depending upon which state is involved. The following statements give an indication of the range of opinions.

- Responsibilities will be cooperatively decided by representatives of the school districts and the teacher training institutions.
- Student teaching may include those duties granted to a teacher and any other part of the school program for which the supervising teacher is responsible.
- Student teachers may be granted responsibilities identical to those of regular teachers.
- Student teachers may exercise the same authority in the control of pupil conduct as regularly certified teachers.
- Student teachers will assume classroom responsibilities as delegated by the classroom supervisor.
- Student teachers can perform only under the direction of a regular teacher and may not legally take charge of a classroom in the absence of the regular teacher.
- Student teachers are given the opportunity to prepare and present lessons, but the cooperating teacher at all times has a duty to exercise proper supervision over the pupils in his charge.

The above list indicates that the question concerning student teachers' legal duties and responsibilities is difficult to answer. The majority of the states offer no legal direction in the formulation of the answer to this question. The laws and legal opinions in the states that do approach this topic do not possess enough commonalty to provide general guidelines. Many of these states either permit or expressly provide that the student teacher be granted a large degree of authority, while other states provide that this authority be very restricted. The university should provide specific requirements or general guidelines to the cooperating teacher. If such information is not presented, the cooperating teacher should ask for them.

Case Study No. 65: Let Me Try Teaching Alone

Ted's student teaching assignment is approximately two-thirds completed. You have been pleased with his progress. His plans have been fully developed and submitted for approval well in advance. Except for one minor incident relating to pupil control, you have never felt compelled to become involved while he is teaching, although you have never left the classroom for a substantial period of time.

One day, in a candid comment, Ted said to you that he wished you would let him "try his own wings" for just a week without monitoring his plans or his teaching. How do you reply to him?

1. Suggest an alternative that would give him more freedom but allow you to maintain supervision.
2. Indicate that you will check into the legal ramifications of such action.
3. Agree to the request and let him teach for a week.
4. Reject the suggestion on the basis that you have responsibility for the class.
5. _____

Comment

Generally, the student teacher should be given some time for independent teaching, as noted in Chapter Seven. The cooperating teacher is responsible for all that happens in the classroom, but there are ways to maintain responsibility and still allow more freedom for the student teacher.

Questions

1. Would this request be legal in the state where you teach?
2. Aside from legal considerations, are there any professional or ethical questions involved in this request?
3. How can a cooperating teacher permit more freedom and still meet his obligation to supervise?

Tort Liability
Who Defends the Student Teacher?

Tort is defined simply as a wrong or injury that someone has committed against another party (Martin, et al. 2001). Tort liability is grounded in the following:

Every person is responsible for his or her own negligent acts and, thus, teachers are responsible for their actions in relationships to their pupils.

Student teachers stand in a teacher-like relationship to their pupils. Most states hold student teachers accountable for injuries to pupils by requiring or allowing them to be given protection under school district policies or state liability laws. While the extent of protection varies from state to state, most state laws stipulate that, to be covered, student teachers must be acting without malicious intent and must be acting within the scope of their assigned duties. Most attorney general opinions have asserted that student teachers would be protected or indemnified against legal action under state laws (Hall, 1989).

Student teachers are responsible for their actions with pupils. The mere fact that they are not regularly certified does not absolve them of this responsibility. However, there have been very few lawsuits against student teachers, perhaps because they generally are not of sufficiently high stature to serve as defendants in suits by pupils or parents (Hazard, 1976). In a national survey of student teaching programs, Johnson and Yates (1982) found that there were only 47 responses to their question, "To the best of your knowledge, has your student teaching program or have any of your student teachers ever been involved in a lawsuit growing out of any aspect of student teaching?" The following summary identifies those responses that could be considered to be against a student teacher:

- Controversy over grade in student teaching--4 cases.
- Student teacher accused of hitting a pupil--4 cases.
- Student teacher accused of negligence resulting in injury to a pupil--8 cases.
- Student teacher accused or convicted of a felony--2 cases.
- Use of corporal punishment by student teacher--2 cases.

Considering the small number of lawsuits and even smaller number of court cases arising from student teaching, tort issues do not seem to be the most compelling legal aspects of student teaching experiences (Guyton and McIntyre, 1990). Although the possibilities of a student teacher being sued are slim, some of the states have anticipated civil liability for student teachers and made provisions for it. Most of these states have provisions in their statutes on student teaching granting them the same protection as regularly certified teachers.

It can be concluded from the literature and cases that risk exists, although not to the extent to that of teachers. Again, it is a good policy to check the provisions for student teacher liability in your state. Even though such events are rare, it would still be prudent to take reasonable precautions. The next section addresses the major issues that could confront student teachers.

Reasonable Precautions Regarding Legal Issues
Twelve Conditions

While teachers and student teachers should not be expected to be experts on educational law, they should have a working knowledge of legal issues that impact their professional actions and duties. To this end, Monts (1998) surveyed public school administrators to identify laws in which they believed student teachers should be well versed as they begin their professional experience. Listed below are the twelve legal topics that superintendents and principals reported most critical for preservice teachers to be aware of:

- Corporal punishment and discipline.
- First aid and medication.
- Rights of children with disabilities.
- Physical contact.
- Negligence.
- Time spent alone.
- Permission slips.
- Family Education Rights and Privacy Act.
- Child abuse.
- Liability insurance.
- Search and seizure.
- Due process.

Each of these items will be discussed in the sections that follow. The review is not intended to be exhaustive but rather to serve as representative examples of issues that could arise during a typical student teaching assignment.

Corporal Punishment and Physical Contact

Corporal punishment has been outlawed by the majority of states in this country. Kohn (1996) stated that inflicting physical force on students imparts the inappropriate message to students that use of power and aggression are appropriate means to resolve conflicts. Aside from the physical discomfort that results from corporal punishment, psychological damage can also result. But since the United States Supreme Court has ruled that corporal punishment does not meet the standard of cruel and unusual punishment as defined by the Eighth Amendment, its practice is still legal and used in some states and the Supreme Court has established guidelines that need to be followed when corporal punishment is administered. Corporal punishment is usually thought of as striking or spanking a student. But Burns, Roe, and Ross, (1989) reminded readers that corporal punishment has been interpreted in some courts as any disciplinary measure that inflicts pain or discomfort upon a student even though no physical contact occurred between the student and teacher. Requiring a student to stand on his tip toes to place his nose in a circle drawn on the chalkboard for an extended length of time would be an example of "noncontact" corporal punishment.

It is strongly suggested that student teachers never use corporal punishment. It is not an effective method to bring about long term change in student behavior and can result in detrimental ramifications. The cooperating teacher should help the student teacher find other methods of behavior modification that are more productive and humane.

Physical contact between teachers and students is strongly discouraged in many school districts. Unfortunately, even a hug for a distraught student or a pat on the back for a job well done could be misinterpreted. To protect themselves against accusations of child abuse most teachers practice a "no physical contact policy" with their students (Del Prete, 1996). DiGiulio (2000) suggested that avoiding all but the most superficial physical contact between students and teachers would be a prudent rule of thumb to follow.

Case Study No. 66: Struggle With A Student

You left your student teacher alone with a class and are occupied in another part of the building. During a study period, a girl left her seat and your student teacher asked her to sit down. When she refused, your student teacher sent her to the dean's office where she was told to return to class the next day and apologize to the student teacher.

The pupil returned the next day and talked with the student teacher but did not apologize. After some talk, the two went into the hall and an argument resulted. The student teacher took the pupil by the arm to take her to the office, but the student jerked away. A conflict resulted and the student teacher accidentally struck the pupil in the head, breaking her glasses.

The parents came to school in a hostile mood. The student teacher apologized for her behavior, but that may not be sufficient. As the cooperating teacher, what do you do?

1. Nothing. This is now in the hands of the school administration and possibly the courts.
2. Try to bring the student teacher, pupil and parents together to attempt to reconcile the problem.
3. Check to see if you are legally responsible in any way since you are responsible for the class.
4. Talk with the pupil and see if you can determine the cause of her behavior.
5. _____

Comment

One of the many questions to be addressed is whether the student teacher was acting legally by being alone in the classroom. Second, one needs to examine whether proper procedure was followed by the student teacher in dealing with the problem. Although the major decisions will probably rest with the school administration and the parents, the cooperating teacher, who probably knows the pupil and why she acted that way, might try to find a solution that would be acceptable to all parties without litigation or serious damage to the student teacher's future.

Questions

1. Does the fact that the student teacher is alone in the classroom have any significance to the basic question in this case?
2. What guidelines can be developed to prevent a matter such as this from happening?

Suspected Child Maltreatment

Nothing can be more devastating to a child or teen's well-being and self-image than maltreatment from individuals who should be sources of support and affection. Krantz (1994) defined maltreatment as any adult behavior that intentionally or unintentionally causes harm to children. In severe cases, maltreatment can cost a youngster his life. Feldman (1999) reported that more than three million children and teens in the United States fall victim to child abuse each year. Frequently the perpetrators of abuse are parents or close family members. Since abuse often takes place in the privacy of a child's home, many people are reluctant to become involved and report suspected cases to authorities. Teachers are among the most likely people to notice signs of abuse and all 50 states have passed legislation that require teachers to report suspected cases of abuse (Anspaugh and Ezella, 2001).

Abuse can occur in all kinds of families regardless of race, ethnicity, locality, or socio-economic position. People who regularly work with children should avoid jumping to conclusions over every bump and bruise exhibited by youngsters, but if a student teacher observes a pattern of injury or trauma, she should discuss her concerns with her cooperating teacher. If the cooperating teacher agrees that the evidence suggests a pupil is likely a victim of maltreatment, then a report should be made to the designated school authorities.

Maltreatment can surface in many forms. Childhelp USA (2000) identified the following as major categories of maltreatment:

- Physical Abuse.
- Emotional Abuse.
- Sexual Abuse.
- Physical Neglect.
- Emotional Neglect.

Child abuse is difficult to detect with certainty, but Robbins (1990) provided the following list of symptoms that might indicate a child is a victim of abuse or violence. A cooperating teacher should review these indicators with a student teacher.

- Visible, serious injuries that have no reasonable explanation.
- Bite or choke marks.
- Burns from cigarettes or immersion in hot water.
- Feelings of pain for no apparent reason.
- Fear of adult or care givers.
- Inappropriate attire in warm weather (possibly to conceal injuries).
- Extreme behavior - highly aggressive, extremely passive, withdrawn.
- Fear of physical contact.

Health and Safety Issues

Safety of pupils should always be paramount in the minds of teachers. Cooperating teachers need to impress upon student teachers the need to carefully monitor the well being of youngsters in their care.

Many pupils have medical conditions that require regular treatment with prescription drugs. Student teachers should be made aware of any regulations concerning the possession and distribution of medication. Most likely the dispensation of medication, including over the counter medications is done in the clinic by the school nurse.

Complaints of headaches and playground bumps and bruises also should be treated by the properly licensed medical staff of the school. The American Federation of Teachers (1997) maintains that teachers should not be providers of health care services for pupils. Only during extreme emergencies should the student teacher administer first aid.

Case Study No. 67: A Dangerous Laboratory Experiment

Ashley had designed a water study for her science class to complete. Pupils were to collect water samples from a nearby pond and do a microscopic observation and analysis of the organisms found in the sample. During the laboratory session, one of the boys in the class sliced his finger with a cover slip. Instead of observing pond water, the boy and several of his peers gathered drops of his blood to view under the microscope. Nearly twenty minutes elapsed before Ashley discovered that the laboratory exercise had taken a detour for some of her pupils. How should you and Ashley respond to the situation?

1. Ignore it since there seems to be no serious injury.
2. Tell those involved to place their slides in a plastic bag for proper disposal, wash their hands thoroughly and get back on task.
3. Send the pupil who suffered the cut to the school nurse.
4. Send all the students involved to the school nurse.
5. _____

Comment

Safety issues, especially in a high risk environment such as a science laboratory, must always be a priority. In recent years there has been heightened concern about the health risk of exposure to bloodborne pathogens such as the virus that causes hepatitis B and HIV/AIDS. In 1992, the Office of Occupational Safety and Health Administration (OSHA), under the United States Department of Labor, published a Bloodborne Pathogens Standards Summary that applies to schools. Among other things, this OSHA summary mandates that schools develop a plan to reduce students' exposure to bloodborne pathogens and to formulate strategies for dealing with exposure should it occur (Martin, et al, 2001). Student teachers should be made aware of such regulations.

Questions

1. What reasonable safety precautions would be appropriate in such a laboratory setting?
2. Are there any concerns about proper supervision in this situation?

Permission to Take Pupils Off Campus

Learning can be enhanced by taking students out of the classroom and exposing them to real world settings. Student teachers should be encouraged to use field trips and other community resources to augment their pupils' educational experiences. But as Howe and Jones (1998) attested, field trips do not just happen and require time in preparation and attention to detail. Gerlovich and Hartman (1998) compiled a 19 point checklist to which educators should adhere when taking students off campus. Among the details to be attended is acquiring permission from the parents or guardians of the pupils to be taken away from school. If educators make sufficient plans and follow the proper procedures, the quality of the learning experience should be enhanced and the possibility of litigation should be decreased if an accident occurs.

Rights of Students With Disabilities

In 1975, Congress passed Public Law 94-142 that gave all children with disabilities, regardless of handicap, the right to a free and appropriate public education. Over the years, PL 94-142 has been amended and is now called the Individuals with Disabilities Education Act (IDEA). According to Santrock (2001) the IDEA outlined several mandates for services that need to be provided for children and youth with disabilities. These services include evaluation and eligibility requirements, individualized educational program (IEP), and a least restrictive learning environment for each student. The IDEA also requires schools to work closely with parents of children with disabilities by informing the family of proposed actions that would impact the child, encouraging parental involvement and attendance at meetings regarding the child's placement or progress, and the right to appeal decisions made by the school regarding their child's program.

Many schools have responded to the "least restrictive environment" clause by educating the child with special learning needs in the regular classroom. The pupil's education is guided by specific accommodations that are recorded on the child's IEP. Full inclusion means that student teachers will be required to respond to a wider range of learning abilities and behaviors in the classroom. Preservice and practicing teachers need ongoing professional development to keep abreast of ever-changing special education law. As an example of such ongoing education, Culverhouse (1998) described a course offered by Teachers College, Columbia University to help teachers serve special needs students in the regular classroom as mandated by federal law. Citation for the description is in the Useful References section at the conclusion of this chapter.

Family Education Rights and Privacy Issues

Conn and Zirkel (2001) reminded teachers they need to be aware of provisions in the Family Educational Rights and Privacy Act (FERPA) that protects the confidentiality of students' educational records and gives the right of parents to inspect and challenge the content of such records. While one might assume that educational records mean numbers in a grade book or folders in a file cabinet, Conn and Zirkel revealed that some courts have determined any public disclosure of student performance can be considered a student record. This legal interpretation of FERPA may make classroom practices such as having students exchange papers for grading or having a student volunteer hand back graded papers in violation of federal legislation.

Case Study No. 68: Public Recognition

Mark has just completed teaching a sculpture unit in his fine arts class. Several of his students created excellent products and Mark decided to put them on exhibit in the display case outside your classroom. The students' names were prominently displayed beside their art work. Mark was excited about the exhibit. He thought his students would appreciate the recognition and the display would draw attention from parents who would attend the school open house later in the week. How do you respond to Mark's display of his students' creations?

1. Congratulate him on implementing a good idea and showing initiative.

2. Suggest to him that all students' work should be displayed, not just the best.
3. Ask Mark to get written permission from the students and their parents before displaying their art work.
4. Check with the school personnel to determine whether they have a policy regarding public display of student work.
5. _____

Comment

Mark's idea of wanting to reward excellence by placing quality works of art on display seems like an admirable notion. Yet, publicly displaying students' work if their names are identifiable may be in violation of FERPA regulations. One alternative is to secure written permission from students and their parents before displaying work or publishing names, even for positive accomplishments.

Questions

1. Why would students or their parents object to public recognition for positive accomplishments?
2. What are other ways to recognize excellent work of students?

Search and Seizure

The Fourth Amendment of the United States Constitution protects individuals from unreasonable search and seizure. With recent emphasis on making schools drug and violence free learning environments, school personnel frequently are caught between preserving individual freedom and providing a safe and secure setting for all. Burns, Roe, and Ross (1989), simply defined search as looking for illegal goods such as weapons or drugs and seizure as confiscation of such contraband. They recommend student teachers discuss the situation with their cooperating teacher if they suspect a student of being in possession of dangerous or banned items.

While desiring to preserve safe learning environments, the courts have upheld the rights of school officials to conduct searches of students if there is reason to believe they might be in possession of dangerous items or substances. Krumm and Thompson (1998) advised school personnel who are charged with maintaining a safe and orderly learning environment, not to trample on students' Fourth Amendment rights by conducting indiscriminate or mass searches without just cause. Student teachers should defer search and seizure duties to the principal or person designated to carry out such responsibilities if the need arises.

Due Process

Many states have enacted "due process laws" that are intended to protect students' rights in severe disciplinary cases which could result in suspension or expulsion from school. For example, Chapter 5 "Due Process and Pupil Discipline" of Indiana Code 20-8.1, section 3(c) states:

"No rule or standard shall be effective with respect to any student until a written copy thereof is made available or delivered to the student or his parent, or is otherwise given general publicity within any school to which it applies."

Most due process laws specify how rules, regulations, and policies are established, areas of prohibited student conduct, how disciplinary measures will be administered, courses of action to be taken to correct student behavior, and the student and parents' right to appeal. Student teachers should be familiar with the due process laws in the state and the school district to which they are assigned.

Negligence

Teachers are expected to protect their students from harm while they are in school. Burns, et al (1989) stated that courts determine one negligent if a child is injured and the person in charge failed to exercise reasonable care and act sensibly. Martin, et al. (2001), asserted that teachers can protect themselves from negligence charges by exercising reasonable and prudent judgment in performing their duties, avoiding exposing pupils to all foreseeable dangers and hazards, and ensuring proper supervision.

Case Study No. 69: Five Minutes Of Risk

Your student teacher, Eric, failed to make enough copies of a worksheet his pupils needed to complete a homework assignment. He left his students alone while he went to the teachers' room to make the copies he needed. When he returned a few minutes later, the floor in the back of the room was covered with broken glass. In Eric's absence, two of his students got out of their seats and were "showing off" for their classmates. During their stunt, one of the students fell through the glass front of a display case. Miraculously, the student was not badly injured but did require a trip to the emergency room to close a gash in his arm. Upon learning of the incident, the pupil's parents contacted the school's principal and informed him they were filing negligence charges against the student teacher and the school district. What should you do?

1. Make sure an accident report was filed concerning the incident.
2. Call your attorney.
3. Try to schedule a conference with the pupil's parents.
4. Contact the college supervisor.
5. _____

Comment

This case has all the earmarks for a successful negligence suit. The fact that the students were unsupervised and that the accident likely would not have occurred if Eric had been present puts him and the school in legal jeopardy. Leaving pupils unsupervised, even for a brief period of time, is a dangerous practice and puts educators in legal peril.

Questions

1. How do you instill in a young preservice teacher a sense that he is responsible for the welfare of pupils in his care?
2. What legal responsibilities do you have if an accident occurs while your pupils are being taught by a student teacher in your classroom?

Liability Insurance

Student teachers might want to consider purchasing liability insurance because the school district's insurance may not cover them. Liability insurance could possibly be obtained through a rider on one's existing homeowners' or renters' policies. But many traditional student teachers may not be at a station in life where they possess such insurance. Coverage also may be obtained through education professional organizations. Cooperating teachers should determine a student teacher's legal status before authorizing any activity which might result in liability.

Legal Rights Of Student Teachers
Do They Exist?

The laws of the majority of the states are silent as to the rights of student teachers. However, approximately one-fifth of them have enacted statutes directly granting student teachers the same legal protection as regular teachers. Most of these states use almost identical language in the applicable sections of their statutes. The Nebraska statute (1975) is a good representation of the conditions:

> A student teacher or intern under the supervision of a certificated teacher, principal, or other administrator shall have the protection of the laws accorded the certificated teacher, principal, or other administrator and shall, while acting as such student teacher or intern, comply with all rules and regulations of the local board of education and observe all duties assigned certificated teachers.

The key phrase in this and the other statutes, relevant to the discussion here is "protection of the law." While these statutes do not specifically explain the meaning of this phrase, student teachers enjoy the same degree of protection in covered areas as that granted to certificated teachers. The term "law" as used here would appear to include the Constitution of the United States, federal laws, state laws, state board of education and local school district policies and regulations.

Fourteen states permit student teachers to be compensated for personal injuries incurred during the course of their clinical experience under workmen's compensation laws or school district medical plans (Hall, 1989).

A small number of states, while not granting the general "protection of the law" to student teachers, provide them with the protection of workmen's compensation insurance to cover injuries arising out of and in the course of their assignment. Such protection has been given in these states by statutes and court decisions. Wyoming (1975), one of the states granting it by legislative enactment, has a law that is illustrative of those in other states and reads in part:

> "The student of teaching, during his field experience, is deemed an employee of the school district . . . for the purpose of workmen's compensation . . . insurance as provided for other district employees."

Courts in at least two other states have granted student teachers the right of workmen's compensation. In a California case a student teacher was injured while supervising students on the playground. The Industrial Accident Commission held and the state supreme court concurred that the student teacher was an employee of the school district and as such was legally entitled to compensation from the school district in which he was student teaching if he were injured while so engaged.

Mulhern (1979-80) reported on a case in Michigan in which a physical education student teacher, in the absence of the cooperating teacher, was tossed in the swimming pool by his students. During this time he was struck in one eye by his whistle, causing loss of sight in the eye. The student teacher sued the school district under the Workmen's Compensation Act. The Compensation Board granted him benefits and the supreme court of that state upheld the Compensation Board.

Provisions for Dismissal

While institutions have discretion in dismissing student teachers, courts have recognized that student teachers have the right to be treated fairly and to not be dismissed without reasonable cause (Hall, 1989). In a West Virginia case (1971) a student was denied the right to teach because of his reputation as a militant on and off campus and the publicity he had received associating him with violent incidents at his university. The teacher education center had attempted to place him in several school districts and all of them refused to accept him. The student sued the West Virginia Board of Regents to recover damages for his having been deprived of the right to teach. A federal district court dismissed the suit in a landmark decision that reaffirmed school officials' right to reject a student teaching candidate so long as customary procedures and uniform guidelines were followed in a reasonable and nondiscriminatory manner.

A federal district court, in a North Carolina case (1971), also dismissed the suit of a student who had been denied application for a student teaching assignment by university officials who had serious questions about his character in terms of suitability for teaching. He had admitted to smoking marijuana and had been arrested for drug possession. The court held that the university officials did not act in bad faith and were not arbitrary in their discretion. It further held that university officials are entitled to wide discretion in the regulations of the training of their students.

In another North Carolina case (1973), a federal district court held that the dismissal of a student teacher from his assignment without warning violated the First Amendment of the United States Constitution, particularly freedom of speech, and due process of law under the Fourteenth Amendment. The student teacher had been dismissed because he made statements that approved the Darwinian theory of evolution, indicated his personal agnosticism, and questioned the literal interpretation of the Bible. The court in the decision set forth the following principles:

- A student teacher under the supervision of a certified teacher or principal shall have the protection of the law accorded the certified teacher.
- Unpaid student teachers have the same right to protection as a certified teacher and should not be relieved of his teaching duties for unconstitutional reasons.
- A hearing held with only 20 minutes notice before a hostile ad hoc committee without eyewitness testimony or factual inquiry denies due process and equal protection.
- Although academic freedom is not one of the numerated rights of the First Amendment, the Supreme Court has on numerous occasions held that the right to teach, to inquire, to evaluate, and to study is fundamental to a democratic society.
- The university and the school authority had duly agreed that he (the plaintiff) would have a term of practice (sic) teaching at the school in question. He had the reasonable expectations that this opportunity for practice teaching would continue until the end of the fall term as required by his university curriculum.

In a Missouri case (1979), the Dean of a School of Education administratively dropped a student teacher from his assignment after receiving criticisms from the student's cooperating teacher and university supervisor. The student teacher was dismissed for deviating from lesson plans, having difficulty accepting criticism, failing to detect and correct grammatical errors, over identifying with students, and exhibiting other inappropriate behaviors. A meeting was arranged to include the student teacher, university supervisor, cooperating teacher, and assistant principal to discuss and try to resolve the problems. During the meeting, the student teacher was uncooperative and did not respond to the questions being raised.

The student teacher was ordered out of the school by the assistant principal. The university supervisor wrote a letter to the Associate Dean of Education expressing his concern about his "strange behavior" and his possible "need of psychological help." After reviewing the deficiencies outlined in the letter, the Associate Dean requested that the student teacher withdraw voluntarily from student teaching.

Twelve days later, the student teacher, who had not withdrawn, received a letter advising him that he had been dropped administratively from the course. The student sued, alleging that his due process rights were being violated, decisions were arbitrary and the note written about him would impose a stigma to his reputation.

The court ruled against the student teacher, stating that his due process rights were not violated. There is no requirement for a hearing when a student is being dismissed for academic deficiencies.

The court also concluded that the decision made by the dean to drop the student from the course was made in good faith, not arbitrarily.

The case should alert supervisory and administrative personnel to the need to understand and practice due process. As a follow-up to this case, personnel at the University of Missouri at St. Louis identified practices necessary to ensure due process. The following list summarizes the essential elements:

- Clinical education students must be provided a specific and complete statement of requirements and expectations.
- The student must be provided a specific description of the competencies by which he or she will be evaluated, detailing the processes to be employed.
- Actual supervisor practice at both the school and college level must be consistent with published policy available to the student in advance.
- Orientation of students should provide, in writing, supervisor and institutional requirements.
- Supervisory observations should be frequent, comprehensive, recorded, and followed up.
- Conferences should be held after observations and include a detailed written summary, with copies retained by student and supervisor.
- Adequate conferring time must be provided throughout the program.
- Evaluation must be within the context of improvement of stated competencies.
- Grades awarded must relate directly to the stated criteria for those grades.
- Supervisors should maintain continuing, factual, objective, written records on each clinical student they supervise, and the students should always receive a copy.
- Students should be informed in advance of the steps that will ensure due process for them.
- It should be made clear that clinical experiences are courses within the curricular framework of the university and, as such, removal from student teaching does not require a full hearing if it is for academic reasons.
- Every effort should be made to let students participate in decisions made about them and to know the data upon which those decisions were made.
- Students may continue in the clinical experience as long as they complete established requirements and demonstrate at least the stated minimum levels of competence.

- Students may be removed from the clinical experience if it is determined that the pupils assigned to the setting are suffering from their presence.

Although most of these procedures apply to university supervisors, a joint approach is necessary with the cooperating teacher to insure that due process is met. The possibility of problems such as the ones described in this section are remote, but it is a good idea to be aware of the conditions that insure due process exists.

In conclusion, student teachers in some states enjoy by statute the same legal rights as certificated teachers. In all states they enjoy the same civil and constitutional guarantees as all teachers and other citizens. The student teaching situation is unique in that it is primarily a curriculum responsibility and as such is subject to different interpretations.

Case Study No. 70: Error In Judgment

Two weeks before the scheduled completion of student teaching, the principal calls you to the office and informs you that the superintendent has instructed him to dismiss your student teacher from school. It seems she and a teacher consumed drugs with some students who were participating in a school sponsored activity in another town. Although she was not at the event in an official capacity and the students were not in her classes, the superintendent felt this indiscretion should not be ignored. Since your student teacher's pupils were not involved and since her performance was satisfactory, what kind of response do you make?

1. Implement the superintendent's decision.
2. Appeal for consideration on the basis of her good performance in class.
3. Check with the university supervisor to determine the legal implications.
4. Talk with the student teacher and secure her point of view before you take any action.
5. _____

Comment

It has been established that student teachers can be withdrawn from student teaching for academic reasons, which are rather loosely defined. The success of any litigation in court may depend upon the documentation of the event by either the plaintiff or defendant and whether due process was followed. Obviously the student teacher committed an error of judgment, but the question is whether she should be suspended for that indiscretion when the act was not on school premises and in the presence of students for whom she was not responsible. However, the fact that she was in possession of a controlled substance with minors cannot be ignored.

Questions

1. What would be the appropriate due process procedures for the school system?
2. How much should an illegal or immoral act committed away from the school influence the decision of whether to retain or dismiss a student teacher?

Substitute Teaching
Can A Student Teacher Legally Serve?

The question of whether a student teacher can serve as a substitute teacher has largely gone unanswered by the various states. Generally states will not permit student teachers to serve as substitute teachers because they are not licensed. However, at least one state has indicated that "student teachers may serve as substitute teachers and be compensated after they have been recommended for substitute certification by the chief school officer of the district to which they are assigned" (Delaware, 1970).

Most judiciary and attorney general opinions have inferred that student teachers have no authority to substitute teach (Hall, 1989). The basic question seems to be whether student teachers can teach without supervision. The critical definition here is to determine what constitutes supervision. Generally, student teachers are not legally allowed to serve as substitute teachers because they are not licensed and still in a training program and because substitute teaching implies the absence of a teacher and, hence, have no supervision.

The diversity of interpretations among the states indicates that the role of a student teacher as a substitute is unclear. It may vary within states depending upon university policies and contracts between teachers and individual school districts. The best course of action is to seek clarification before any consideration is given to the employment of a student teacher as a substitute.

Case Study No. 71: On Strike!

Mr. Gray's school district and the local teachers' association have been entangled in bitter contract discussions. Negotiations were at an impasse and the teachers voted to go on a "work stoppage." Early the morning that the strike was scheduled to begin, Mr. Gray received a phone call from Melissa, his student teacher. She has just received a call from the school principal requesting her to come to school and serve as Mr. Gray's temporary replacement until the strike ended. The principal told her that her substituting would be beneficial to the pupils since they were used to her being in the classroom and she already knew the classroom procedures. The principal also pointed out that teacher strikes were illegal in the state. Melissa was calling Mr. Gray for advice as to how she should respond to the principal's request. What should he tell his student teacher?

1. Tell her to remain out of school until the dispute is settled.
2. Advise her to call her college supervisor.
3. Suggest she use her own judgment.
4. _____

Comment

Student teachers occupy a unique niche in a school. They often develop a fierce allegiance to their cooperating teacher. At the same time, they recognize the importance of making a good impression with the school's administration. The principal's request puts the student teacher in a very awkward position as Melissa has obligations to factions on both sides of the controversy. Having the student teacher call the college supervisor for assistance is good advice. Most teacher education institutions do not want their students involved in labor disputes and strikes. If such an event occurred early in the student teacher's experience another site likely would be sought which does not have such conflicts.

Questions

1. What ramifications might there be for a student teacher placed in such a dilemma?
2. What is your reaction to the principal's request in this case?

Ethics In Teacher Education
Doing Things Right or Doing the Right Thing?

There is often a difference between "doing things right" and "doing the right thing." In examining the two phrases above, the difference between legal and ethical behavior becomes apparent. While teachers need to operate within the law at all times (doing things right), there are many times when ethical considerations (doing the right thing) need to guide the behavior of educators.

Thorndike and Barnhart (1974) defined ethics as "the study of the standards of right and wrong; the part of philosophy dealing with moral conduct, duty, and judgment." While not every individual will come to the same conclusion about what is the ethical course of action when faced with a difficult decision, Freeman (2000) stated that professional organizations have established codes of ethics that its members have agreed will be used to guide their practice. At a time when educators are striving to have teaching recognized by society as a full fledged profession, Kipnis (1986) asserted that adherence to a strict code of ethical behavior is a distinguishing characteristic of a true profession. So those who aspire to raise the status of education should be advocates of teachers following a prescribed ethical behavior.

In 1975, the National Education Association (NEA) composed a general code of ethics. The *Code of Ethics of the Education Profession* contains a preamble which admonishes educators to honor the dignity of students, provide access to learning opportunities for all students, and to work respectfully with all members of the learning community. Principle I outlines the educators' *Commitment to the Student* while Principle II delineates the teachers' *Commitment to the Profession*. A copy of the code should be available from the local NEA representative.

Freeman (2000) was adamant that aspiring teachers should be well versed about educational ethics and ethics should be the centerpiece of preservice teacher education. Yet, Goodlad (1990) found that the moral and ethical aspects of teaching were largely ignored in the curricula of most teacher education institutions. Student teachers likely will come across numerous situations that will require them to make ethical judgments and difficult decisions for which they may feel ill equipped. Cooperating teachers can play an important function by helping student teachers grapple with the gray areas of ethics as they arise in their clinical experience. And an excellent way for the cooperating teacher to help student teachers form ethical dispositions is to model exemplary behavior in his interactions with pupils, parents, and colleagues.

Case Study No. 72: An Unethical Response

Your student teacher was in the middle of a presentation when he observed a note being passed among students in the back of the room. He continued his monologue but moved to the area of the room where the note was being circulated. He confiscated the note before it arrived at its destination, unfolded it, and read its contents aloud to the class. The note contained several expressions of affection directed toward another student in the class. As he continued to read the note, both the author and the intended recipient were thoroughly embarrassed. When you asked him about the episode, he told you that he believed his actions were justifiable because students should not pass notes if they did not want the contents to be made public. How do you respond to the situation?

1. Review the NEA Code of Ethics and point out his possible violation.
2. Ask him to apologize to the students involved.
3. Let him deal with any repercussions that arise from the incident.
4. _____

Comment

Many children and adolescents report the worst thing that could ever happen to them is to be embarrassed in front of their peers. It is not professional conduct for teachers to intentionally place pupils in such an uncomfortable position. One of the responsibilities of cooperating teachers is see that incidents such as this do not occur.

Questions

1. What does the NEA Code of Ethics say that is pertinent to this case?
2. What impact does the teacher's use of humiliation as a classroom management technique have upon the learning environment?

Case No. 73: Fishing Buddies

You and your student teacher, Jeff, have gotten along very well all term. One of the reasons for your compatibility is that you have many things in common, your joint love for the outdoors among them. Jeff works on weekends as a fishing guide for a local outfitter. His boss asked him to take their new drift boat for a "shake down" run before they used the craft with paying customers. Jeff invited you to come along for the maiden voyage that was to be taken on a prime stretch of a river that you have always wanted to fish. How do you respond to Jeff's invitation?

1. Accept Jeff's invitation.
2. Accept the offer but insist on paying the usual guide fee.
3. Decline the invitation.

4. Make an excuse for not being able to go.
5. _____

Comment

It is wonderful when student teachers and cooperating teachers are compatible. Yet it is important to maintain a professional relationship that does not become encumbered with too much fraternization. It can be problematic if one's professional judgment becomes clouded by too much familiarity. But it would seem possible that the cooperating teacher could accompany Jeff without jeopardizing a professional relationship since this is a mutual interest and an occasion which will not be a continuing process.

Questions

1. What does the NEA Code of Ethics say that is pertinent to this case?
2. Where should the line between one's personal and professional relationships with student teachers be drawn?

Case Study No. 74: Personal Passions

Amanda has a passion for animals and is an avid animal rights advocate. She is completing her student teaching assignment under your supervision and has been very enthusiastic about everything she has taught to date. As a culminating activity for a unit on persuasive writing, Amanda planned to require all of her students to write to their state legislators asking them to support pending legislation to prohibit the use of leg-hold steel traps. You are not comfortable with Amanda's judgment in making the assignment. How do you get her to rethink her assignment?

1. Simply tell her that such an assignment is not appropriate.
2. Ask her if there are other sides of the issue to be considered.
3. Ask her how she would feel if she were required to support a cause in which she had no interest.
4. _____

Comment

This case underscores again the importance of having student teachers' plans reviewed by the cooperating teacher before they are taught. Getting students actively involved in real issues and putting their academic skills to use is a very effective instructional strategy, but imposing one's personal convictions upon students is inappropriate.

Questions

1. What does the NEA Code of Ethics say that is pertinent to this case?
2. How can student teachers be encouraged to share their passions with students without being accused of indoctrination?

On Monday afternoon, Miss Bennett and Brian met with Mr. Williams, the principal, to discuss the legal ramifications of student teaching that might relate to them. Mr. Williams, after apologizing for not dealing with this question earlier, proceeded to describe the authority and responsibility of Brian as a student teacher and Miss Bennett as a cooperating teacher.

It is now Friday afternoon. The last students have left the classroom and Miss Bennett and Brian are unwinding from the long week.

Brian says, "Even though I am tired, I certainly feel more relaxed than I did when the week began. That story I heard about a student teacher being sued really had me upset."

Miss Bennett replied, "I must admit that I was somewhat apprehensive after hearing of that incident. However, I feel more reassured now that we have talked with Mr. Williams."

Remember:

- **Existing laws and regulations regarding supervised student teaching vary from state to state.**
- **The cooperating teacher should be familiar with any applicable laws and regulations concerning student teaching in his state and school district.**
- **The student teacher should be apprised of all legal guidelines which affect her.**
- **The cooperating teacher, not the student teacher, is charged with the care of pupils and their well-being.**
- **It is incumbent upon the cooperating teacher to be fully aware of the student teacher's planned activities.**
- **The student teacher, like any other teacher, is responsible for her negligent acts and may be held liable for them.**
- **The student teacher enjoys the same civil and constitutional guarantees as teachers.**
- **Using student teachers as substitute teachers is generally not legally authorized and is not recommended as a sound educational practice.**

- The student teacher and cooperating teacher should be knowledgeable of the "due process' procedures of the university and the cooperating school.
- There is a difference between "doing things right" and "doing the right thing".
- Modeling moral and ethical behavior for your student teacher may be the best way to help her develop exemplary professional behavior.

Useful References

American Federation of Teachers (1997). *The Medically Fragile Child in the School Setting*. ERIC ED 420128.

Anspaugh, David J. and Gene Ezella. (2001). *Teaching Today's Health*. Needham Heights, MA. Allyn and Bacon.

Balch, Pamela M., and Patrick E. Balch. 1987. Legal Issues Related to Student Teaching and Supervision. Chapter 13 in *The Cooperating Teacher: A Practical Approach for the Supervision of Student Teachers*. Lanham, MD. The University Press of America.

Burns, Paul C., Betty D. Roe, and Elinor P. Ross, (1989). *Student Teaching and Field Experience Handbook*. Columbus, OH. Merrill Publishing Co.

Childhelp USA. 2000. Child Abuse. www.childhelppusa.org/abuse.htm.

Conn, Kathleen, and Perry A. Zirkel. 2001. Teachers, Schools and the Law: Ignorance is Not Bliss. *Association of Teacher Educators Newsletter*. 34 (March): 4-7.

Culverhouse, Gay. 1998. Inclusion: Professional Development of General Education Teachers and the Impact on Special Education. ERIC ED 426976.

Del Prete, Tony. 1996. Hands Off? The Touchy Subject of Physical Contact with Students. *Our Children* 22(Nov-Dec): 34-35.

DiGiulio, Robert C. 2000. *Positive Classroom Management*. Thousand Oaks, CA. Sage Publications Ltd.

Drowatsk, John N. 1980. The Cooperating Teacher and Liability During Student Teacher Supervision. *Journal of Physical Education and Recreation* 51 (February): 79-80.

Feldman, Robert S. 1999. *Child Development: A Topical Approach*. Upper Saddle River, NJ. Prentice Hall.

Freeman, Nancy K. 2000. Professional Ethics: A Cornerstone of Teachers' Preservice Curriculum. *Action in Teacher Education*, 22 (Fall) 12-18.

Gerlovich, Jack A., and K. Hartman. 1998. *The Total Science Safety System: Elementary Edition,* Computer Software. Waukee, IA. JaKel, Inc.

Goodlad, John I. 1990. *Teachers for Our Schools.* San Francisco, CA. Jossey-Bass.

Greene, Jim 1998. How Teachers Can Avoid Being Sued: Law and American Education. ERIC ED 437381.

Griffin, L. E. 1980. Who Is Accountable for the Student Teacher: The Public Schools or the Universities? *Journal of Physical Education and Recreation* 51 (April): 18.

Gullatt, David, and John Tollett. 1995. Educational Law: A Relevant Course for All Teacher Education Programs. Paper presented at the Annual Spring Conference of the Louisiana Council of Professors of Educational Administration, Natchitoches, LA. March 29-30. ERIC ED 389695

Guyton, Edith, and John D. McIntyre. 1990. Student Teaching and School Experiences. Chapter 29 in Houston (Ed) *Handbook of Research on Teacher Education.* New York. Macmillan Publishing Company.

Haberman, M., and P. Harris. 1982. State Requirements for Cooperating Teachers. *Journal of Teacher Education* 33 (April-May): 45-47.

Hall, Gayle. 1989. Legal Relationship of Student Teachers to Public Institutions of Higher Education and Public Schools. ERIC ED 344078.

Hazard, W. R. 1976. Student Teaching and the Law.ERIC SP 009 739.

Henderson, Martha V., David E. Giatt, Dawn T. Hardin, Catherine Jannik, and John R. Tollett. 1999. *Preventive Law Curriculum Guide.* ERIC ED 437366.

Howe, Ann C., and Linda Jones. 1998. *Engaging Children in Science.* Upper Saddle River, NJ. Prentice-Hall. Inc.

Johnson J., and J. Yates. 1982. A National Survey of Student Teaching Programs. ERIC ED 232-963.

Kipnis, Kenneth. (1986). *Legal Ethics.* Prentice-Hall Series in Occupational Ethics. Englewood Cliffs, NJ. Prentice Hall.

Knickerbocker, Joan L., and Geraldine H. Roberts. 1983. Student Teaching Supervision: Legal Implications for Cooperating Teachers in Illinois. *Illinois School Research and Development* 19 (Winter): 22-27.

Kohn, Alfie. 1996. *Beyond Discipline: From Compliance to Community.* Alexandria, VA. The Association for Supervision and Curriculum Development.

Krantz, Murray. 1994. *Child Development: Risk or Opportunity.* Belmont, CA. Wadsworth Publishing Company.

Krumm, Bernita L., and John R. Thompson. 1998. *Student Search and Seizure: 1998 Update.* Paper presented at the Annual Meeting of the Educational Law Association, November 19-21, Charleston, SC., ERIC ED 427432.

Long, Bruce E. 1984. Ensuring Due Process in Clinical Education Experiences. *The Teacher Educator* 19 (Spring): 29-33.

Martin, Ralph, Colleen Sexton, and Jack Gerlovich. 2001. *Teaching Science for All Children.* Needham Heights, MA. Allyn and Bacon, Inc.

Monts, Dana R. 1998. Student Teachers and Legal Issues. Paper presented at the Annual Meeting of the Mid-South Educational Research Association, New Orleans, LA. November 3-6. ERIC ED 428039.

Morris, John E., and K. Fred Curtis. 1983. Legal Issues Relating to Field-Based Experiences in Teacher Education. *Journal of Teacher Education* 34 (March-April): 2-6.

Mulhern, John D. 1979-80. Student Teaching and the Betts Decision. *Viewpoints* 2 (Fall/Winter): 6-7.

Robbins, M. W. 1990. Sparing the Child: How to Intervene When You Expect Abuse. *New York Magazine* 10 (December): 42-53.

Santrock, John W. 2001. *Adolescents.* Chapter 7. New York, NY. McGraw-Hill Companies, Inc.

Swalls, Fred. 1976. *The Law on Student Teaching.* Danville, IL. Interstate Printers and Publishers, Inc.

Thorndike, E. L., and Clarence L. Barnhart. (1974). *Thorndike Barnhart Intermediate Dictionary.* Glenview, IL. Scott, Foresman and Company.

Wood, Craig. 1976. The Current Legal Status of Student Teaching in the United States. ERIC ED 127 283.

11

Problems Of Student Teachers

Miss Bennett and two colleagues attended a conference for cooperating teachers hosted by the university Brian attended. She welcomed this experience because it would be her first opportunity as a supervisor to communicate and share ideas with teachers from other schools.

The participants were to spend one session sharing problems that they were encountering in working with their student teachers. Miss Bennett assumed this would be a dull session because she had experienced no real difficulties with Brian. How wrong she was! As soon as the chairperson opened the meeting for discussion, concerns and requests for assistance came from every section of the room. One teacher commented that her student teacher was lazy, and another complained that his student teacher was so busy with work and campus activities that he missed several days and was usually unprepared when he was in school. Miss Bennett shifted in her seat as she heard another teacher describe her student teacher's apathy, and she was really surprised to hear that two supervisors had been faced with the problem of student teachers who did not have the minimum skills necessary to work with pupils.

"You are all lucky," commented one teacher who had remained silent up to this point. "One day my student teacher told a class how easy it was to secure drugs." This was followed by a number of teachers who shared a variety of problems. The discussion time elapsed before all of the problems could be identified or solved. Miss Bennett left the room wondering what she would do if she were faced with a problem student teacher . . .

Student Teacher Problems
Exceptions or Routine?

Student teaching is not free from problems. This chapter is written for the small number of cooperating teachers who will find themselves coping with student teachers who are experiencing difficulty to the extent that it interrupts classroom learning, requires considerable effort to solve, or possibly leads to a decision of whether a student teacher would be recommended for certification. A secondary purpose is to identify those problems that are most predominant so that cooperating teachers can help student teachers make adjustments to improve their performance.

Researchers have devoted considerable attention to problems of student teachers. According to Harwood and others (2000), the most frequent reason for student teachers to unsuccessfully complete their clinical experience or withdraw from student teaching was the revelation that they lacked the aptitude for the profession. This may be caused by such things as a lack of knowledge about a teacher's life, unrealistic expectations of student performance, or failure to comprehend the amount of time and effort consumed by activities beyond the school day.

In this chapter, the authors address problems that seem to be most prevalent and possibly contribute to the lack of aptitude for teaching. Individual problems are described and discussed in terms of how student teachers may be assisted by their supervisors. No effort is made to prioritize the problems in terms of difficulty.

Economic Concerns

Student teaching can be more expensive for students than any other phase of their college program. Costs of transportation and housing may cause additional expenditure when a student teacher has to commute or move to a community away from campus. Clothes and their care may be more expensive. Even incidental expenses, like the price of lunch, may be regarded as significant by student teachers. Teacher examinations mandated in many states are expensive and may be required during student teaching. The results of economic problems may be shown through worry, fatigue, appearance, or avoidance of situations which require spending money.

Cooperating teachers should make every effort to be understanding and should refrain from making requests that might cause financial complications for the student teacher. They may be in a position to offer money-saving ideas if the communication about the matter is open and frank.

On the other hand, a cooperating teacher should not allow a student teacher's preoccupation with financial concerns to deter his performance while teaching. If financial matters seem to become excuses for not meeting obligations, then a conversation with the university supervisor may be necessary. In some cases, student teacher priorities may have to be adjusted.

Family Problems

Conflicts in this area may include a wide range of possibilities. Some students may be adjusting to being away from home while others may be experiencing marital complications. Single parents may have child care and custody issues that might limit their effectiveness. Problems of this nature may affect the classroom behavior of a student teacher by lack of preparation, irritation or even depression. This type of problem may be extended beyond family and include relationships with peers or significant others.

This is an area where it is often difficult for the cooperating teacher to render assistance. However, when it is apparent that these problems are affecting the student teacher's performance, they must be addressed. It is important that the cooperating teacher establish empathy with the student teacher and discuss the problem or refer him to someone who can help.

Case Study 75: Problems At Home

Connie, a non-traditional student teacher, has been working in your classroom for about a month. She has been reasonably effective in her work with the pupils, but she was frequently distracted by unpleasant family issues. She finally confides in you and shares that she is going through a nasty divorce, embroiled in custody issues, and is dealing with a suicidal teenager who is in danger of being expelled from school. Connie is requesting a two weeks' leave of absence to get her family life in order. How do you respond to her request?

1. Contact the university supervisor.
2. Permit her to stay and do the best she can.
3. Support her request.
4. _____

Comment

Connie is definitely in a difficult situation. Telling her that she will just have to cope with the situation would be inappropriate. But the thought that the severe personal crisis would be "fixed" in a couple of weeks is unrealistic. Withdrawing from student teaching and concentrating on getting her family life in order would seem to be the top priority in this case.

Questions

1. How does a cooperating teacher remain supportive of a student teacher without becoming too emotionally involved in personal issues?
2. What other issues might need to be considered in this case?

Feelings of Inadequacy and Insecurity

This pattern of difficulties focuses on self-concept and the ability to readily adjust to situations that may be potentially threatening. Benson, Larson and Nierenberg (1994) found that "high maintenance" student teachers (student teachers experiencing problems that require considerable attention from superiors) were likely to possess the following personality traits:

- Lack of self-confidence.
- Non-assertive behaviors.
- Lack of initiative.
- Apathy.
- Low display of energy.
- Lack of sense of humor.
- Unwilling to take risks.
- Unrealistic perceptions of self-efficacy.
- Lack of enthusiasm and motivation.
- Negative attitude.
- Inability to manage mood swings.
- Immaturity.
- Inflexibility.
- Self-centeredness.
- Frequent procrastination.

A student teacher who has feelings of inadequacy may become frustrated, withdraw, become apathetic, be moody, or even show signs of depression. These feelings may be prevented through planned activities which allow a student teacher to experience success and to gain confidence. The use of positive reinforcement by the cooperating teacher may help to establish desirable behaviors and eradicate the more inappropriate ones.

Case Study No. 76: Three Students With Headaches

You have asked Todd to teach a complete unit. His pupils become lost and bored after four days. He lectures to the class in a monotone voice that is inaudible in the back half of the room. He practically reads his entire lecture to the students and rarely makes eye contact with his charges. While you are in the office making a telephone call, three students from your class come to the office complaining of headaches. They obviously were trying to escape Todd's uninspiring class. What do you do?

1. Nothing. Let Todd deal with the fallout from his poor presentation.
2. Make specific suggestions about how he can improve his delivery.
3. Encourage Todd to try more interactive and engaging teaching strategies.
4. _____

Comment

Todd exhibits classic symptoms of insecurity. Encouraging him to take some risks by trying a variety of instructional strategies would likely improve the motivation of his pupils. If their interest and enthusiasm increases, Todd's level of security should improve as well.

Questions

1. What could teachers do to help student teachers to be more secure in their roles?
2. What other possible explanations can their be for Todd's lack luster performance.

Immaturity

The immature person fails to display the behavior that is expected from a student teacher. In most cases immaturity is apparent when the person resorts to the behavior which is acceptable to a younger group, most likely that of college associates, in order to gain acceptance. The person may possess all needed attributes for teaching except the ability to relate to pupils and teachers in an adult manner.

Symptoms of immaturity are usually easily recognizable. The following are some of the more obvious ones:

- Tends to dominate conversation.
- Poses answers to any complex problem that is discussed.
- Frequent informal contacts with students.

- Appearance that identifies with college students or public school pupils.
- Vocabulary that is punctuated with popular phrases and clichés.
- Has difficulty accepting responsibility.
- Social behavior inconsistent with adult norms.

The immature student can change. A single activity or encounter can bring about the realization that a change is needed. A frank talk may achieve significant results. There are several other procedures that can be successful in helping the student to abandon immature behavior. Consider the following:

- Put the student teacher in situations where he can be accepted as an adult by both pupils and faculty.
- Encourage association with mature teachers.
- Stay close to the student teacher in situations where immature actions are likely to surface.
- Insist that the student teacher's work be of professional quality.
- Monitor the student teacher's association with pupils.
- Reinforce mature behaviors if they occur.

Case Study No. 77: Breach Of Confidentiality

Your student teacher mentioned to you that a pupil in another class has demonstrated weird behavior that he attributes to the effects resulting from listening to rock music. His comment was overheard by a student standing close by. Word spreads throughout the school and eventually to the parents that the student teacher thinks that the boy is weird. Some of the students start teasing him and he resents it. The parents have come to the school and complain about the student teacher's "inappropriate" comments. They want some action taken. The principal talks with you first. What kind of response would you make?

1. Agree to talk with the student teacher.
2. Suggest that the principal and you talk with the student teacher.
3. Agree to investigate the matter and then report back.
4. Confront the student teacher and tell him that he should make amends.
5. Talk with the parents and attempt to allay their concerns.
6. _____

Comment

Whether or not the accusation is true, the student teacher has made an allegation in an improper way. Was it caused by his immaturity or by an attempt to compensate for his own sense of insecurity? First the parents have to be considered and then a plan of action must be devised to see that the student teacher does not make such accusations again.

Questions

1. How can you communicate to the student teacher that such comments are unethical?
2. What signs could a supervisor look for which would cause her to anticipate that the student would make an unfortunate remark?

Problems Relating to School Adjustment

The transition from a university to a public school setting may not be as smooth as one would assume in spite of an increasing number of field experiences prior to student teaching. A student teacher must assume a new role of teacher without having the credentials or experience. Tension can result from the new environment resulting in some adjustment problems. These problems may peak quickly, and a cooperating teacher should be alert for symptoms. Many can be corrected early in the experience.

Stress

Stress is likely to be experienced by student teachers and may originate from a number of sources. Abebe and Shaughnessy (1997) identified the following factors which student teachers reported as producing stress:
- Unmotivated students.
- Working with peers.
- Supervisor's visits.
- Discipline issues.
- Preparing for the unexpected.
- Relationships with parents.
- Time management.
- Relationships with students.
- Selection of appropriate teaching material.

Whitfield (1995) found that stress was a major area of concern for student teachers and observed that stress was manifested in following ways:

- Family problems.
- Crying almost every night.
- Poor health.
- Exhaustion.
- Panic.
- Sleep difficulty.
- Doubt about choosing the right profession.

These situations may confront cooperating teachers and university supervisors when they occur. Not all symptoms of stress are highly visible, but the cooperating teacher should be alert to the possibility when he notices some of the above behaviors.

Morris and Morris (1980) make a number of suggestions for cooperating teachers in helping student teachers cope with stress:

- Establish and maintain open communication among the student teacher, cooperating teacher, and university supervisor.
- Encourage student teachers to schedule some time each day for themselves.
- Provide opportunities for student teachers to share their experiences.
- Encourage student teachers to get sufficient amounts of exercise, rest, and sleep.
- Encourage or even require that student teachers prepare unit and lesson plans well in advance.
- Encourage student teachers to engage in regular, in-depth self-evaluation.
- Provide a comprehensive orientation program to student teaching.

More recently, Murray-Harvey and others (2000) found that student teachers reported that a positive relationship with their cooperating teachers was the most significant factor that helped them deal with stress during their clinical experience.

Worry Over Possible Failure

The accountability movement has its impact on the concerns of student teachers. With the expanding number of tests that must be passed and criteria that must be met, student teachers may be anxious because it poses another roadblock to certification. Student teaching is the final test in many programs and a student teacher may initially feel unable to succeed. If so, the completion of a degree may be in jeopardy. A student teacher may either feel inadequate or have no valid frame of reference to evaluate performance. These feelings may lead to concerns about passing student teaching.

One of the best methods of coping with the problem is to make certain that some sort of success is experienced as soon as possible. If the student teacher quickly perceives that there is a good chance of success, many apprehensions should disappear.

Adjusting to the School

Student teachers may experience school adjustment problems. Potential causes of concern include:

- Being assigned to a school that is in a different cultural environment than the one the student teacher knows.
- Lack of acquaintance with faculty.
- Lack of knowledge of school procedures.
- Lack of knowledge about pupils.

The result may be that they feel as if they do not belong. If this is the case, they may show symptoms of confusion or stress.

Cooperating teachers need to be sensitive to any feelings of not belonging or of being confused about prevailing practices. If these feelings continue to exist, review the suggestions in Chapter Two regarding adjustment to the school.

Problems of Acceptable Appearance

The difference between the accepted patterns of dress in the public schools and the prevailing pattern on campus may create a breach that is difficult to reconcile. A student teacher may have some difficulty accepting the fact that appearance is a factor in teacher-student relationships. When this occurs, problems are likely to focus on casual dress and the difficulty that it may present in being accepted by faculty, students, and administration. It may not be easy for a student teacher to understand that it is sometimes necessary to dress more formally than teachers in order to gain the same degree of acceptance from students or to be distinguished between students and faculty.

Sometimes there is temptation to impose personal standards upon a student teacher without giving due consideration to individual preference. The criteria for judgment should be whether the student teacher's appearance affects professional relationships with pupils. If appearance must be discussed, the following guidelines may be helpful in approaching the problem:

- The student teacher will usually prefer to have the cooperating teacher discuss the subject with him.
- An early explanation of school dress policy, if one exists, can avoid an inadvertent violation of the rules.
- Reasons for standards of appearance should be explained.
- Criticism of styles as such should be avoided if possible.

Physical appearance and dress in the classroom are somewhat analogous to the wearing of a uniform in that it is a symbol indicating that the person who wears it has certain skills, responsibilities, and authority. If a student teacher becomes aware that appearance can help to achieve acceptance as a professional person, the more informal or unacceptable patterns of appearance may be voluntarily abandoned.

Case Study No. 78: Distracting Dress

Your school does not have a dress code for faculty members. Some teachers wear rather formal attire but most are more casual, although they dress in good taste. Unfortunately your new student teacher's choice of clothes borders on the outrageous. Her attire is even drawing comments from those who dress casually. It has come to the point that the students notice it and are making comments. The teachers have implied that her appearance is "different." What can you do to see that her dress is more appropriate?

1. Talk with her about her appearance and point out that it may be a barrier in her establishing good relationships with the students.
2. Quote some of the comments that you are hearing.
3. Look for reasons other than appearance that might be causing pupil distraction.
4. Talk with the university supervisor about the matter.
5. _____

Comment

The choice of clothes is a personal matter and dress codes for teachers have virtually disappeared. However, an individual, particularly a student teacher, should be aware that appearance can affect how persons respond to her. A student teacher should be aware that her appearance can either enhance or lower the perceptions that others have.

Questions

1. What guidelines should be used to determine acceptable appearance?
2. Should a cooperating teacher ever mention the choice of clothes to a student teacher?

Student Adjustment

The school environment takes a student teacher away from a relationship with peers and places him in an adult-student mode. This may be an uncomfortable role for the student teacher, especially one who does not look much older than some of the students. Student teachers will be attempting to establish working relationships with students that will involve some degree of respect between the two groups. Problems result when mature judgments are not made.

The sometimes narrow age span between secondary student teachers and their students can lead to mutual attraction. Problems occur when a student teacher fails to react to such situations in a mature manner. A male student teacher may be flattered by the attention given to him by a high school girl and be tempted to find time to be with her. Such contacts may extend past the school day into evening and weekend meetings. If the relationship becomes obvious, a student teacher will begin to lose the respect of students and may incur the displeasure of his cooperating teacher or building administrator.

A female student teacher may find that male attraction is displayed through some type of annoying behavior. It may appear to her to be a discipline problem and she will be likely to respond accordingly. She may find it hard to believe that such behavior stems from their desire to secure her attention.

A cooperating teacher must intervene whenever such problems start to surface. Several alternatives are available when consideration is being given to such a move:

- Explain to the student teacher why certain pupils are acting as they are.
- See that the problem is discussed before it gets out of hand.
- Alert the student teacher to sensitive situations.
- Talk to the pupils involved and ask for their cooperation.

- Make suggestions about how to appear more mature in the eyes of the students.
- Make your presence known in social situations.

Case Study No. 79: You Are My Favorite!

You left your student teacher alone with your classes one Friday when you attended an inservice workshop out of the school building. Jeffrey knew in advance that you would be gone and, without consulting with you, decided to give each student a personal card with a note written in it. The following Monday two girls from one class sought you out to discuss the written comments. They felt that the comments were inappropriate because the tone was, at best, juvenile, but more specifically leering and sexist. For example, he wrote his address and phone number on a girl's card and asked her to call him to talk about "life, art, and literature." He also wrote that she was his "favorite". Another girl was embarrassed because of his comments about her physical appearance. Jeffrey had admitted to writing the cards and says that he wanted to establish better rapport with the students. He did admit to liking a few of the girls. Given this incident and this admission, what is your next step?

1. Withdraw him from his classes until you have had time to investigate the matter more fully.
2. Explain the damage that he has done and ask him to devise a plan to correct his indiscretion.
3. Contact the university supervisor, the school administrator, and possibly the school counselor.
4. Allow him to continue teaching but monitor him closely.
5. _____

Comment

This is the case of a student who has let his emotions race ahead of his professional responsibility and who may have some problems that need to be solved before he is certified to teach. Incidents such as this could cause a sexual harassment suit and could cost him a career in teaching. This is a situation where immediate action should be taken to prevent someone from taking more drastic action.

Questions

1. How could a cooperating teacher have failed to notice the student teacher's strong personal interest in female students?

2. What preventive measures can a cooperating teacher take to see that such an incident does not occur?

Extended Schedule

Many of the problems affecting a student teacher have their roots in activities that consume time outside the school day and prevent the allocation of sufficient time to teaching. Unfortunately many of these outside diversions have deadlines and probably take priority over student teaching. The amount of time devoted to outside responsibilities may reflect in mediocre teaching performance and a poor evaluation.

The following indicators may be clues that the student teacher is spending a considerable amount of time with activities other than preparation for student teaching:

- Inadequate preparation.
- Reluctance to go beyond the minimum requirements.
- Completion of requirements at the last minute.
- Absence from school.
- Fatigue.
- Requests to be excused from meetings.

The above conditions do not necessarily indicate that a student teacher is involved with other activities, but it would be well to be aware of that possibility. These behaviors should be dealt with as soon as they appear in order to determine the cause and seek a solution. A frank discussion of the potential consequences from not giving total effort may be worthwhile. The cooperating teacher will need to isolate the problems, identify the consequences and try to work with the student teacher to develop strategies for avoiding a serious situation.

Additional Course Work

Most educators associated with student teaching are opposed to student teachers completing any course work while student teaching, but for a variety of reasons they are occasionally confronted with that reality. The demands of an intensive college course can consume hours of time. The responsibilities of student teaching may seem less important than the immediate need to meet course requirement deadlines.

A student teacher who is involved in a day-long program of teaching should be discouraged from enrolling in formal course work. Although the cooperating teacher may not be in a position to determine whether course work is taken, she should point out the consequences in the event that performance is not meeting expected standards.

Part-time or Full-time Employment

Financial problems are real to a great number of college students. Some may completely finance their education by employment while others seek jobs in order to live more comfortably. In a study of 250 education students, Ransom (1994) found that 49 had worked at least part time during their student teaching experience. Elementary education student teachers worked an average of 15 hours per week while their secondary education counterparts worked 20 hours per week.

The student teacher who has been able to work while successfully managing college requirements will likely anticipate that the same can be done in student teaching. Part-time employment is likely to be detrimental to a student teacher's performance at school but the student teacher may feel that there is no other choice.

The conflict of demands for time can create problems. The cooperating teacher must first protect her class and then point out the possible consequence of a student teacher's performance if he fails to devote more effort to student teaching. It would be well to try to explore some course of action that will enable a student teacher to reconcile his need to work with the intensive demands of a student teaching schedule.

College Activities

If a student teacher is assigned to a school close to the college campus, there may be the temptation to continue with normal extracurricular activities. Such participation competes for time but a student who occupies an established position at college may be reluctant to surrender some of that esteem to the uncertain promises of student teaching. Directive behaviors on the part of the cooperating teacher may be necessary in this situation.

Case Study No. 80: Problems With Time

It is school policy for teachers to report at school by 8:00 a.m. It is past 8:15 and your student teacher has not yet arrived. When it is time to begin class, you proceed to teach the student teacher's lesson.

The school secretary notifies you later in the day that the student teacher had called at 9:00 saying that she would not be in today because she had some things she needed to get done at the college. She has been late before but this is the first time that she has not shown up at all. How would you deal with this situation?

1. Ignore it unless it occurs again.
2. Discuss the matter with her college supervisor.
3. Have a frank talk with the student teacher and tell her that she is dealing with her obligations in an irresponsible way.
4. Have an administrator talk with her about the need for meeting a time schedule.
5. _____

Comment

The attendance rules of a school are probably going to be more rigid than the guidelines that students experience at a university. It seems that it must be communicated to the student teacher that she is expected to meet her responsibilities without prompting and that unexplained absences can cause difficulty for the program of the school.

Questions

1. What are reasonable expectations in regard to attendance and promptness?
2. How can a cooperating teacher insure that attendance expectations are adequately communicated to a student teacher?

Confronting Extended Schedule Problems

A student teacher has too much at stake to deliberately risk a low evaluation. It is not fair to permit a student teacher to jeopardize this report. When a cooperating teacher feels that outside activities are threatening a student teacher's success or pupil progress, the following points should be discussed with the student teacher:

- Learning about teaching cannot be accomplished by doing as little as possible.
- A student teacher who is not thoroughly prepared is being unfair to the pupils.
- The competing demands are only temporary while the results of student teaching are more permanent.

• The requirements of student teaching must be met.

Case Study No. 81: Off In The Corner

Your student teacher is having problems with classroom control. She is not well organized, does not get along with students, or mix with teachers. In addition, she is enrolled in a university course and is in the corner of the library studying for the class in any spare moments at school. This makes it difficult for you to work with her because she seems to avoid her problems and take refuge in the demands of the campus course. Some changes are going to have to be made. What course of action should you take?

1. Lessen her teaching responsibilities so that she will have more discretionary time.
2. Indicate that you cannot recommend that she pass student teaching unless she improves.
3. Confront her with the problem and suggest that it appears that she must either discontinue student teaching or withdraw from her university class.
4. Team teach with her so that she can make it through the experience.
5. _____

Comment

It should be quite apparent to the reader by this time that the authors feel that a student teacher must devote full time to teaching in order to be well qualified. The situation above indicates that the student teacher needs to be spending time trying to improve. Another college course simply is a distraction. If she continues with this kind of schedule, there could be no successful ending.

Questions

1. What is the teacher's obligation to the class at this point?
2. Should the university supervisor be involved in this situation?

Case Study No. 82: Tennis Or Teaching?

Kathy has a predicament. She is on the university tennis team and receives a full athletic scholarship. She is student teaching during tennis season and has an obligation to be at the school full time. Her tennis coach wants her to be absent for several days in order to make trips to other universities to compete with the team.

She also wishes to have her available by 3:00 each afternoon when the matches are played on campus. You resist this request on the basis that anything other than a full-time assignment is disruptive to your class and that there is need for after school participation. The tennis coach tells you that she will not win a match without Kathy and she should have some rights since she has invested $20,000 in the girl through athletic scholarships. She implies that a day away from school now and then is really not that important. What is your response?

1. Make the necessary adjustments that will accommodate the tennis program.
2. Indicate that she will have to decide between tennis or teaching.
3. Contact the university supervisor for a decision.
4. _____

Comment

This is a classic illustration of the conflict between the demands and expectations of athletic requirements and student teaching obligations. The supervisor's first priority must be the impact of such a schedule upon the students in the class, but another pressing question is in regard to the relative importance of teaching requirements verses athletic competition. Consideration must also be given to which skills are going to be more important after the student teacher graduates.

Questions

1. Is it fair for a cooperating teacher to be placed in the position of having to make a decision about this matter?
2. Is there any type of approach that can insure that tennis and teaching requirements can both be met?

Instructional Problems

Instructional problems range from difficulties in processing cognitive matters through problems with technique. In looking at the major problems reported, the authors noted that those related to discipline, classroom management, and planning seemed to be the most prevalent. The problems subsumed below are summaries of the difficulties that seem to be most frequently experienced in the instructional domain.

Student Motivation

Student teachers want to be able to combat apathy, incomplete assignments, negative attitudes, excessive absences, and other symptoms of the lack of motivation. They want to know how to secure the attention of pupils and to arouse interest in their studies. Difficulties can arise when the student teacher uses the wrong procedure, such as the threat of denying grades and privileges until goals have been met. Students may not respond to this type of motivation.

Student teachers must learn to take a more positive approach to student motivation. Linking lessons to the pupils' real life experiences, crafting objectives to pupils' interests, and engaging students in active learning are effective strategies to improve student motivation. Others believe that many students are under challenged. Rinne (1998) asserted that students will often rise to a challenging learning experience because they feel the need to say they could accomplish a task that would stretch their limits.

Difficulties in motivation may be prevented or corrected through attention to the fact that teacher behavior influences pupil behavior. A student teacher must be aware of the potential for influencing students as well as have a knowledge of specific techniques that can be used for motivation.

Adapting Subject Matter to Pupil Level

Student teachers may not be aware of the level of subject matter understanding that pupils have. Thus, they often experience difficulty in adapting the subject matter to the needs and interests of their pupils. This may be compounded by a student teacher's not knowing the basic structure of knowledge and how it can be interpreted to learners.

In addressing this problem, the cooperating teacher should assist the student teacher in understanding that the subject matter must appear relevant to indifferent students and be appropriate for all pupils. This may involve analysis of what has been taught and what should be taught. It also will likely come with the establishment of priorities so that the material considered to be the most important is stressed.

Classroom Management and Discipline

Studies have indicated that problems with class control and discipline create the greatest anxieties in student teachers (Reed,

1989). Doebler and Roberson (1987) report eight areas of problems associated with classroom management and discipline:

- Classroom control.
- Class monitoring.
- Maintaining on-task behavior.
- Organizational skills.
- Interacting with students.
- Management of groups.
- Transition.
- Time management.

During a three-year period, Reed (1989) investigated discipline problems of 300 student teachers who were enrolled in a weekly, on-campus seminar at Virginia Commonwealth University. The problems were subsumed into 17 categories that are summarized in rank order.

- Excessive talking.
- Uncooperative behavior.
- Instructional issues.
- Not doing work.
- Insolent/rude behavior.
- Breaking rules.
- Aggressive behavior.
- Inattentiveness.
- Lack of motivation.
- Problems with parents.
- Not staying in seat.
- Not being prepared.
- Using abusive language.
- Stealing.
- Sexual harassment
- Class clown.
- Racial harassment.

A study by Kher and others (2000) identified strategies that preservice teachers viewed as effective in dealing with pupil misbehavior. Student teachers most frequently said that they would send students to the office, give verbal instructions to stop misbehavior, lecture or reprimand the students involved, talk to individuals separately, or involve the principal or parents as measures to curtail inappropriate behavior. Yelling at students and threatening punishment were reported as ineffective management strategies. The researchers noted that the student teachers polled lacked any notion of how to prevent problems from surfacing in the first place and how to encourage pupils to cooperate with the teacher.

Whitfield (1995) found that management/discipline was one of the four major causes of concern for student teachers (the other three being stress, relationship with cooperating teachers, and sense of competence). Confronted with classroom management problems, they struggled with students off task, loss of control, frustration with cooperating teachers' management systems, a perceived lack of student respect, and unaccustomed moments of personal "temper."

Although student teachers have had previous discussions about discipline in course work, it is not until they are bodily in the classrooms for extended periods of time that the issue of discipline becomes real. It is then that anxiety sets in, and they begin looking for answers to specific problems (Reed, 1989). Student teachers generally tend to equate the success of their experience with the ability to maintain discipline. The concern about the ability to discipline must be addressed because in most cases student teachers will have first-year assignments that will demand more control than that needed in the cooperating teacher's classes.

Student teachers should be assisted in the establishment and maintenance of an effective learning environment. Cooperating teachers may offer practical tips for coping with discipline problems, but they will have to go further if they are to have a significant impact on the future management skills of their student teachers. It would be well to share a management system with the student teacher so that he feels in control and has some model from which to respond when problems arise.

Threat of Violence

While our nation has been jarred by a rash of tragic acts of school violence in recent years, the *2000 Annual Report on School Safety* maintained that schools were still safe places for pupils and teachers. Nevertheless, preservice teachers frequently express concern over the problem. They frequently ask what can be done to prevent violent acts from occurring and how they should respond if they are aware that the threat of violence arises in their classroom.

The student teacher should be well informed of any school safety programs and emergency procedures that the host school has in place. They should be involved in helping to carry out any aspect of the program that falls within the domain of student teaching.

Case Study No. 83: School Lockdown

A gun shop located just a few blocks from your school was burglarized two days in advance of the anniversary of a nationally publicized school shooting. Weapons and ammunition were stolen. Upon hearing the news, the school administration feared a similar act of violence and instructed teachers to be on high alert. All exterior doors were locked. Outdoor activities were curtailed. Security guards patrolled the halls. No one was permitted to enter or leave the building. Pupils begin to ask your student teacher to explain what was taking place. How should she respond?

1. Tell the pupils that she does not know.
2. Tell the pupils the truth about what is happening.
3. Give few specific details but assure them that their safety is being guarded.
4. _____

Comment

As in any emergency, panic must be avoided. The demeanor of the adults in the school sets the tenor for how the pupils will react. Pupils need to be reassured that all precautions are being taken to assure the safety of everyone. The specific details revealed should be dictated by the age and maturity level of the pupils. In many cases the administration will draft a common message to be announced or relayed to the students. Such a uniform response should help reduce the number of rumors that often swirl around such events.

Questions

1. What specific steps would you take if your school came under threat of assault?
2. What can teachers do to help pupils feel safe during a crisis situation?

Lack of Basic Teaching Skills

Most candidates for a teaching certificate demonstrate that they possess the minimum competencies to be a successful teacher. But occasionally, student teachers complete their clinical experience and serious doubts remain about their teaching ability. Making decisions on incompetence is difficult, but the recent emphasis on performance criteria is making it more simple. Any of the following traits could be indicators of inadequacy:

- Timidity.
- Insecurity.
- Immaturity.
- Lack of organizational skills.
- Ineffective planning.
- Failure to consistently meet responsibilities.
- Weak interpersonal skills.
- Poor communication skills.
- Inability to manage a classroom independently.
- Students not showing any measurable progress.
- Problems with expressing thoughts.
- Lack of the basic techniques of teaching.
- Inadequate content knowledge.
- Lack of interest in teaching.
- Lack of ability to demonstrate reflective thinking.

Many of the above weaknesses can be improved through recognition and concentrated effort. If the problem is identified early and the student teacher is aware of it, a successful corrective plan may be devised. Although each problem needs an individual diagnosis and plan of action, the following procedures by the cooperating teacher seem to have potential for helping the student teacher improve:

- Work together with the student teacher in classes.
- Insist on thorough planning.
- Inquire about other activities that might be competing for a student teacher's time and energy.
- Arrange for situations where a student teacher can experience some success and then reinforce appropriate behavior.
- Demonstrate effective teaching styles.
- Provide continuous feedback.
- Identify problems early in the program whenever possible.
- Recognize even small improvement in performance.

When it appears that little or no progress is being made, the college supervisor should be contacted. He can take the initiative in confronting the student teacher with the fact that performance is unsatisfactory. Sometimes his presence alone can be the catalyst that brings about change. He may be able to motivate a student teacher or suggest a plan of action that will be beneficial.

The cooperating teacher should document a student teacher's poor performance. If the difficulty is such that it can be identified on videotape, secure a recording of the performance for the college supervisor's use. Written information and other forms of record will give the college supervisor a better idea of what has happened. The supervisor can work more effectively if there is a complete record of past activities and an accurate description of deficiencies.

The greatest oversights on the part of supervisors may be failure to keep complete records and reluctance to notify the college supervisor when it becomes apparent that a student teacher may not have the skills necessary for certification. Closely behind may be the failure to identify the problem early enough to permit any kind of remedial procedures.

Case Study No. 84: Ineffective Oral Communication

You have agreed to host Sally as a student teacher in your classroom. During your initial interview you noticed that she had an unusual voice. When she began working with your pupils, they had difficulty understanding her. They often had puzzled looks on their faces and asked her to repeat what she said. Communication problems exist. What action do you take?

1. Ask the college to assign her elsewhere.
2. Ask the school's speech therapist about the problem.
3. Do nothing and hope that your pupils will get used to her voice quality.
4. Suggest that she get professional help.
5. _____

Comment

The cooperating teacher's first responsibility is to ensure a quality educational experience for her pupils. If the student teacher is proving to be detrimental to the growth and progress of the pupils, steps need to be taken to protect their development. The challenge here is to create a solution that will promote the professional growth of the student teacher without hindering classroom learning.

Questions

1. At what point does a cooperating teacher request that a student teacher be removed from her classroom?
2. What problems would you have in dealing with this situation?

Helping Student Teachers With Problems
Going the Extra Mile

Each problem is unique and demands an individualized plan. It is important to know how to approach each situation so that the problem may be identified and solved. Problem solving is also a very human enterprise and will call for understanding and concern. This chapter will close with a model for the analysis of problems and some general suggestions for supervisors that may be reviewed when a difficult situation arises.

Problem Analysis

One approach to a problem is to develop a procedure for analysis that has some consistency. The model below is a step-by-step procedure for looking at a problem and working toward a solution:

Step 1: Get The Facts.

a. What has happened?
b. Why did the problem occur?
c. What principles or issues are involved?

Step 2: List And Evaluate Alternative Courses Of Action.

a. How will each alternative affect the participants involved?
b. Are the alternatives feasible?
c. Which will most likely prevent the situation from occurring again?

Step 3: Take A Course Of Action That Seems Most Defensible.

a. Why is it a better alternative?
b. How will it benefit the student teacher?
c. Is it likely to prevent a problem from occurring in the future?

Establish a Climate for Problem Solving

The style and behavior of a cooperating teacher can contribute to the successful remedial procedures of student teaching problems. Generally a positive, understanding demeanor contributes to a better climate for dealing with difficulties and conflicts. The following behaviors may be considered in establishing the desired climate for problem solving:

- Discuss the problem with the student teacher in an objective manner.
- Treat the student teacher as a colleague.
- When possible, demonstrate confidence in the student teacher's ability to manage problems.
- Provide opportunities for the student teacher to succeed.
- Be encouraging whenever possible.
- Be available for conversation and discussion.
- Be a good listener.
- Be sincere.
- Know the facts before action is taken.
- See that the student teacher feels accepted.
- Capitalize on special skills or interests.
- Try to put problems in context.
- Be flexible.

The discussion of problems had been rather depressing to Miss Bennett initially, but then she began to realize that this background would probably be beneficial to her if she should ever encounter difficulties with a student teacher. She felt better prepared now in the event that such a situation should ever happen to her.

She returned to school the next day wondering about Brian's solo experience. "How did it go yesterday?" she asked.

"Great," replied Brian. "I arrived at school late, but that did not matter. I was an instant success with them since I wore my baggy jeans and my ear ring. I told them how to obtain soft drinks in the lunch room without getting caught, and I even had them sing a couple of songs that I learned at an all-night party."

Miss Bennett was confused until she spied Tom Larson, her associate from across the hall and fellow supervisor, who had attended the conference with her. His innocent face told the story. She broke into a smile, somewhat relieved to know that Tom had told Brian about the frustrations expressed at the meeting. She was inwardly convinced that many problems could be solved if the cooperating teacher and student teacher were comfortable enough with each other to inject a little humor into the professional environment.

Remember:

- **The greatest amount of stress and anxiety may come prior to and early in the student teaching experience.**
- **Each problem is unique.**
- **The problem student teacher should be given an opportunity to overcome his difficulties.**

- **Open communication is a great asset in the prevention of difficulties.**
- **Many awkward situations result from incorrect or poorly considered reactions to stimuli.**
- **Problems often come to the forefront when success is denied.**
- **It is better to prevent a problem than it is to solve one.**

Useful References

Abebe, Solomon and Michael F. Shaughnessy. 1997. Strengthening the Teaching Profession: Preparing Educators to Cope with Stress. ERIC ED 411239

Alilunas, Leo. 1977-78. Some Case Studies of Unsuccessful Student Teachers: Their Implications for Teacher Education Changes. *The Teacher Educator* 13 (Winter): 30-34.

Annual Report on School Safety. 2000. Department of Education and Department of Justice, Washington, DC. ERIC ED 436860.

Bacon, Beth. 2001. Increasing Safety in America's Public Schools: Lessons from the Field. ERIC ED 452285.

Balch, Pamela M., and Patrick E. Balch. 1987. Special Problems and Discipline and Classroom Management Problems. Chapters 10 and 11 in *The Cooperating Teacher: A Practical Approach for the Supervision of Student Teachers*. Lanham, MD. University Press of America.

Benson, Sheryl, Ann Larson, and Iris Nierenberg (University of Illinois). 1994. High Maintenance Student Teachers: Putting the Pieces Together. Paper presented at the Annual Meeting of the Association of Teacher Educators. Atlanta, GA. February 15.

Bents, Mary, and Eugene Anderson. 1991. Failure in Student Teaching. *The Teacher Educator* 26 (Winter): 26-32.

Bowers, Henry C., B. Keith Eicher, and Annabel L. Sacks. 1983. Reducing Stress in Student Teachers. *The Teacher Educator* 19 (Fall): 19-24.

Coombs-Richardson, Rita. 2000. Violence in Schools: Causation and Prevention. Paper Presented at the Annual Convention of the National Association of School Psychology. New Orleans, LA. March 28-April. ERIC ED 440317.

DiGiulio, Robert C. 2001. *Educate, Medicate, or Litigate? What Teachers, Parents, and Administrators Must Do About Student Behavior*. Thousand Oaks, CA. Corwin Press, Inc.

Doebler, Leland K., and Terry G. Roberson. 1987. A Study of Common Problems Experienced by Secondary Student Teachers. *Education* 107 (Spring): 234-243.

Edwards, Steven W. (2000). Strategies to Maximize School Safety. *Impact: Connecticut's Journal for Middle Level Educators.* 7 (Fall): 2-4.

Gorn, Susan (1999). *What Do I Do When . . . The Answer Book on Discipline.* Horsham, PA. LRP Publications. ED ERIC 443264.

Guyton, Edith, and D. John McIntyre. 1990. Student Teaching and School Experiences. Chapter 29 in Houston (Ed.), *Handbook of Research on Teacher Education.* New York. Macmillan Publishing Co.

Harwood, Angela M., Laura Collins, and Mary Sudzina. 2000. Learning From Student Teacher Failure: Implications for Program Design. Paper presented at the Annual Meeting of the American Educational Research Association. New Orleans, LA. April 24-28. ERIC ED 442777.

Kher, Neelam, Lorna Lacina-Gifford, and Sonya Yandell. 2000. Preservice Teachers' Knowledge of Effective Classroom Management Strategies: Defiant Behavior. Paper presented at the Annual Meeting of the American Educational Research Association, New Orleans, LA. ERIC ED 444941.

Knowles, J. Gary, and Virginia B. Hoefler. 1989. The Student Teacher Who Wouldn't Go Away: Learning from Failure. *Journal of Experiential Education.* 12 (Summer): 14-21.

Knowles, J. Gary, and Mary R. Sudzina. 1992. Addressing "Failure" in Student Teaching: Some Practical and Ethical Issues. ERIC ED 353238.

Maxie, Andrea Peters. 1989. Student Teachers' Concerns and the Student-Teaching Experience: Does Experience Make a Difference? Paper presented at the Annual Meeting of the American Educational Research Association, San Francisco, CA, March 27-31. ERIC ED 308164.

Morris, John E., and Geneva Morris. 1980. Stress in Student Teaching. *Action in Teacher Education* 2 (Fall): 57-61.

Morrow, John E., and John M. Lane. 1983. Instructional Problems of Student Teachers: Perceptions of Student Teachers, Cooperating Teachers and College Supervisors. *Action in Teacher Education* 5 (Spring/Summer): 71-78.

Murray-Harvey, Rosalind, Phillip T. Slee, Michael J. Lawson, Halia Silins, Grant Banfield, and Alan Russel. (2000). The Concerns and Coping Strategies of Teacher Education Students. *European Journal of Teacher Education.* 23: 19-35.

Phelps, Patricia H. 2000. Mistakes as Vehicles for Educating Teachers. *Action in Teacher Education* 4 (Winter) 41-49.

Ransom, Peggy E. (1994). Student Teaching "Moonlighting": Does It Have an Impact? ERIC ED 379262.

Reed, Daisy. 1989. Student Teacher Problems With Classroom Discipline: Implications for Program Development. *Action in Teacher Education* 11(Fall): 59-64.

Rickman, L., and J. Hollowell. 1981. Some Causes of Student Teaching Failure. *Improving College and University Teaching*. 29 (4): 176-179.

Rinne, Carl H. (1998). Motivating Students is a Percentage Game. *Phi Delta Kappan*. 79 (April): 620-628.

U.S. Department of Education (2001). Studies Report Declining Rate of School Violence: Secret Service Study Explores Early Detection in School Shootings. *Community Update*. U.S. Department of Education 85 (March/April). 1-2.

Whitfield, Patricia T. 1995. Assimilating the Culture of Teaching: The Student Teaching Experience. Chapter 3 in Slick (Ed.), *Making the Difference for Teachers: The Field Experience in Actual Practice*. Thousand Oaks, CA. Corwin Press, Inc.

12

Evaluating The Student Teacher

Brian Sims' performance as a student teacher had exceeded Elaine Bennett's hopes. He was pleasant, cooperative, liked by the students, and well prepared in his teaching area. His plans were submitted on time and he seemed to be effective in teaching students at all ability levels. Since he was doing well, Miss Bennett felt that she might be doing a disservice to Brian if she delved into a great number of critiques.

She began to have some reservations about this view after the last visit from Dr. Douglas, Brian's college supervisor. He inquired about the amount of time spent in evaluation, and whether Brian was beginning to develop the ability to evaluate himself. Dr. Douglas wanted to know if they had used the evaluation checklist in the university guide for student teaching. Miss Bennett's responses were brief and evasive because she felt such procedures were unnecessary since Brian's progress was satisfactory.

Dr. Douglas stressed that the best evaluation occurred when there was frequent analysis of teaching, emphasizing strengths and discussing teaching problems. Although she did not protest to Dr. Douglas, Miss Bennett felt such techniques might cause Brian to lose confidence. Still she resolved that she would discuss this matter with some of the other teachers who had supervised student teachers, and she also intended to ask Brian about his feelings concerning the type of evaluation he expected . . .

Student Teacher Evaluation
Judgment Day, Pay Day, or Just Another Day?

The evaluation of student teachers is different from the usual evaluations a cooperating teacher is accustomed to making. There are no quizzes, examinations, or term papers. There may even be no letter grades. Evaluation involves an analysis of performance for the dual purposes of formative growth while student teaching and of determining the potential of the individual to succeed as a teacher.

Although a university supervisor may be the evaluator of record, most higher education supervisors rely heavily on the assessment of the cooperating teacher. This individual spends the most time with the student teacher and is in the best position to observe the performance of the teaching candidate. The student teacher generally places more reliance upon the cooperating teacher's professional judgments than any other individual associated with student teaching. The cooperating teacher's evaluation is probably studied more intently by a potential employer than any other material in a placement file.

It is clear that the cooperating teacher's role in evaluating the performance of student teachers is critical. Yet Ramanathan and Wilkins-Carter (1997) found that most cooperating teachers received little, if any, training to be supervisors although many reported that such training would be welcomed.

Because evaluation is complex, it should be no surprise to learn that cooperating teachers and student teachers have different perspectives on evaluation. Williams (1995) found significant differences between cooperating teachers and student teachers in their perceptions of student teachers' performance on 23 survey items, although they do not necessarily lead to conflict. Similarly, Wile (1999) noted that student teachers and their cooperating teachers frequently differed in their views concerning the effectiveness of portfolios as an assessment tool. Such differences have the potential to cause a rift in the relationship between the cooperating teacher and his understudy when the cooperating teacher holds the dual position of coach and judge. This lends support to the findings of Zheng and Webb (2000) that the major role of the cooperating teacher should be that of a mentor, and the final evaluation, or "grade," be determined through collaboration with the university supervisor.

If indeed the major role of the cooperating teacher is to be a guide and mentor for the preservice teacher, then a wide variety of formative assessment strategies should be employed. The summative evaluation criteria usually identified by the college are often dictated by state professional licensing requirements. The assessment techniques used should help the student teacher gain the skills and competency necessary to achieve mastery of those criteria.

Evaluating the merits and quality of the work of another person is a difficult task. There are many problems with evaluation that the cooperating teacher must confront. The first is that of objectivity. Brucklacher (1998) stated that cooperating teachers might rate student teachers too high because they fear that lower evaluations could damage the relationship between them. Second, a cooperating teacher must confront the problem of consistency. She must guard against allowing her own proclivity to lead her away from a set of evaluation criteria or guidelines. Finally, a cooperating teacher must deal with the acquired skills and knowledge of evaluative procedures that she possesses. These include observation and conferencing skills as well as a knowledge of the instruments and techniques that may be used for successful evaluation.

The above considerations will prompt a cooperating teacher to consider the best approach for evaluation. There are a variety of ways that student teachers can be assessed. The descriptions below present common concepts of evaluation and then a recommended procedure to foster the ideal goals for evaluation.

Subjective Evaluation

A subjective approach involves a qualitative analysis of performance from the perspective of the more knowledgeable and experienced person who is sitting in judgment of the trainee. This type of evaluation points toward a terminal process, i.e., once the judgment has been made, it is over. The final evaluation is the only evidence that attention was given to analysis of teaching.

Chiarelott (1980) pointed out that the content of the evaluations may have more to do with the cooperating teacher's biases and idiosyncrasies than the candidate's actual teaching performance. In most cases, the supervisor's biases lean to the positive side. Guyton and McIntyre (1990) point out that cooperating teachers tend to base evaluation on a single overall affective impression rather than on distinct professional competencies. Funk (1982) comments that evaluators tend to overrate those student teachers with whom they are familiar. This may be pleasing initially to a student teacher, but the eventual outcome will be an inaccurate picture of the student teacher's ability.

The problems resulting from subjective judgment are rather obvious. Complete reliance on such an approach can create a good-bad dichotomy where a student teacher may work for approval rather than for growth as a teacher. It places disproportionate emphasis on the final decision, whether it be grade, evaluation checklist, or some other criterion, and may make both parties uncomfortable. Thus, a subjective approach is not sufficient for a comprehensive program of evaluation.

Criterion Referenced Evaluation

The criterion referenced concept of evaluation may be associated with the concept of pay day. There are numerous lists of performance criteria available as standards for assessing the capability of a student teacher. They ostensibly are based on indicators of quality that can be observed and measured by a supervisor. Robertson (1986) indicates four functions of criterion referenced instruments:

- They provide a precise body of skills and abilities that the student teacher and her supervisors can work with to facilitate teaching.
- They provide skills that the teacher is expected to exhibit.
- They provide criteria against which the student teacher's performance can be judged.
- They make an evaluation of individual abilities possible.

The concept of criterion referenced evaluation is to assess the mastery of a number of competencies associated with effective teaching. If a person satisfactorily performs a given number of criteria, certification to teach is granted. This tends to provide specific evidence of achievement as opposed to the more abstract concepts implied in grades or written statements of evaluation. The stated criteria, when accompanied by descriptions, can help focus on specific ways of achieving competency for teaching. This in turn can lead to analysis and skill development.

Although there are promising possibilities with this approach, performance assessment can present problems. Phelps (1986) found that a performance-based report does not, in and of itself, provide enough objective data to combat the difficulties encountered with Likert-type rating scales. The Likert scale permits an assessment of specific skills ranging from highly positive evaluation to highly negative evaluation. The validity of this type of evaluation can be hindered by halo effects which occur when raters are unduly influenced by a single trait or behavior that, in turn, colors their judgment regarding other traits.

If performance assessment is used alone, the result may be an evaluation program that is a summary of teaching criteria with the context skewed. This type of assessment can become a process of verifying that some of the more specific teaching tasks have been completed.

In an effort to overcome the limitations of criterion referenced assessment outlined above, the Interstate New Teachers Assessment and Support Consortium (INTASC) has identified the following principles as necessary for the beginning teacher regardless of the content or grade level being taught:

The Professional Educator:

- Understands content.
- Understands human development and learning.
- Understands differences.
- Designs instructional strategies.
- Manages and motivates.
- Plans and integrates instruction.
- Evaluates.
- Reflects on practice.
- Participates in the professional community.

Using the INTASC principles, Ball State University developed, and Phi Delta Kappa International (2000) published, a popular assessment program to guide the preparation and licensing of preservice teachers. To overcome the problem of subjectivity inherent with many criterion referenced evaluations, a rubric was designed to identify specific teaching quality indicators at four performance levels. Both formative and summative evaluation were stressed in the assessment program.

By the same token, there has been a concerted effort to identify and standardize the traits of quality field experiences for preservice teachers. Byrd and Guyton (2000) edited a publication for the Association of Teacher Educators which identified twelve standards, complete with quality indicators and performance outcomes that described the optimum environment in which preservice training should take place. Although they address the entire scope of preservice teacher education, there are implications for the process of evaluation used by the cooperating teacher. Copies of the publication may be secured from the Association of Teacher Educators.

Continuous Evaluation

The concept of continuous evaluation is that evaluation is a routine part of the developmental process and should be performed by both the cooperating teacher and the student teacher on an ongoing basis. Evaluation is a tool instead of an end product, stressing analysis and reflection rather than criticism and faultfinding. A comprehensive program of evaluation involves an analysis of plans, procedures, alternatives, and implications for the improvement of teaching.

The student teacher needs to learn how to make valid judgments because self-assessment will be the major method for evaluation throughout her professional career. The cooperating teacher's goal, therefore, is to instill within the student teacher the ability to accurately evaluate her own teaching.

Effective evaluation focuses on concern for a student teacher's progress in particular and the improvement of teaching in general. A simultaneous analysis of both is more likely to produce acceptance by the student teacher. If a student teacher approaches evaluation feeling that she and the cooperating teacher are working on a problem, she should be more objective about the analysis. In general evaluation should:

- Be designed to provide the student teacher a valid frame of reference for objective evaluation.
- Focus on those skills and techniques that are essential for good performance as a teacher.
- Identify specific areas that need improvement as well as recognize those that are satisfactory.
- Provide guidelines for the next steps in learning about teaching.
- Furnish a prospective employer an objective description of the student teacher's ability and potential for teaching.

A successful student teaching experience should prepare a teaching candidate to meet minimum professional standards. The cooperating teacher is responsible for helping the student teacher reach that level of proficiency. The goal is to make evaluation an implicit and routine part of the teaching process.

Case Study No. 85: To Coach Or Teach?

You and a fellow cooperating teacher have completely different philosophies of how to supervise a student teacher. You view a cooperating teacher as a nurturer who works with a student teacher so that she emerges more competent. Your colleague believes that a student teacher grows best if a cooperating teacher observes and evaluates performance. If the student teacher is not succeeding, it is up to the supervisor to determine what is wrong and correct it. He encourages you to use formal summative procedures of evaluation of the student teacher rather than the more collegial style that you prefer. What kind of response do you make?

1. Make no response. You have no obligation to please this person.
2. Try a combination of the two approaches, but make certain the student teacher understands whether you are being formative or summative.

3. Confirm with the university supervisor what type of evaluation is expected.
4. Ask the student teacher which style she would prefer.
5. _____

Comment

Perhaps your colleague is insecure or feels the formal approach is less hassle. In either case, the cooperating teacher's obligation is to use an evaluative style that enhances the progress of the student teacher.

Questions

1. What style of evaluation do you prefer from your supervisors?
2. What do you consider to be the objective of evaluation?

Criteria For Effective Teaching
Evaluating the Right Competencies and Behaviors

For decades debate has raged concerning the aptitudes, behaviors, and skills that effective teachers should possess. Colleges and universities that train prospective teachers have devised checklists and rating scales which have been used to evaluate the performance of student teachers. Horton, Thacker, and Thompson (1998) reported the following categories of teacher competency were most often evaluated by teacher training institutions:

- Behavior management.
- Effective interaction and questioning skills.
- Communication skills.
- Establishing set.
- Giving clear directions and assignments.
- Planning long and short range objectives.
- Giving positive reinforcement.
- Using good testing and work analysis procedures.
- Classroom management.
- Current professional and subject knowledge.

Many states have developed documents that outline what competent teachers should know and be able to do. The Vermont Department of Education (1999), for example, adopted five broad standards against which certified teachers were evaluated. Those standards are listed below:

- **Learning**
  Content Expertise
- **Professional Knowledge**
  Methodology and Pedagogy
- **Colleagueship**
- **Advocacy**
- **Accountability**

Sixteen guiding principles for educators were derived from the Vermont Standards for Educators, and quality indicators were developed to describe what each principle would look like when translated into classroom practice. Student teachers are required to demonstrate competency commensurate with that expected of a beginning teacher before licensure is granted. Other states may have, or be developing, similar standards.

Day and Martin (2000) reviewed the current interest in performance-based assessment of student teachers and its endorsement by the National Council for Accreditation of Teachers (NCATE). The authors listed the following attributes student teachers must demonstrate to be recommended for licensure:

- Planning.
- Organization.
- Methods of instruction.
- Creativity.
- Assessment practices: daily monitoring.
- Assessment practices: variety.
- Instructional focus.
- Content mastery.
- Classroom management.
- Awareness of students.
- Rapport with students.
- Professional demeanor.

While efforts have been made recently to reach professional consensus on what constitutes exemplary teaching, conventional wisdom and experience of the supervisor likely will continue to play a role in the evaluation decision. For example, the evaluator may focus on the personal attitudes of the student teacher. McDermott and others (1998) found that highly effective teachers, especially in urban and low-income school districts, had a strong sense of efficacy, took pride in their profession, and embraced their role as an advocate for pupils. The evaluator also may focus on specific personality traits of the prospective teacher. Camperell and Stoddart (1998), reported that the most effective teachers generally were outgoing, emotionally stable, conscientious, agreeable, and open-minded. Finally, the evaluator may take a more practical approach and focus on traits such as teaching skills, work habits, character, personality, and educational preparation that, according to Horton and others (1998), are criteria sought by superintendents when reviewing the resumes of potential new hires.

It is apparent that no single list exists that clearly defines the behaviors and practices of effective teachers. Yet care must be taken to ensure that the criteria used to evaluate the performance of student teachers have their roots in valid educational theory and pedagogy and are not skewed by the evaluator's personal predilections or bias.

Case Study No. 86: Too Busy To Evaluate

Your student teacher is now responsible for the maximum teaching load suggested by the university. This has given you some time to catch up on activities that you have been unable to do when you have a full schedule. Since you have confidence in your student teacher, you have not observed or made any evaluative analysis in some time. You thought that this was proper until heard that your student teacher was complaining that she does not know how well she is doing because you never evaluate her. What do you decide to do?

1. Tell her that you feel her teaching is satisfactory.
2. Review an evaluation form with her so that she will have some tangible assessment of performance.
3. Gradually begin evaluating again by concentrating on one or two factors.
4. Share your ideas with her in a conference.
5. _____

Comment

This scenario speaks to the importance of continuous evaluation. From the outset, student teachers should receive some type of formative evaluation. Silence does not necessarily communicate positive feelings to the student teacher when it comes to evaluation. Although it is logical to take acceptable performance for granted, it often needs to be reinforced.

Questions

1. How can a cooperating teacher compromise evaluation with spending time outside of the classroom?
2. If a student teacher is progressing satisfactorily, what should be stressed in evaluation?

Case Study No. 87: Poor Lesson

Your student teacher has just completed the poorest lesson that he has taught. He was impatient, talked too rapidly, and was incorrect with some of the information presented. There are several problems to deal with and you have to decide how to communicate them to the student teacher. What is your best strategy?

1. Give him your considered appraisal in a subjective manner.
2. Compare what he has done with criteria that define effective teaching.
3. Concentrate on improving one area at a time.
4. Start with a self evaluation in order to get an understanding of how he feels.
5. _____

Comment

Obviously this situation demands some response from the cooperating teacher. Before any move is made, it might be beneficial to determine whether such performance is routine or the exception. If this is just a one-time situation, it may not be as serious as it appears and may be due to such factors as lack of planning or loss of sleep. If poor lessons are recurring, a supervisor needs to take a more serious look at the problem. The approach may depend also on how the student teacher has responded previously to evaluative discussions and how he perceives the cooperating teacher. Several decisions will have to be made before an effective evaluation can be planned.

Questions

1. Which of the problems should be approached first?
2. How can a cooperating teacher establish confidence needed by the student teacher to make the evaluation effective?

Evaluation Techniques
Choosing the Right Procedures

A cooperating teacher who evaluates a student teacher must be articulate, specific, understanding, and tactful. Evaluation can be emotional and an ill-chosen word or poor sense of timing can create a negative mood and affect rapport. Non-verbal cues may be more important than verbal ones. In the evaluation process, the goal is for the cooperating teacher and student teacher together to objectively assess performance.

Effective evaluation involves a variety of methods. The type of technique will vary with the task, the student teacher, the cooperating teacher, available time and physical conditions. A student teacher who is open can probably be evaluated more directly. The insecure student teacher will require a different approach. Some ideas may need to be transmitted through written communication while others need to be developed through conversation. There is no one procedure, and a cooperating teacher will have to choose the techniques that best fit the given situation.

The techniques that follow are presented as alternatives for effective evaluation. Supervisors will probably find that a combination of practices will be the most effective in evaluating student teachers.

Conference

The conference is one of the standard models for evaluation. This method, which was the topic of Chapter Eight, allows for discussion of areas of concern. Conferences provide immediate reinforcement or correction of mistakes and allow a quick exchange between the two parties.

Written Comments

Written comments in the evaluative process have great value for student teachers, possibly because they are more formal and permanent. A written analysis provides a tangible record of student growth that can be reviewed periodically. Many universities encourage some type of written communication between a cooperating teacher and a student teacher.

Written comments can be made when conversation is not possible, allowing a cooperating teacher to provide a more comprehensive reaction without having to rely on memory. Statements can be more carefully worded for greater clarity. This procedure is a beneficial way to offer criticism because written statements may be considered to be more objective than oral reviews.

Supervisors who choose to use written comments in evaluation may wish to review the section of Chapter Seven devoted to that topic. As indicated, evaluation can be a part of a comprehensive exchange of written ideas.

Structured Observation

The use of structured observations gives student teachers feedback on specific teaching behaviors or techniques. In this type of observation, the evaluator focuses on a prearranged area of performance and provides feedback and analysis for the student teacher. For example, Johnson and others (1998) explained a process that gave the student teacher quantitative data concerning the equity of interactions with students. Their instrument provided focused feedback on three variables:

- The type of questions asked.
- Whether interactions were academic or non-academic.
- Whether interactions were student initiated.

Such information gave student teachers a basis upon which they could make appropriate modifications in their practice and instruction.

Rating Scales and Analysis Forms

The majority of teacher education institutions use rating scales for evaluation. Reyes and Isele (1990) studied 368 evaluation forms of elementary student teachers from NCATE accredited institutions and found a general lack of a frame of reference for evaluation and diversity among institutions. They did observe that 70 percent of the evaluative criteria were related to instructional concerns and 30 percent to non-instructional areas. They further found that 64.5 percent of the items were high inference items that mean a high degree of subjectivity is involved in completing an evaluation form.

Rating scales, or checklists, permit a flexible method of evaluation and can generate additional comments on the student teacher's progress (Ediger, 1987). A quality checklist will contain a comprehensive set of knowledge indicators, teaching skills, and attitudinal behaviors pertaining to effective teaching. It is almost a certainty that a cooperating teacher will be asked to use a checklist of some type in the evaluation of student teachers.

There are some obvious advantages to checklists. One very positive argument for them is that they force consideration of some skills and traits that might otherwise be overlooked or ignored. Another productive evaluative activity that can be developed through analysis forms and scales is the sharing of perceptions by the student teacher and the cooperating teacher who complete the forms independently and then compare the results.

A great number of rating scales exist for use in evaluating student teachers. One example is reproduced in the Appendix as Worksheet Number Fourteen. The reader may wish to review and analyze it in terms of the validity of its criteria and its potential use in the evaluation of student teachers.

Audio and Video Feedback

Audio and videotapes provide realistic feedback to the student teacher. Tapes can be particularly helpful in analyzing such skills as questioning techniques, word usage, voice inflection, content organization, and management skills. A playback is sometimes all that is necessary for identifying positive teaching qualities or weaknesses. The evidence from the tape can provide concrete illustrations of concepts under discussion.

The authors have pointed out previously that videotapes help provide analysis and feedback to student teachers. This method can be equally effective for evaluation.

Pupil Evaluation

Pupil evaluations offer a perspective on the effectiveness of a student teacher's performance in that they reveal the impressions of the persons directly impacted by the student teacher's instruction. Pupils may be able to make suggestions to the student teacher that the cooperating teacher cannot convey. Older students, obviously, can be more articulate in their evaluations than younger ones. Pupil evaluations are probably more reliable if they are made anonymously.

The student teacher's reservations about pupil evaluations may be an obstacle to overcome when using this technique. The student teacher may suspect that the pupils will submit harsh or unfair criticisms. Other student teachers will be looking for praise only and can become quite concerned if there is even one poor evaluation.

There are various ways of soliciting pupil evaluations. One of the simplest and most popular methods is the administration of pupil rating forms that can be completed quickly. These structured forms have the advantage of focusing on the particular concerns of the student teacher. Perhaps the most informative and revealing pupil evaluations come from open-ended questions such as the following:

- What did you like best about the class or the student teacher?
- What did you dislike about the class or the student teacher?
- If the student teacher were to teach the class again, what changes should be made that would be more helpful to you?

The open-ended type of question lets students express ideas in their own words. It is less restrictive and permits pupils to communicate their prevailing thoughts.

Case Study No. 88: Concern Over Pupil Evaluation

Your student teacher decided to have his pupils evaluate him using an open-ended technique. Most of the comments were constructive but three were critical statements that were upsetting to the student teacher. Although the negative comments were blunt, they did identify problems that the student teacher should seek to correct. How do you discuss these negative comments with him?

1. Place the negative comments in context by reviewing all the positive comments that were made.
2. Look at the criticisms in an objective manner and develop a strategy for improvement.
3. Suggest that he ignore the comments.
4. Ask him to write a self evaluation and compare it with the comments that were made by the pupils.
5. _____

Comment

While pupils assessments can be revealing and helpful, remind the student teacher that they may be painfully honest. An elementary pupil was asked by his grandmother how the student teacher assigned to his classroom was performing. Trying to couch his appraisal positively he replied, "My teacher needed some help and this guy was the best she could get." Not many pupil comments are this diplomatic.

Perhaps a good beginning would be for the cooperating teacher to convince the student teacher that he understands his feelings. If he knows that the cooperating teacher is aware of his thoughts, he may be in a better position to engage in objective appraisal of his skills. Ultimately, one would hope that the conversation would turn to a reasonable consideration of the specific complaints.

Questions

1. What techniques can be successful in establishing empathy toward the student teacher's feelings?
2. How can a few critical comments be put in context with the total number of evaluations?

Self Evaluation

If a student teacher is to become a responsible teacher, she must be able to evaluate herself accurately. She should begin to develop and refine this ability during student teaching. The procedures described above should all lead to the goal of self evaluation.

Elkind (1976) suggests that self evaluation should begin by asking the student teacher to evaluate her own behavior. He found that there were differences between the perceptions of cooperating teachers and student teachers. Hungerman (1984) reported that student teachers rated themselves more modestly in the beginning of the student teaching experience and perceived themselves as making greater progress than did the teachers, who ranked the student teachers higher at both points with less progress in the interim. On the other hand, Nelson (1986) reported that, in general, both elementary and secondary school student teachers accorded themselves higher self-ratings than either field or college supervisors. Supervisors generally agreed in their ratings of secondary school teachers, but not elementary school teachers. Females' ratings tended to agree with supervisors' ratings more than males' ratings.

The message seems to be that cooperating teachers may find their perceptions differing from those of the student teachers and that part of the evaluation process will be the reconciliation of the two points of view. This should not eliminate the use of self evaluation.

Portfolio Evaluation

One of the most comprehensive tools to document the professional growth of preservice teachers is the portfolio (Diamantes, 1996). The portfolio is intended to provide a process by which preservice teachers can document the ways they will meet initial licensure requirements. In the process, students learn many self-assessment skills that will continue to be important as a life long learner (Swetnam, 1997). Ball State University (2000) developed a portfolio handbook that outlined the value of the portfolio to the student teacher, evaluator, prospective employer, and educational institution. The document also described types of portfolios that could be used at various points during teacher training. Artifacts were suggested that would demonstrate competence in meeting INTASC standards. More information about this handbook should be available from the institution.

Other author's have praised portfolios as a superb evaluation tool. Dutt, Kayler, and Tallerico, (1999) identified increased student teacher reflection, enhanced opportunities to engage in professional dialogue, and a mechanism for student teachers to validate growth as benefits of using portfolios as an assessment instrument.

Johnson (1999) also lauded portfolios as valuable tools that not only provided documentation for professional growth for preservice teachers but also gave them a head start in learning a documentation process for professional development that many states and school districts are requiring for relicensure purposes.

Evaluating According To Ability Level
Looking at the Quadrants

In Chapter Seven, an outline of developmental supervisory approaches was presented. Quadrant One student teachers would be supervised differently from those with higher levels of professional skills. In like manner, evaluation should also take into account the developmental level of the student teacher. The following suggestions give guidelines for differentiating the evaluative techniques.

Evaluating the Quadrant One Student Teacher

The evaluation of the Quadrant One Student teacher (low abstraction and low commitment) would take a more directive approach. A cooperating teacher might review the lesson with the student teacher and indicate whether it was successful according to specified criteria. This could be followed by a listing of expectations for the next lesson.

Evaluating the Quadrant Two Student Teacher

With Quadrant Two student teachers (low abstraction and high commitment) evaluation could take the form of providing a limited frame of reference for the student teacher and then asking for analysis. A supervisor might say, "I would rate you as needing more clarity in your directions, needing better organization at the beginning of class, and needing to spend more time on task. Which are you going to begin with and what improvement will you try to make tomorrow?" This is still a directive approach, but it gives the student teacher the option of making a decision. The cooperating teacher is gently urging the student teacher to take more control of evaluation.

Evaluating the Quadrant Three Student Teacher

The Quadrant Three student teacher is high in abstraction but low in commitment. Generally, a more collegial approach works best. Evaluation would involve both parties offering a critique and then negotiating any differences. The conclusion would be one that is mutually determined and based on consensus about what improvements need to be made.

Evaluating the Quadrant Four Student Teacher

In Quadrant Four (high abstraction and high commitment), a cooperating teacher would be more indirect. The supervisor should provide evaluation through thoughtful questions that cause the student teacher to be more thorough in self-analysis. An example might be something like, "Why are you successful in motivation?"

Major Evaluations
Focusing on the Checkpoints

Any evaluation procedure should emphasize at least two formal processes, the mid-term evaluation and the summary evaluation. Some teacher education institutions require more frequent evaluations. The mid-term evaluation will likely focus on a set of criteria to be judged either formally or through an extended conference. The final evaluation will require the completion of a written assessment that will become a part of the student teacher's evaluation or permanent record.

Mid-term Evaluation

The midpoint affords a good opportunity for a more comprehensive look at the student teacher's progress. She has been in the school long enough for patterns to emerge but has enough time remaining so that concentrated effort can be devoted to improvement. A comprehensive evaluation can be reassuring both in terms of progress and in allowing time for strengthening weak areas.

Some universities require a mid-term report. A discussion of this report can be enlightening for the student teacher, especially if she is allowed to participate in the evaluation. Such a tangible form of evaluation can provide a great amount of reassurance for the student teacher as well as outline goals for the remaining weeks of the experience.

The Summary Evaluation

The summary evaluation will likely be a written report to the university. The discussion of the summative evaluation between the cooperating teacher and the student teacher may be the final opportunity for them to communicate formally. The student teacher will be vitally interested in knowing what the supervisor has to say.

A discussion of the final report can be a rewarding terminal experience for the student teacher provided that there are no last-minute surprises. The final report should be a summary of criteria that have been considered during student teaching. Such a conference should result in the student teacher formulating a profile that indicates both strong points and weaker traits. It also can serve as the time when recommendations may be discussed concerning the type of teaching position to pursue as well as the skills and traits that continue to need improvement.

Legal Considerations
Following Due Process

The legal implications for student teaching were discussed in Chapter Ten, but the unique nature of the final evaluation warrants additional comments. With increased legal awareness in all facets of our society, the question of the legality of student teacher evaluation sometimes arises. Case law seems to affirm the principle that professionals have the right, obligation, authority, and ability to evaluate teacher candidates. The courts only insist that due process must be exercised. Due process was discussed in Chapter Ten in regard to the obligations to the student and those criteria should be reviewed. In addition to those factors, the following five processes constitute due process in student teacher evaluation:

- Review the evaluation instrument and its interpretation with the student teacher.
- Observe the student teacher.
- Critique and analyze the student teacher.
- Evaluate the student teacher continuously.
- Discuss the completed final evaluation form with the student teacher.

The question concerning confidentiality of the final evaluation is often raised. Since 1974, when Congress passed the General Evaluation Provision Act and an amendment, commonly known as the Buckley Amendment, confidentiality of student teacher evaluations is prohibited in teacher education institutions receiving federal funds. The essence of the amendment is that students are given an absolute right to see education records maintained by the school.

The key to good evaluation, as well as due process, seems to be open communication. When evaluation becomes an integral part of student teaching and the student teacher is informed of, and participates in, the process, the outcome is almost certain to be a wholesome approach to self evaluation based on sound criteria.

Case Study No. 89: Minimum Competency

Your student teacher is nearing the end of his clinical experience. He has been dependable, responsible, and has developed a good rapport with the pupils. Yet nearly all the written communications he has generated contained numerous grammatical and spelling errors. You are dismayed that a college student and prospective teacher is so deficient in basic writing skills. His final evaluation is scheduled in two weeks. How do you respond to his poor writing skills?

1. Minimize the poor quality of his written work and hope he improves with experience.
2. Recommend that he complete some remedial work in grammar before being recommended for certification.
3. Work to help him improve his grammar.
4. _____

Comment

The ability to use the language effectively may be considered as one basis for the evaluation of competency. It is unfortunate that the student teacher was permitted to get to this level of teacher preparation without demonstrating ability to use correct grammar. The issue must be addressed even though it comes near the end of student teaching. Some sort of procedure should be put in place to insure that the future teacher uses both written and oral language correctly.

Questions

1. Why would a cooperating teacher be hesitant in addressing a glaring deficiency in a student teacher's performance?
2. What are the ramifications of waiting too long to call attention to substandard work by a student teacher or, worse yet, ignoring it?

Case Study No. 90: Doing Everything Well

You feel that Laurie is doing so well teaching your classes that you find it difficult to think of her as a student teacher. There seem to be no areas where any type of criticism is warranted. How do you go about establishing any kind of evaluation procedures in this situation?

1. Focus discussions on why her teaching is so effective.
2. Make sure the criteria you are using to evaluate her performance are valid and essential for good teaching.
3. Ask Laurie to identify areas of her teaching that could be refined.
4. Use evaluation time to analyze what the pupils are learning.
5. _____

Comment

If Laurie is performing at the level that one would expect of a second or third year teacher then she is obviously a Quadrant Four student teacher. Such talented student teachers are ready to consider how their actions impact their pupils. This procedure, focusing on the product of teaching rather than the process, coupled with good conferencing techniques may lead to a more meaningful assessment of the distinguished student teacher. May there be many student teachers like Laurie!

Questions

1. What criteria should be used to determine that a student teacher is doing well?
2. What more sophisticated teaching techniques could be used by outstanding student teachers?

Miss Bennett and Brian sat down to review the evaluation report that she would send to the university for his record. It would be the last formal evaluation session and both parties were relaxed and confident as they talked.

Miss Bennett began, "Brian, I think you have excellent potential for teaching and I would be pleased to have you work here if there is a position available. You are poised and superior in establishing student rapport. You are certainly better than average in subject knowledge, use of voice, and creativity. You are less effective in the areas of organization and in fostering more logical and creative thinking in the classroom discussions. However, you showed improvement and will correct these difficulties as you gain experience. They are not serious enough to cause any need for any remedial action, of course."

Brian agreed, "I want to work on the techniques of questioning, and I must remember that these students are not as well informed as they sometimes appear. Organization has been a problem for me, but I realize now how important it is for teaching. I agree with your analysis and would suggest that, if anything, you are too kind. I appreciate all the help you have given me in reaching this point in my professional development. I also feel that I can now make valid appraisals of my teaching and this will allow me to continue to improve. You have been most helpful in getting me to this point."

Remember:

- The goal of evaluation is skill in self evaluation.
- The conference is basic to the evaluative process.
- Evaluation should involve a variety of techniques.
- Identification of weaknesses should be accompanied by an explanation.
- Evaluation should begin when the student teacher starts teaching and continue throughout the experience.
- Evaluation is more than passing judgment; it is a process of honest interaction between two adults.
- If a supervisor withholds his views concerning a student teacher's progress, the student teacher may interpret the silence as criticism or indifference.
- The student teaching experience presents the final opportunity for teacher appraisal by a person who can observe performance frequently.
- Evaluation at all levels should stress growth.
- Good communication is good due process.

Useful References

Balch, Pamela M., and Patrick E. Balch. 1987. Evaluating a Student Teacher. Chapter 8 in *The Cooperating Teacher: A Practical Approach for the Supervision of Student Teachers*. Lanham, MD. University Press of America.

Ball State University, 2000. *Student Teacher's Portfolio Handbook*. Published by Phi Delta Kappa. Bloomington, IN.

Brucklacher, Barry. 1998. Cooperating Teachers' Evaluations of Student Teachers: All "A's"? *Journal of Instructional Psychology* 25 (March): 67-72.

Byrd, David, and Edith Guyton, editors. 2000. *Standards for Field Experiences in Teacher Education*. Association of Teacher Educators. Reston, VA.

Camperell, Kay, and Pat Stoddart (Utah State University). 1998. The Evolution of Criteria for Evaluating Student Teachers Over 30 Years. Paper Presented at the Annual Meeting of the Association of Teacher Educators, Dallas, TX.

Chiarelott, Leigh, Leonard Davidman, and Corey Muse. 1980. Evaluating the Pre-service Teacher Candidate. *Clearing House* 53 (Feb): 295-99.

Day, Roger, and Tami S. Martin. 2000. Performance-Based Assessment of Secondary Mathematics Student Teachers. *Action in Teacher Education*. (Fall): 86-94.

Diamantes, Thomas. 1996. Using Portfolios to Assess Student Teacher Progress. ERIC ED 405360.

Dutt, Karen, Mary Kayler, and Marilyn Tallerico. 1999. Assessing Student Teachers: The Promise of Developmental Portfolios. *The Teacher Educator* 34 (Spring): 201-215.

Ediger, Marlow. 1987. Evaluating Student Teaching Performance. ERIC ED 282927.

Elkind, Barbara. 1976. Going to Be a Cooperating Teacher? Be the Best! *Instructor* 86 (October): 81.

Ellwein, Mary Catherine, M. Elizabeth Graue, and Ronald E. Comfort. 1990. Talking About Instruction: Student Teachers' Reflections on Success and Failure in the Classroom. *Journal of Teacher Education* 41 (Nov-Dec): 3-14.

Funk, F. F., J. L. Hoffman, A. M. Keithley, and B. E. Long. 1982. Student Teaching Program: Feedback from Cooperating Teachers. *The Clearing House* 55 (March): 319-321.

Guyton, Edith, and D. John McIntyre. 1990. Student Teaching and Field Experiences. Chapter 29 in Houston (Ed.), *Handbook of Research on Teacher Education*. New York. Macmillan Publishing Co.

Henry, Marvin A. 1995. Supervising Student Teachers: A New Paradigm. Chapter 2 in Slick (Ed.) *Making the Difference for Teachers: The Field Experience in Actual Practice.* Thousand Oaks, CA. Corwin Press, Inc.

Horton, Dan, Della Thacker, and Jim Thompson (Indiana State University). 1998. Improving A Teacher Education Program: PDS Schools, Field Experiences, Teacher Evaluation, and Standards Throughout the Profession Blend Together to Provide More Effective Classroom Teachers. Paper Presented at the Annual Meeting of the Association of Teacher Educators, Dallas, TX.

Hungerman, Ann D. 1984. Competency in Classroom Management: Conflicts in Assessment. Paper presented at the annual meeting of the Association of Teacher Educators, New Orleans, LA. ERIC ED 244951.

Johnson, Ellen, Barbara Borleske, Susan Gleason, Bambi Bailey, Kathryn Scantlebury. 1998. Structured Observations. *Science Teacher* 65 (Mar): 46-49.

Johnson, J. 1999. Professional Teaching Portfolio: A Catalyst for Rethinking Teacher Education. *Action in Teacher Education* (Spring): 37-49.

Kratzner, Ron, and Ted Bitner. 1991. Validity and Reliability Measures for a Student Teacher Evaluation Instrument. *The Teacher Educator* 27 (Summer): 8-13.

Lloyd, Randall, Marilyn Moore, S. Rex Morrow, Susan Nierstheimer, and Fred Taylor. 2000. Infusing INTASC Principles into Teacher Preparation at a Professional Development School: Assessing Benefits to Stakeholders. *Action in Teacher Education* 33 (Fall): 47-55.

McDermott, Peter. 1998. The Best Teachers in Low Income, Urban Schools: How Do They Maintain Their Enthusiasm and Excellence? Paper presented at the Ethnography in Education Forum. Philadelphia, Pa. March 5-7. ERIC ED 419027.

Nelson, David., and Wesley Sandness. 1986. Self-Evaluation in Student Teaching: A Reanalysis. Paper presented at the annual convention of the Midwest Educational Research Association, Chicago, IL. ERIC ED 288843.

Phelps, Le Adelle, Charles D. Schmitz, and Deborah Lee Wade. 1986. A Performance-based Cooperating Teacher Report. *Journal of Teacher Education* 37 (Sept-Oct.): 32-35.

Phi Delta Kappan, 2000. *Evaluation of Student Teachers Guidebook.* Phi Delta Kappa International. Bloomington. IN.

Ramanathan, Hema and Elizabeth Wilkins-Carter. 1997. Training for Cooperating Teachers and University Supervisors in Their Role as Evaluators in Early Field Experiences. Paper

presented at the annual meeting of the Midwestern
Educational Research Association, Chicago, IL. ERIC ED
414260.

Reyes, Donald J., and Fred Isele, Jr. 1990. What Do We Expect from
Elementary Student Teachers: A National Analysis of Rating
Forms. *Action in Teacher Education* 12 (Summer): 8-13.

Robertson, Blaine P. 1986. Student Teacher Evaluation:
Development of a Summative Evaluation Instrument for Use
at the Secondary Level. ERIC ED 271420.

Smith, Edwin R., and Patricia K. Smith. 1991. Assessment of
Student Teachers: An Alternate Model. *Teacher Education
Quarterly* 18 (Fall): 39-46.

Sudzina, Mary R., and J. Gary Knowles. 1993. Personal,
Professional and Contextual Circumstances of Student
Teachers Who "Fail": Setting a Course for Understanding
Failure in Teacher Education. *Journal of Teacher Education* 44
(Sept -Oct): 254-262.

Swetnam, Leslie. 1997. Teacher Candidate Portfolios: A Continuum
of Assessment for Professional Development and Institutional
Accountability. Paper presented at the Annual Meeting of the
American Association of Colleges for Teacher Education,
Phoenix, AZ. ERIC ED 405338.

Vermont Department of Education. 1999. *Five Standards for
Vermont Educators: A Vision for Schooling.* 120 State Street,
Montpelier, VT.

Wile, J. M. 1999. Professional Portfolios: The "Talk" of the Student
Teaching Experience. *Teacher Educator* 34 (Winter): 215-231.

Williams, John Carl, and Wally S. Holmes. 1983. Student Teacher
Grades: What Do They Mean? *School and Community* 69
(May): 15.

Zheng, Binyao and Linda Webb. 2000. A New Model of Student
Teacher Supervision: Perceptions of Student Teachers. Paper
presented at the Annual Meeting of the Mid-South
Educational Research Association, Bowling Green, KY. ERIC
ED 447136.

Epilogue

The period of student teaching seemed to pass in an unbelievably brief time. Brian Sims finished his last day as a student teacher and said farewell to his pupils. He was unprepared for the emotional reactions of some of his students and he was visibly touched by their expressions of regret that he was leaving. He conveyed his final appreciation to Miss Bennett and the other school personnel, vowing he would keep in touch. He left the school as a confident and competent young professional who liked teaching, but he realized that he was a much different person from the insecure young man who timidly walked into the building a few weeks ago. At this moment he was convinced this experience had made a more profound impact on him than any other block of academic or professional study at the university.

Elaine Bennett felt she was a different person, too. She was certain she was a better teacher for having had the experience of sharing her classroom with a student teacher. She had done considerable reflecting about her own teaching during the past few weeks, and she had learned much from Brian. Her professional background had been enriched due to the university contacts associated with student teaching. Most of all, she felt that the presence of two teachers in the classroom caused her students to receive more attention. She may have helped shape the destiny of a young teacher, but she also had refined her own teaching skills and developed a number of supervisory techniques. She allowed herself a final look down the hall as Brian disappeared into a crowd of students and then turned back into her classroom where she gazed for a moment at his empty desk . . .

Becoming A Supervisor
Do It the Professional Way

Brian Sims is the composite of many student teachers and Elaine Bennett represents hundreds of beginning supervisors. Both were as typical as they could be in illustrating what can be accomplished in an experience where no two situations are alike. Brian's problems and achievements were the ordinary ones, and Miss Bennett made the decisions that would usually be appropriate. Their example suggests that a teacher and student teacher who are aware of their roles and responsibilities can bring about decisive changes in teaching skills.

The content of this book was designed to broaden alternatives rather than to prescribe specific techniques of supervision. The number of possibilities for experiences is virtually unlimited.

However, Worksheet Number Fifteen in the Appendix summarizes a number of typical activities of student teachers. The checklist can assist in assessing the totality of the experience and provide some direction for any future supervisory activities.

A teacher is a decision-maker who has to choose from alternatives rather than rely on a pat response to situations that appear to be similar. Judgments are based on awareness of the dynamics of a given situation, the personalities of the people involved, and knowledge of practices and their effects. The inevitable outcome of such decision-making is manifest by the behavior of those whom he instructs. The individuals who came under the influence of a teacher are now making our laws, manufacturing and selling goods to us, living happy lives and making homes, erecting buildings, repairing our automobiles, accessing the Internet, providing us with health care, and guiding our children. The teacher is not the sole person responsible for molding our society, but there is at least one moment when this individual can touch another person in such a way that a life may be changed. One opportunity for cooperating teachers is presented in the student teaching experience.

The purpose of this book is to expand the teacher's concepts of options and techniques for guiding student teachers. The pages and chapters are designed to increase the number of choices for making wise decisions concerning the development of a future teacher. Within a given context, nearly any statement or procedure suggested in this book can be right, wrong, or irrelevant. The teacher must consider all significant factors and then determine an appropriate course of action. The more that is known about the field, the better the possibility of making sound judgments.

The cooperating teacher alone has to supervise student teachers. Other teachers can offer advice, and materials can provide background for making a judgment, but ultimately the decisions must be made by the cooperating teacher. Success depends on how well knowledge and values are applied in a professional situation. If they are put together correctly, a cooperating teacher will affect teacher education in a lasting way.

Appendix

Worksheets for
Professional Supervision

Permission is given by the authors for the reader to copy any of the forms and use them for professional supervisory activity. Most worksheets are contained on the CD, *Supervising Student Teachers the Professional Way: Book Supplement* which is distributed by Sycamore Press and may be printed from the disk for classroom and supervisory use.

Worksheet Number One

Checklist for a Student Teacher's Arrival

The list below may serve as a guide for insuring that a cooperating teacher has completed the activities necessary to assure a smooth beginning for a student teacher.

1. Prepare the pupils for a student teacher's arrival.
   ___ Inform pupils of the impending arrival.
   ___ Tell pupils something about the student teacher.
   ___ Create a feeling of anticipation for a student teacher's arrival.
   ___ Other
2. Learn about the student teacher's background.
   ___ Subject knowledge.
   ___ Pre-student teaching field experiences.
   ___ Special interests or skills.
   ___ Other
3. Read the university student teaching handbook.
   ___ Understand basic responsibilities.
   ___ Review requirements and expectations for cooperating teachers.
   ___ Other
4. Become aware of the legal status of student teachers.
   ___ Responsibility of cooperating teacher when a student teacher covers the class.
   ___ Rights and responsibilities of the student teacher.
   ___ Other
5. Become familiar with school policy concerning student teacher responsibilities.
   ___ Reporting to school.
   ___ Absences.
   ___ Attendance at faculty meetings.
   ___ Supervisory activities.
   ___ Other

6. Make a pre-teaching contact with the student teacher.
   _____ Letter of introduction.
   _____ Student introduction.
   _____ Encourage pre-teaching visit.
   _____ Other
7. Secure copies of materials to be used in orienting the student teacher.
   _____ School handbook.
   _____ Daily schedule.
   _____ Class Rosters.
   _____ Seating charts.
   _____ Other
8. Make necessary arrangements for the student teacher to be comfortable in the classroom.
   _____ Arrange for a desk or table.
   _____ Have necessary supplies.
   _____ Prepare a file of necessary and informative materials.
   _____ Other
9. Secure teaching resources for the student teacher.
   _____ Textbooks.
   _____ Curriculum guides.
   _____ Resource books.
   _____ Computer availability.
   _____ Other
10. Develop a plan for the student teacher's entry into teaching.
    _____ Introduction to the class.
    _____ Introduction to the faculty and support staff.
    _____ Initial teaching activities.
    _____ Other

Worksheet Number Two

Preparing for the First Few Days
of Student Teaching

The following responsibilities usually must be assumed by a cooperating teacher during the first few days of student teaching. This form may be used either as a planning guide or as a review of preparation activities in meeting these responsibilities.

1. Prepare for the special needs of the student teacher in adjusting to a different environment.
    Planned procedures: _____
    _____

2. Introduce the student teacher and create situations early so that the student teacher can earn status in the eyes of students.
    Planned procedures: _____
    _____

3. Establish a partnership arrangement.
    Planned procedures: _____
    _____

4. Introduce the student teacher to other faculty members and the administrative staff.
    Planned procedures: _____
    _____

5. Acquaint the student teacher with the classroom routine and management techniques.
    Planned procedures: _____
    _____

6. Apprise the student teacher of the class work that is currently under way.
    Planned procedures: _____
    _____

7. Involve the student teacher in the activities of the classroom.
    Planned procedures: _____
    _____

8. Provide the student teacher with necessary teaching resources and a place to work.
    Planned procedures: _____
    _____

9. Orient the student teacher to the school building and its facilities.

   Planned procedures: _____

   _____

10. Discuss school policies and regulations with the student teacher.

    Planned procedures: _____

    _____

11. Assist the student teacher in learning pupil names.

    Planned procedures: _____

    _____

12. Delegate responsibility and authority to the student teacher.

    Planned procedures: _____

    _____

13. Plan for the student teacher's gradual assumption of teaching responsibilities.

    Planned procedures: _____

    _____

14. Orient the student teacher to the community.

    Planned procedures: _____

    _____

15. Help the student teacher acquire background information about the students.

    Planned procedures: _____

    _____

Worksheet Number Three

List of Basic Requirements
for Student Teachers

Many student teachers and cooperating teachers feel that it is beneficial for a cooperating teacher to make a list of specific requirements that will be expected of student teachers. For those who wish to develop such a list, the requirements below can serve as a point of departure in determining a specific set of expectations. But do make sure such activities are consistent with the expectations of the college.

- Submit lesson plans in duplicate two days in advance.
- Submit evaluation tools for approval at least two days in advance.
- Prepare at least one set of grades.
- Spend some time going over the files of the students.
- Ride the entire route of a school bus that has a number of your students on it.
- Prepare at least one bulletin board display.
- Plan to have students complete an activity that involves their use of the media center under your supervision.
- Review and show at least one videocassette, operating the equipment without assistance.
- Utilize the overhead projector in at least one of your classes.
- Attend at least three extracurricular activities.
- Write frequent self evaluations.
- Have conferences with a minimum of three students.
- Sit in on a parent conference.
- Observe a minimum of 25 classes in a variety of grade levels or disciplines.
- Video tape and analyze three formal class sessions.
- Try a variety of instructional strategies.
- Incorporate appropriate technology into your teaching.
- Attend a school board meeting.

Worksheet Number Four

Personal Competencies
of Cooperating Teachers

Cooperating teachers serve as role models, facilitators, and sometimes counselors for student teachers. The criteria below provide indicators for determining the extent to which one serves as a supportive guide for a student teacher.

1. Accepts the student teacher as a professional colleague as evidenced by:
   ___ showing respect for the student teacher's decisions.
   ___ allowing the student teacher to assume responsibility.
   ___ listening to the student teacher's ideas and concerns.
   ___ using relevant ideas submitted by the student teacher.
   ___ permitting the student teacher to assume the same privileges as a cooperating teacher.
2. Accepts the usual mistakes of the student teacher as evidenced by:
   ___ refraining from overreacting to mistakes.
   ___ allowing the student teacher to continue with responsibilities.
   ___ stating that mistakes are normal and most are not irrevocable.
3. Restrains from prescriptive directions as evidenced by:
   ___ discussing options with the student teacher before a decision is made.
   ___ allowing freedom of choice on the part of the student teacher.
4. Conducts professional discussions with the student teacher, as evidenced by discussions about:
   ___ learning problems of students.
   ___ teaching methodologies and their applications.
   ___ use of authentic assessment strategies.
   ___ student behavior.

5. Allows a student teacher to observe and discuss the cooperating teacher's activities and teacher effectiveness as evidenced by:
   ___ student teacher analysis of a supervisor's lesson.
   ___ student teacher suggesting alternative procedures to the cooperating teacher.
6. Diagnoses learner's interests and needs, develops learning strategies and shares these procedures with the student teacher, as evidenced by:
   ___ discussing diagnostic procedures.
   ___ explaining why conclusions were reached.
   ___ encouraging the student teacher to be involved in the development of Individual Education Plans (IEP).
   ___ explaining why certain teaching techniques will be used as a result of the diagnosis and analysis.

Worksheet Number Five

Analysis Form for Student Teachers Who Have Difficulty Relating to Pupils

This worksheet may be used by a student teacher to analyze personal relationships with pupils. After the form is completed, it may be used for review and discussion with the cooperating teacher.

                                                          Yes No

1. *Do I show sufficient enthusiasm so that my students are aware of the interest that I have in specific subjects and teaching in general?*   ____ ____
   Supporting information: _____
   _____
   Enthusiasm could be improved by: _____
   _____

2. *Am I courteous to pupils and show them respect and, in turn, command respect from them?*   ____ ____
   Supporting information: _____
   _____
   Respect could be improved by: _____
   _____

3. *Do I insist that my pupils treat others with courtesy and respect?*   ____ ____
   Supporting information: _____
   _____
   I could appear to be more courteous by: _____
   _____

4. *Do I recognize good work as much as or more than I criticize poor student accomplishment?*   ____ ____
   Supporting information: _____
   _____
   I could better recognize student work by: _____
   _____

5. **Do I make assignments that are clear and specific and justify those assignments in terms of their value to students?** ___ ___
   Supporting information: _____

   _____

   Assignments would be acceptable if: _____

   _____

6. **Do I make an effort to provide for individual differences?** ___ ___
   Supporting information: _____

   _____

   I could further individualize my teaching by: _____

   _____

7. **Do I employ a variety of teaching procedures in order to avoid monotony and to appeal to student interests and learning styles?** ___ ___
   Supporting information: _____

   _____

   I could improve variety by: _____

   _____

8. **Do I attempt to make every student in my classes feel some personal responsibility for the effectiveness of my class?** ___ ___
   Supporting information: _____

   _____

   I could increase students' feelings of responsibility by:

   _____

9. **Do my students really believe that my main purpose is to help them to learn?** ___ ___
   Supporting information: _____

   _____

   I could better convince my students by: _____

   _____

10. **Do I believe that my main purpose in teaching is to help students and be an advocate for them?** ___ ___
    Supporting information: _____

    _____

    I can further refine my beliefs through: _____

    _____

Worksheet Number Six

Student Teacher Readiness Assessment

The purpose of this document is to provide preservice education students with feedback concerning professional, ethical, and interpersonal competencies that our experience tells us are critical to the success of classroom teachers.

STUDENT _____ DATE _____ COURSE _____ INSTRUCTOR _____

Student Self-Evaluation

COMPETENCY	Excellent	Satisfactory	Unacceptable	COMMENTS
1. Attendance				
2. Punctuality				
3. Oral expression				
4. Written expression				
5. Interaction with others				
6. Reliability/ Dependability				
7. Self-Initiative/ Independent				
8. Collegiality				
9. Professionalism and Judgment				
10. Responsive to feedback				

Faculty Evaluation

COMPETENCY	Excellent	Satisfactory	Unacceptable	COMMENTS
1. Attendance				
2. Punctuality				
3. Oral expression				
4. Written expression				
5. Interaction with others				
6. Reliability/ Dependability				
7. Self-Initiative/ Independent				
8. Collegiality				
9. Professionalism and Judgment				
10. Responsive to feedback				

Worksheet Number Seven

Student Teacher Visitation Request

TO: _____

FROM: _____

RE: Permission for Student Teacher to Visit Your Class

WHEN: Date _____

_____

Time: _____

_____

Class: _____

_____

_____ Student Teacher

_____

_____ Cooperating Teacher

If the above time is satisfactory, will you please sign and return one copy to the cooperating teacher and keep the other copy for your information.

Sign here for approval _____

Worksheet Number Eight

Lesson Analysis Form

Teacher _____

Date_____Time_____Subject or Grade _____

_____

_____ **Planning:** Outline or lesson plan prepared and followed.

_____ **Introduction of Lesson:** Gains students' interest and attention.

_____ **Strategies and Materials:** Appropriate to content and class, effectively used, questioning techniques.

_____ **Classroom Management:** Classroom organized, students involved, effective discipline.

_____ **Momentum of Lesson:** Well paced, smooth transitions.

_____ **Delivery:** Voice, articulation, enthusiasm, vocabulary, grammar, nonverbal communication, teacher mobility, humor, student names, responses to students, eye contact.

_____ **Closure:** Summarization, relating content to future lessons.

Comments:

Instructional Observation Checklist

Yes No N/A

1. Were the objectives and standards clearly identified? — — —

2. Did the students appear to be correctly diagnosed? — — —

3. Were previously learned concepts and skills reviewed? — — —

4. Were students motivated before and/or during the lesson? — — —

5. Was reinforcement appropriately used? — — —

6. Was the lesson sequenced (easy to difficult, narrow to global, general to specific, etc.)? — — —

7. Were the students on task during the entire lesson?

8. Were directions clearly given? — — —

9. Were the students actively involved in their own learning? — — —

10. Was there evidence of teacher monitoring for comprehension during the lesson? — — —

11. Were students given an opportunity to practice or apply skills taught? — — —

12. Were techniques for retention used? — — —

13. Was transfer of learning built into the lesson? — — —

14. Did use of materials and activities facilitate the lesson? — — —

15. Did the teaching style fit the lesson? — — —

16. Were provisions made for evaluating the students prior to the end of the lesson? — — —

17. Were students given knowledge of results? — — —

18. If needed, were provisions made for reteaching or extension? — — —

19. Were the lesson objectives and standards achieved? — — —

Worksheet Number Ten

Checklist for Guiding Planning

The following procedures are recommended as ways of guiding planning more effectively.

1. Planning should be done cooperatively with both cooperating teacher and student teacher suggesting activities and ways to present relevant learning experiences.
   Analysis of cooperative planning: _____

   Possible improvement: _____

2. The cooperating teacher should acquaint the student teacher with his yearly plans, reviewing what occurred before the student teacher's arrival and projecting what will likely occur after she leaves.
   Analysis of planning review: _____

   Possible improvement: _____

3. The cooperating teacher should explain her procedures for pupil-teacher planning.
   Analysis of pupil-teacher planning procedures: _____

   Possible improvement: _____

4. The cooperating teacher should review the teaching plans made by the student teacher, raising questions and offering suggestions.
   Analysis of review process: _____

   Possible improvement: _____

5. The cooperating teacher should provide evaluative sessions in which the student teacher gains skill in judging the effectiveness of her plan.
    Analysis of evaluative procedure: _____

    Possible improvement: _____

6. The cooperating teacher should make certain that the student teacher's plans are submitted in advance so that they may be reviewed and changed, if necessary.
    Analysis of planning requirement: _____

    Possible improvement: _____

7. The cooperating teacher should encourage creativity and allow freedom in planning.
    Analysis of creative planning: _____

    Possible improvement: _____

Worksheet Number Eleven

TEACHER CLASSROOM ACTIVITY PROFILE

TEACHER _____

CLASS _____ SUPERVISOR _____

Date _____

3 Minute Intervals

Teacher Activity	Time	1	2	3	4	5	6	7	8	9	10	11	12	13	14	15	16	17	18	19	20	Summary Approx. Min.	Summary Approx. %
MN Management—Non-Learning																							
ML Management—Learning																							
D Random Discussion																							
P Presentation																							
R Recitation/Drill																							
LT Logical Thinking																							
TP Thinking Process																							

Explanatory Notes

Comments

Completed Teacher Classroom Activity Profile

TEACHER CLASSROOM ACTIVITY PROFILE

Department of Secondary Education
Indiana State University

TEACHER ___ Sims ___

CLASS ___ US History ___ SUPERVISOR ___ Bennett ___ Date ___ 10/25 ___

3 Minute Intervals

Time	9:03	:06	:09	:12	:15	:18	:21	:24	:27	:30	:33	:36	:39	:42	:45	:48	:51	:54			Summary	
	1	2	3	4	5	6	7	8	9	10	11	12	13	14	15	16	17	18	19	20	Approx. Min.	Approx. %
Teacher Activity																						
MN Management—Non-Learning																						
ML Management—Learning																						
D Random Discussion																						
P Presentation																						
R Recitation/Drill																						
LT Logical Thinking																						
TP Thinking Process																						

Explanatory Notes

1. Attendance check and distribution of papers
2. Introduction to Colonial Williamsburg
3. Videotape: "Where It All Began"
7. Questions about tape and assignment review
8. Interruption from Intercom
10. Students who have visited Williamsburg share their experiences
12. Discussion question: How is Williamsburg life similar to and different from life in the United States today?
16. Discussion questions: Is life better now than it was then? What was good and not so good about Williamsburg?
18. Assignment: Are there any "colonies" at the present time in our nation? Compare your ideas with the stage of development that we find in colonial Williamsburg.

Comments

1. Class began quickly and efficiently.
2. Perhaps you could have spent a little more time telling the students what to look for in the video.
3. It is good for students to share their experiences, but do not let them get you off track.
4. Your comparison of Williamsburg to today was good because it caused the students to use reasoning skills.
5. You may want to move around in the room more so that you are in closer proximity to more students.
6. Do not be annoyed by the Intercom. You will have to put up with it.
7. The summary and the assignment happened too quickly. Allow more time for closure.
8. Regarding the assignment: Many students have access to computers. I suggest that you ask them to do some information searches on their software or the Internet to see if they can access any good information or ideas.
9. Interesting class. It had a variety of activities and involved different levels of cognitive activity. The students seemed attentive and motivated.

Worksheet Number Twelve

Examples of Written Communication

Student Teacher   **Supervising Teacher**

IDEAS

How do you plan for discipline?

1. Always be prepared
2. Have at least three different activities each day
3. Explain rules so that students know what is expected

AGREEMENTS

When do you want the bulletin board display ready?

Try to have it on the board Monday morning.

EVALUATION

I will work on that. The students gave little response to my questions, as you observed.

Questions such as, "How about roots?" are hard for students to answer. Try to be more specific.

Student Teacher	Supervising Teacher
What did you think of the introduction to the new unit?	You did this well. The students remained attentive. Word usage was at students level of understanding. The events were nicely coordinated. Did you notice that students needed more time to get pen and pencil ready? When there is time remaining as there was today, use it for review or for explaining the assignment.

PROFESSIONAL INFORMATION

Neal acted strangely today. Why?	He is being treated for a manic-depressive syndrome. He may not have taken his medication today.

| **Student Teacher** | **Supervising Teacher** |

THINKING ABOUT TEACHING

John is not making any progress. I wonder if persons like him should even attend school.

In spite of poor academic work, he is acquiring attitudes and values. This is part of teaching, too.

DETAILS AND PROCEDURES

Thank you.

1. Get the attendance check out by 8:15.
2. See that the door is closed (noise down the hall).
3. Let pupils at the end of each row pass the books. This saves time
4. Check window shades on sunny days.

Worksheet Number Thirteen

Participation Activities for
Teacher Education Candidates

The following worksheet provides the opportunity for the cooperating teacher or student teacher to either plan or record activities related to typical participation activities that are expected of student teachers.

1. Faculty Responsibility Other Than Instruction

2. Supervision Activity

3. Social Activity

4. Athletic Activities

5. Subject Matter-Related Activities

6. Community-Related Functions

7. Communication with Parents

8. Professional Activity

9. Co-Curricular Activities

Worksheet Number Fourteen

Student Teacher Evaluation Checklist

Student Teacher Information:					Student Teaching Experience:				
Name: _____					School: _____				
SS #: _____					Address: _____				
Subject(s): _____									

1 = Above Average, 2 = Average, 3 = Below Average, NB = No Basis For Judgment									
Academic and Instructional Competencies	1	2	3	NB	**Personal Characteristics**	1	2	3	NB
1. Manages instructional time effectively					16. Appearance and grooming				
2. Manages student behavior effectively					17. Written communications				
3. Uses effective instructional strategies and activities					18. Voice qualities				
4. Monitors student performance					19. Oral communications				
5. Provides effective instructional feedback					20. Initiative				
6. Exhibits effective human relations skills					21. Responsibility				
7. Performs non-instructional activities adequately					22. Commitment to the profession				
8. Uses appropriate levels of questions and questioning					23. Potential ability to lead				
9. Uses effective lesson plans					24. Self-confidence and poise				
10. Uses a variety of resources and activities to motivate students					25. Potential for growth				
11. Uses instructional objectives to plan and implement instruction					26. Empathy				
12. Displays knowledge and understanding of subject matter					27. Reaction to suggestions and criticism				
13. Maintains accurate records					28. Professional relationships				
14. Maintains a supportive environment					29. Self evaluation				
15. Adjusts teaching strategies after evaluating teaching effectiveness					30. **SUMMARY EVALUATION**				

Please type comments: Include evaluative, elaborative, and supportive comments concerning the student teacher's strengths, areas needing improvement, and growth patterns during student teaching.

Typed Name _____   Title _____

Signature _____   Date _____

Worksheet Number Fifteen

Final Checklist of Student Teacher Activities

This summary worksheet lists a number of activities that are considered to be beneficial for student teachers. Although every experience cannot provide activities in all areas, the checklist below can serve as a guide in assessing the extent of a student teacher's involvement and in projecting activities for future student teachers.

	Adequate	Less Than Adequate	Notes
Planning and Organization			
1. Prepared unit plans			
2. Prepared daily plans for a minimum of four consecutive weeks.			
3. Located and used supplemental reference materials			
4. Prepared a file of resource materials			
5. Studied student records			
Teaching and Analysis			
6. Practiced at least five techniques of teaching whole groups			
7. Worked with individuals and small groups			
8. Used a variety of media devices			
9. Video taped one or more lessons and studied the playback			
10. Taught several classes without the cooperating teacher being present			
Classroom Management and Discipline			
11. Prepared a seating chart			
12. Learned pupil names quickly			
13. Shared in routine teaching skills, i.e., roll, attendance			
14. Regulated temperature, lighting, and other physical aspects of the room			
15. Helped with disciplinary problems			
Conferences			
16. Conferred regularly with cooperating teacher			
17. Conferences covered a wide range of topics related to teaching			

	Adequate	Less Than Adequate	Notes
18. Conferred with the university supervisor			
19. Conferred with parents			
20. Used conferences as one method of evaluating teaching process			
Observations			
21. Observed a number of teachers			
22. Observed during the entire block of time			
23. Observed in more than one school			
24. Observed different subject and age levels			
25. Showed evidence of teaching improvement through observation			
Participation			
26. Attended activities and functions in the community			
27. Assisted with extraclass activities			
28. Helped supervise playground, cafeteria, and corridors			
29. Participated in pupil groups such as home rooms and clubs			
30. Contributed unique skills to the extraclass settings			
Faculty and Administration Participation			
31. Learned about the work of special teachers			
32. Learned about the responsibilities of other staff members			
33. Attended faculty meetings			
34. Became acquainted with a cross section of the faculty			
35. Conferred with the building administrator			
Professional Activities			
36. Discussed pupil records with guidance personnel			
37. Participated in professional meetings			
38. Studied a teacher code of ethics			
39. Became familiar with professional journals			
40. Learned about the role of teacher associations and unions			
Evaluation			
41. Prepared, administered, and scored classroom tests			
42. Evaluated homework and other assignments			
43. Kept a grade book and built a record of work completed by pupils			
44. Assisted in determining and reporting pupil progress			
45. Learned to evaluate self			

	Adequate	Less Than Adequate	Notes
Miscellaneous			
46. Became aware of the legal aspects of student teaching and student teaching supervision			
47. Became aware of the legal aspects of teaching			
48. Made a case study of one or more pupils			
49. Examined several textbooks			
50. Displayed adequate skills in using chalkboard			

Author Index

Subject Index